Patriots & Tories

The Secret Untold History of the United States

Arleen Hartery Martino

ISBN: 0578097206
ISBN 13: 9780578097206

Dedication

This book is dedicated to the memory of John Fitzgerald Kennedy, thirty-fifth President of the United States and pre-eminent hero of my youth, who lost his life in a patriotic attempt to restore the American System of Political Economy.

Rest assured, President Kennedy, that we patriots shall yet prevail!

November 14, 2011

I owe the existence of this book to the genius of Lyndon LaRouche. In 2008, when the stock market was collapsing, in the face of what I perceived to be great danger, I searched the Internet in an attempt to get a quick financial education. That is when I found Lyndon LaRouche and his masterful video, *1932*. Impressed with the patriotic fervor of that video, I then dug deeper on his site and discovered, to my delight, a valuable trove of history lessons. In those history lessons, I recognized the truth---the suppressed truth about my country! Armed with this knowledge, I then determined to pen this book for adolescents, so that they might have a truthful resource to reference. For their protection and for the defense of my country, I want them to understand the great mission of the United States republic.

Ideally, the book is meant to be read with an adult, so that together adult and child can enjoy a shared experience of enlightenment. The book is written as a series of essays and it is suggested that you read them one at a time. Much of the information in the essays is purposefully repeated, so that key facts can be quickly assimilated. The next generation will then be armed with an understanding of the true history of the United States republic.

This is a dangerous world that we live in. Evil men rule it from high echelons of power and other corrupted men, by default, help them promote their evil agenda. These evil men intend to destroy the sovereign nation-state system and return the world to feudalism. Standing in opposition to this ancient evil plan, the United States republic once stood as a lone example for the world. Its government was established under a mandate to live apart from this ancient system of empire and defeat it. Instead, however, this government "by the people and for the people," now faces possible extinction because, unaware, the people have let evil move in and take it over. Ben Franklin once made a foreboding statement in which he predicted that the government of the United States might one day end in despotism because the people, corrupted and ignorant, would just give up their rights as free people. I hope Franklin's prediction does not come true.

Lyndon LaRouche is the modern-day voice for American nationalism. With a dedicated group of patriots helping him, he unceasingly champions world freedom by internationally promoting the American System of Political Economy. I hope that many people will find this truthful sketch of U.S. history, appreciate it and then decide to support Lyndon LaRouche. There is a free daily education waiting for everyone on *www.larouchepac.com*. On that site, anyone can also search through fifteen years of thoroughly researched back-logged articles of the *Executive Intelligence Review*. Or they can actually choose to support LaRouche's work by taking out an online subscription to the periodical. God bless Lyndon LaRouche. May he succeed in his attempt to save the republic!

Arleen Martino
Littleton, Massachusetts

Preface For Adults

Throughout this volume, we will constantly reference the term British Empire (or sometimes we will just refer to "the British" or just "the empire.") So that you don't get confused and start to wonder if you are lost in the wrong century, let us clarify the meaning of the term by giving some pertinent background information. The British Empire exists today as a covert political and financial institution of immense power. It came into existence as a privately owned empire, in 1763, when a "partnership" between the British East India Company and the British Crown was formed at the end of the Seven Years' War in Europe.

The British East India Company had been established in 1600 as a private trade monopoly when a group of London merchants obtained a fifteen-year charter from Queen Elizabeth I that gave them exclusive control over British trade in the Far East. In possession of this royal charter, that company grew immensely rich. The charter also granted this private trading company the right to govern themselves, raise an army to defend themselves against their rivals, and issue their own currency. With these rights, the company functioned like an independent government.

Over a century later, in order to expand its power, the company sought to forge a "partnership" with the British Crown, so it instigated the Seven Years' War, financed the Crown's involvement in it, and then, after bankrupting it, secured an agreement to bail it out under terms favorable to itself. Lord Shelburne facilitated the deal. Under his auspices, the British East India Company thereafter exercised control over the Crown and effectively usurped its government. The entity that emerged from this deal is what we refer to as the British Empire. The British Empire still exists today. Organized as the Inter-Alpha Group of banks, it is now an immense financial empire---the modern world's only empire. It has orchestrated the current world financial crisis.

The British Empire is the extension of a very old system of oligarchy that reaches back into antiquity. Prior empires functioned under the same system. Only the locale of empire has changed over time. Before the British Empire, there was the Venetian Empire. The fourteenth century collapse of its financial usury scheme brought the world into the Dark Ages. Then, after prolonged suffering, Europe emerged into the light of the Renaissance and in Italy a revival of the humanist teachings of Plato reunited the Eastern and Western Rites of the Church. The concept of the nation-state also emerged to challenge the empire's system of financial usury, so, to survive, a core of Venetian bankers sought a new locale for the re-establishment of their banking empire. Initially they moved their operation to the Netherlands, but targeted the British Isles as the long-range locale of operation.

In the Netherlands, they formed Anglo-Dutch trading companies and enlarged them in order to prevail over world trade.

As Venetian-style trading companies began to dominate the economy in the Netherlands, merchants from all over Europe began to congregate in the empire's newly-established financial center. Then the Bank of Amsterdam was founded in 1609 as an empire-controlled central bank. The first bank of its kind, it fused Venetian banking with a speculative stock exchange. Already wealthy merchants then began trading on that exchange in order to enlarge their portfolios. By 1610, Venice had forged the greatest financial empire the world had ever seen. She then proceeded to foment war in order to keep the people down. In the process she destroyed Dutch culture. She then cautiously began to infiltrate England.

In order to escape the horrors of Venetian-style banking, from as far back as the fifteenth century, the Florentine Academy in Italy, under the guidance of the great Cardinal Nicholas of Cusa, had planned for the establishment of a New World republic in the Americas. Then, in order to escape the moral collapse pervading Europe, men steeped in Renaissance culture fled to Tudor England. Gradually, bold colonization leadership developed in England. By the seventeenth century, John Winthrop and other Puritan merchants sent a small advance party of men to Salem, in Massachusetts, to study the needs of their planned colonization project.

In 1629, during a period of great political upheaval in England, and fearing that they might lose their window of opportunity, Winthrop and his Puritan colleagues pulled off a sort of political coup by getting Charles I to sign a charter that gave them the right to go to the Massachusetts Bay in America and rule themselves in the tradition of free Englishmen. With this charter, the Massachusetts Bay colonists secured the right to appoint their own governor, establish laws for themselves, build industry, develop commerce, and create a currency. The principles of free government established in the Massachusetts Bay Colony, in the years prior to 1688, later became the model for the U.S. Constitution.

Almost immediately, after issuing the charter, the Crown realized its mistake and tried to have it returned. But, Governor Winthrop stalled and began to plan for eventual revolution. Afterwards, the Venetian bankers tried to overthrow the Stuart kings, Charles I and Charles II, because they refused to allow them to set up a central bank in England like the one that had been created in Amsterdam.

The use of colonial government scrip continued in Massachusetts until William III of the Netherlands House of Orange, under the direction of the Venetian bankers, invaded Britain in 1688. Then, under his rule, in order to restrict the liberties of the inhabitants of Massachusetts, the Crown again demanded the return of the charter, but, still refusing, the colonists instead engaged in a long protracted political fight with the enemy-infiltrated Crown.

In the following years, Gottfried Liebniz emerged in Europe to orchestrate a broad fight for the principle of the sovereign nation-state. With the support of England's spirited Queen Anne, he had much success forging a republican alliance for progress, but, when Anne was poisoned in 1714, his circle fell apart. Then, by 1763, with the British East India Company in control of the Crown, the prospects for republican government in the colonies became politically hopeless, so Ben Franklin gave the signal for the start of the American Revolution.

The American Revolution raged for seven years, but, finally, with the help of the League of Armed Neutrality---an association of European nations committed to the defeat of Britain, the colonies won that war. The U.S. Constitution was then established as the political outcome of Leibniz's dynamic economic work. With Russia and France allied with the U.S. after the war, for a while, there was the hope of peace. But, in 1782, when Prime Minister Shelburne established the British Foreign Office as a covert arm of the empire and began to promote more warfare, this peace was compromised. Under these conditions, the U.S. was eventually isolated and weakened.

In order to destroy the U.S. alliance with France, the British Empire brought Napoleon Bonaparte to power, incited the Napoleonic Wars, and then decided the outcome of those wars by selectively funding battles. The U.S. alliance with the nations of Europe was then effectively destroyed. In the nineteenth century, as the empires of Europe forged a colonial system of great imperial power, only the United States republic stood as a bulwark against the British Empire's world domination. To defeat the U.S. republic, that empire planned the American Civil War thirty years in advance of its outbreak.

And so it goes down through history, as covert conspiracy has proceeded to manipulate and lead mankind. This book shall document the involvement of the British Empire in the affairs of the United States right from its inception as a nation. Later, when the hero, Lincoln, became president, he not only defeated the British-sponsored Confederacy, but he also forged a great U.S. technology start. The nations of the world then began to emulate the U.S. as planned. But, just as world transformation seemed imminent, the banking empire re-infiltrated the U.S. government and the British Foreign Office forged secret alliances and widespread warfare in order to curtail progress. This eventually led to two world wars.

The British Empire is heir to a long legacy of empire. That legacy can easily be traced to ancient Babylon and on through the empires of Persia, Rome, Byzantium, Venice and, now, Britain. Today's British Empire, however, is a more deadly strain of the old system of usury because it is international in scope. Under masterful leadership, a few notable U.S. presidents embraced the economic principles embedded in the U.S. Constitution, and, for brief periods, prevailed over the empire's usurious game. Except for them, the republican legacy of Plato, Leibniz and Franklin would have early been extinguished. This book shall tell the story of these exceptional patriots.

Preface For Adolescents

Welcome to a fresh new hopeful view of world history! Unlike most histories, this history of the world doesn't start at the beginning, but starts later---at the point where the United States of America is founded. It takes this starting point for a very special reason. You see, in the eyes of its founders, the establishment of the United States was meant to be a fresh start for the world. And it was meant to give birth to new hope. So, this history starts here---at the rebirth of hope.

The history of the world, up to the lawful and free establishment of the United States, is largely the story of the enslavement of people to empire. And, the system of empire is very different from the free nation-state system espoused by the United States. The two systems embrace opposing ideas about people and about money! Everyone knows that money is a medium of exchange and that people need money in order to survive, but in order for happiness to prevail in the world, money must be lawfully regulated. If laws are not enacted to regulate money, a minority of evil men will step in to usurp the control of money in order to enrich themselves and control the rest of the people. In the long history of the world, it has happened over and over again!

This ancient dynamic has, for ages, brought misery to the world at large because it makes the majority of men into the slaves of the few. The people who founded the United States understood the magnitude of the suffering that these horrible conditions created, so they became determined to forge a better way for everyone. This book will show you what that better way is and will give you examples of how, when followed, for brief periods in American history, the lot of Americans improved dramatically in a short length of time. This improvement inspired leaders of other nations to copy the American way, and so, the lives of their people improved, too. It is an inspiring story replete with heroic examples of inspiring men---some of them presidents. Hopefully, it will help you grow in understanding, simplify your life, make you happy and give you the hope of a wonderful future. It is meant to do all of these things and be fun, too!

You might say---we know about freedom. Everyone knows that Americans are free. You may believe this, but a close look at the facts will show you that this is not entirely true. We, as a nation, were founded as a free people, but, except for brief periods, we have actually been largely fooled into relinquishing much of our freedom, and so, we have suffered needlessly! And, we continue to suffer today because we have failed to protect our industry and we have failed to bring back the cherished institution of the National Bank---a bank that was, at one time, the driving force for national prosperity. It still could be such a force! During its two short charters, the Bank of the United States served the interests of the people. It was very different from the Federal Reserve Bank which now unlawfully regulates our finances and serves the interests of the empire. This book will show you how this private central bank gained so much power. It will also tell you about the patriotic presidents and will show you how they attempted to fight for the American system while imposters and rogues promoted its demise. It is an interesting and enlightening story. Have a fun-filled inspiring adventure while reading it.

Table of Contents

PART III   THE THIRD CENTURY

"History is not history unless it's the truth."

ABRAHAM LINCOLN, TO HIS LAW PARTNER,
WILLIAM HERNDON, 1856

1

ENGLAND'S FIRST CANAL

"An investment in knowledge pays the best interest."

Ben Franklin

As the representative of the British colonies in the New World, Ben Franklin sailed from Pennsylvania to England in 1757. He would spend nearly twenty years in Europe engaged with the republican circles of Gottfried Liebniz, planning the freedom of the world. When Franklin arrived in England, he found a backward country with no roads between cities and no canals. London was the center of a world trade empire and it was wealthy, but the countryside was horribly poor. Engaged in cottage-style manufacturing, the people could find a wider market for their goods only by transporting them by horseback to the city in the dry season after horse-beaten paths had become free of mud. All this was about to change with the arrival of Franklin in England.

George II was on the throne, but he ruled in the shadow of his illustrious grandmother, the Electress Sophie of Hanover. She had been the protector and friend of Gottfried Liebniz and his circle of republican allies in Germany. They had arranged for her succession to the English throne upon the death of the spirited Queen Anne. But, Sophie died too soon and her ignorant son, George I, duped tool of the imperial oligarchy, gained the throne. He died in 1727 and was succeeded by his equally ignorant son, George II who died in 1760. Then the notorious George III, who brought so much misery to the British colonies in the New World, gained the throne. His government, completely controlled by the empire, then stifled American commerce and manufacturing and discouraged western expansion on the American continent. Franklin was determined to create a thriving self-sufficient economy in America, but George III thought otherwise. So Franklin, determined to wait for an opportunity in America, instead took a circuitous route to the establishment of American industrial advance by targeting England for his first experiment in economic progress.

Franklin was then already famous in England and its government feared his republican leadership. Established in Europe as American counterintelligence agent, he corresponded with a wide network of intellectual giants. And, as a leading scientist himself, he had published the results of experiments that clarified the nature of electricity. He had also established the American Philosophical Society in Philadelphia, the first organization to unite the American colonies. In England, he would work covertly to plan and strengthen native industries in the outlying regions. The results were to be spectacular.

At the outset of his project, armed with appropriate letters of introduction from world-renowned scientists, Franklin approached local scientists and manufacturers in England to forge a study in electricity, metallurgy and steam power. With this collaboration in place, they then began to create what would become the industrial city of Manchester by connecting it strategically by canal to a source of cheap coal.

Here is how it happened: Franklin became acquainted with the Gilbert brothers, buckle manufacturers, who, in 1757, had been hired to manage the Duke of Bridgewater's lands and mines at Worsley. John Gilbert then convinced the Duke of Bridgewater, Francis Egerton, to cut a canal from his coal mines eastward to Manchester. Periodically flooded, the coal mines there were often shut down, so the idea of building a canal appealed to the young owner of the estate. Not only would the canal free the mine by diverting its flood waters, but the displaced water would operate the proposed canal. When completed, the canal would transport coal-laden barges to Manchester.

The young Duke had inherited the property on which the mines were located and he was an imaginative young guy who had studied engineering at the Lyons Academy. He had seen the canals of Holland and had closely inspected the great Languedoc Canal which crossed a large expanse of France. Leonardo da Vinci had both surveyed for this French canal and designed the locks for it. Then, Jean-Baptiste Colbert, finance minister to Louis XIV, built the canal in the late 1600s. The Duke had been impressed enough with the Languedoc Canal to agree to build a canal of his own and others after it. Preparations for the canal began in secret with an effort to buy up lands surrounding its proposed route. Progressive lobbying efforts directed at the English Parliament then later succeeded in establishing a law that compelled land-owners along the canal route to sell their land to Duke Francis. He then bought up the required land and eventually completed the project.

At one point, when Duke Francis had exhausted much of his funding, the Gilbert brothers sold bonds of low denomination to local merchants to raise more money to fund the canal. Profit-taking was deterred for many years, but eventually the Bridgewater Canal to Manchester became profitable. Duke Francis paid fair prices to landowner displaced of their land, hired many new coal workers at decent wages, and secured decent living conditions for them. The whole project was financed without the help of big banks.

When the canal was completed in 1761, it created an exodus of workers from the countryside to Manchester where jobs became plentiful in the new textile mills which sprang up there. And the canal supplied a cheap supply of Worsley coal to warm the houses of the people. Under a system of protective tariffs, the people then prospered and there was an elevation in the living standard. The success of the Bridgewater Canal inspired a partnership between the Duke, the Gilbert brothers, Josiah Wedgewood, Erasmus Darwin, and Matthew Boulton. They wanted to extend the canal on to Hull, Bristol and London. Erasmus Darwin publically promoted the canals by writing newspaper articles and pamphlets. In them, he extolled the virtues of foreign kings who had promoted commerce through extensive canal systems, some of which traversed very inhospitable country. He then asked the rhetorical question: "If they can do it, why can't we?"

After a bill secured the extension of the canal to Liverpool, Boulton, the Gilberts and the Duke of Bridgewater initiated canal-building projects all over England. Then, for fifty years, the people of England prospered. With access to coal from distant mines, Britain then converted from a wood-burning to a coal-burning economy. All this then made iron and steel manufacturing possible. But fifty years of tariff-protected prosperity and progress proved to be too much for the empire, so its agents organized a systematic lobbying of Parliament and succeeded in removing industry's protection. Then the economy of Manchester and other areas quickly declined to a level of horrible poverty. The enemy blamed the ensuing poverty on the selfishness of entrepreneurs in an attempt to hide the fact that they had themselves caused the collapse. Powerless and, largely unaware, the people were then sadly disenfranchised. We shall speak more about tariff protection during the course of our narrative. We shall also chronicle the sad story of disenfranchisement that has historically repeated itself, over and over again, with the abandonment of tariff protection. It is a story that only awareness can change.

1757-1761

Benjamin Franklin, Genius American Statesman, Diplomat And Inventor

Speaking of the United States republic that he had helped create, he once said: "I believe, further, that this is likely to be well-administered for a course of years, and can only end in despotism, as other forms have done before it, when the people shall become so corrupted as to need despotic government, being incapable of any other."

2

FRANCE AS
AMERICAN ALLY

"As among brute beasts, aquatic creatures have the
least intelligence, so among human beings,
the Venetians are the least just and the least
capable of humanity."

POPE PIUS II IN HIS *COMMENTARIES*

B y the 1770s, Franklin had become prominent in a world movement for self-government and scientific progress. While living in Europe, for intelligence gathering purposes, he had often visited the Earl of Shelburne at his Bowood estate. Shelburne chaired the powerful three-man committee that directed the British East India Company. That committee also included Francis Baring, owner of the powerful Baring Banking House. The East India Company, chartered by the Crown in 1600 as a private joint-stock company, had, by the late eighteenth century, risen to a pinnacle of power in Europe by usurping the British Crown government. As the company's chairman, Shelburne was the most influential of all the financier agents in Europe. The financial oligarchs that ran the East India Company derived their power from exclusive trade monopolies—monopolies over such things as raw materials, commodities, insurance, banking and shipping. The East India Company also employed, in its service, a military force larger than that of the British Crown. Through it, they maintained control over their fiefdoms in India and other parts of the world and operated above all notions of allegiance to any nation.

Shelburne was the "doge" of this financial empire. When he entertained at his luxurious estate, he would engage with Franklin in discussions over colonial rights in America because he knew prudence dictated that he make concessions to the Americans. They were too sophisticated to submit to the brute repression that the empire maintained in other parts of the world.

Soon the Americans declared their independence from Britain and won France over as their ally. With a long history of nation-state building, France had served as a model for the tender new republic being planned for the New World. In 1461, under the bold leadership of Louis XI, a dazzling French nation-state republic had emerged from the Dark Age ruins of enemy-orchestrated war and plague. Prior to the emergence of this republic, there were no better forms of society in the whole world. Before it, ninety-five percent of the world's population existed as slaves or serfs.

France prevailed as the world's foremost nation-state until 1789. Then, threatened by her growing alliance with the young United States, the always well-organized British imperialists, under the direction of Lord Shelburne, counter-attacked and destroyed French sovereignty through the orchestration of a bloody Jacobin revolt and ensuing Reign of Terror. It was followed by revolution and the British-orchestrated Napoleonic Wars.

Louis XI was born in the midst of the Dark Age Black Death Pandemic. In his youth, he received a classic education. Later, he came under the influence of the Renaissance-inspired system of schools called the Brotherhood of the Common Life where he learned about the nation-state teachings of Nicholas of Cusa. As King of France, he later used Cusa's ideas to bring startling prosperity to France.

The great Charlemagne, who had reigned in France from 724 until 814, had actually been the first Frenchman to challenge the enemy's maritime system of exploitation. He did so by developing inland waterways. The enemy routinely used port cities as operational bases for trade, leaving inland areas in a state of underdevelopment because they had no interest in elevating the standard of living of the people. Through enticing local rulers with money and power, agents of empire routinely corrupted these rulers, and they, in turn, allowed the empire to loot their people. But, Charlemagne loved his people and could not be corrupted, so he began to forge the beginnings of progress in France.

With this tradition as a backdrop, when Louis XI became king, France proved to be fertile ground for the emergence of a sovereign nation-state republic. At a distance away from Venice, she was also somewhat removed from the influence of the usurious financiers who had reorganized to revive their rule there after the collapse of their financial usury scheme had brought on the Dark Age.

During the first half of the fourteenth century, beginning with Edward III, France had been invaded by a series of English kings under the direction of the Venetians. These military invasions lasted for one-hundred and twenty years and became known as the Hundred Years War. During the Hundred Years War, the feudal lords of France fought not only the English, but they also fought one another. The Black Death Plague then compounded the effects of this continuous warfare and further decimated the population of

France. As a result, economic production came to a halt and private feudal armies roamed the countryside stealing all they could find, slaughtering the people. Whole towns and villages disappeared.

With France destroyed after the Hundred Years War, the 1420 Treaty of Troyes ceded French sovereignty to the English king, Henry V, so Louis' father, Charles VII, also known as the Dauphin, was deposed. However, by this time, the whole country had come under the influence of the Renaissance-inspired humanist ideas that were rapidly spreading throughout Europe, so great resistance to foreign occupation arose in France and this inspired a loyalty to the Dauphin.

In the midst of this French despair, Jeanne D'Arc emerged to lead the forces of French resistance. In a string of seemingly miraculous military victories, she prevailed over both the forces of foreign occupation and the degenerate French oligarchy that was promoting civil war. Her success led to the coronation of the Dauphin in Reims in 1429, and, even though she was executed by the English two years later, Joan, with her heroism, had began an unstoppable movement for complete French liberation.

Louis XI desired a war of total liberation from the Venetian empire, but his father, the Dauphin, initially hesitated, so this put father and son at odds. Then, in 1447, while Louis was waiting to take the reigns of power in France, his father exiled him to the region of Dauphiné, on the border of Switzerland. There, Louis came into contact with the widening circles of the Florentine Academy and the established schools of the Brotherhood of the Common Life. So, in Dauphiné, Louis began experimenting with economic reform by promoting invention. He also placed agriculture, industry and manufacturing under protection by implementing tariffs for the purpose of developing a home manufacturing base. The small towns in Dauphiné had been badly depopulated by disease and war and high feudal taxation had run many out of the country, especially the Jews, so Louis enticed them all to return by offering them exemption from taxation for a period of twenty years.

Then, in 1456, the Dauphin sent an invading army to Dauphiné and forced Louis to flee to Burgundy. There, Louis remained until his father died in 1461. Then he became King of France.

Louis reigned for only twenty years, but in that relatively short span of time, with all the training his humanist education had afforded him, he reformed France and made it a glorious example of the sovereign nation-state. His model for reform was the city-state of Florence. Louis was a great admirer of Cosimo de Medici. In Florence, the Medicis had established a family-run European-wide banking house to counter the influence of Venice by promoting credit for industry and infrastructure improvements. As a result, Florence emerged as a splendid and prosperous community. After he became King of France, Louis reunited his kingdom by applying the Florentine model for city-state building to his entire nation. In the process, he broke the hold that the banking oligarchs had maintained over his country.

During his reign, Louis furthered the work he had begun in Dauphiné by enacting labor laws to protect the rights of the foreign workers he enticed to come to his country. Engineers, printers, miners, farmers, foundry workers, weavers, dyers, cannon makers and military experts then poured into France. There they were given tools and homesteads with the stipulation that they would make the land productive. Then Louis abolished the right of the state to seize the land or property of foreign workers. He also allowed them to become his subjects if they wished. By establishing living provisions for the army, he removed all incentives for looting.

He also created sanitation standards, water management services and fire departments. He drained swamps to make the land productive and took a census, so that unclaimed land could be redistributed and once more become productive. An edict, issued in 1482, provided for the free circulation of grain, so that no one would go hungry. Military arsenals were built on waterways to keep the enemy at bay. Like the Medicis, Louis believed that banks should serve the nation, so he took steps to regulate them. In order to lure international merchants to trade in his country, he also regularly held major fairs in Lyon and removed restrictions on the international trade conducted there. This lured business away from the city of Genoa, the seat of the enemy's international trade.

Late in his life, Louis wrote a treatise called *The Rosebush of War* for his young son, so that he would have the necessary guidelines for continuing his policies. But, because his son was only thirteen when he acceded to the throne, he failed to continue his father's work. Development of the French nation-state under subsequent kings was also sporadic In order to curtail further progress, the empire then orchestrated the Thirty Years War. When it came to a close in 1648, the great Cardinal Jules Mazarin succeeded in negotiating the Peace of Paris and this peace vindicated the principles by which the nation-state could flourish. War between the France and the British-controlled Habsburgs of Spain, however, continued until 1659. Then, in France, Mazarin officially reinstated the policies of Cardinal Richilieu and this augmented the French Crown's power over the entrenched oligarchy.

Then when Louis XIV came to power in France, he wisely assumed the counsel of a very wise French minister, Jean-Baptist Colbert, and, in 1661, Colbert rescued France's ailing treasury. By 1665, Colbert had bolstered French manufacturing and trade by reestablishing the same principles Louis XI had used to promote French prosperity and independence. This once again made France Europe's leading power. In the next chapter, we shall learn about what later happened to the revived might of France.

1461-1665

3

ALL IN THE FAMILY

"Tyranny is so generally established in the rest of the world that the prospect of an asylum in America for those who love liberty gives general joy, and our case is esteemed the cause of all mankind........We are fighting for the dignity and happiness of human nature. Glorious it is for the Americans to be called by Providence to the post of honor."

BENJAMIN FRANKLIN, 1777

The Connecticut River Valley in New England was the scene in the 1730s of revivalist religious meetings called "great awakenings." Irrational and British-inspired in nature, they stood in contrast to the down to earth pragmatic religion of the region's original settlers. That religion had comforted the people by sustaining their reason. The "awakenings," on the other hand, had been designed to whip the people up into backward emotional frenzies. The leader of these revivalist frenzies was Jonathan Edwards, grandfather of Aaron Burr, one of the most notorious traitors in the history of the United States.

Aaron Burr came from an aristocratic family. Both his father and his grandfather were past presidents of Princeton University, which was then called the College of New Jersey. From 1769-1772, Burr was a student at that college and a classmate of James Madison, the future U.S. President. When colonial interests began to seriously clash with the British, Madison, along with other students, joined the patriotic Whig circle, but, Burr organized a student society in opposition to the Whigs. They spent their evenings in brothels and bars and their days belittling their scholarly counterparts.

Traditional historical accounts tell us that Burr was a daring soldier, but careful research into the background to his nefarious career shows that he was little more than a scheming traitor devoid of any of the character traits that give soldiers courage. Determined to gain entry into the ranks of the newly-formed Colonial army and feigning an air of patriotism, in the summer of 1775, Burr made a trip to Boston where that army was encamped outside the city. There he found General George Washington and presented him with a letter of recommendation he had indirectly obtained from John Hancock. Upon meeting Burr, Washington quickly sized him up and kicked him out of camp.

Yet undeterred, after the Battles of Lexington and Concord, Burr then set out on foot to join up with an expedition of soldiers headed for Quebec. Under the command of Colonel Benedict Arnold, these troops were going to join Montgomery's forces for an assault upon the city of Montreal. When he arrived at Arnold's camp, Burr pulled out Hancock's letter of recommendation, showed it to Arnold, and was accepted as a gentleman volunteer.

As the traditional story goes, Burr became a messenger for Colonel Arnold and went ahead to find General Montgomery who had already captured Montreal. Burr was to alert Montgomery to the approach of Arnold's forces. Burr's own account from after the battle maintains that, while traversing the hostile country, he came up with an "ingenious" idea. Using his best French, he went to a nearby British-allied Jesuit monastery, posed as a priest, and obtained safe passage through the dangerous British-infiltrated countryside to Montgomery's camp. Upon hearing Burr's story, Montgomery is said to have been so impressed with Burr that he made him an aide-de-camp. This allowed Burr to then become a double-agent spy.

The assault upon the British fort at Quebec, by the combined forces of Montgomery and Arnold, was supposed to be a surprise attack, but "somehow" the British learned of the plan. Biographers of Burr have long suspected that he secretly alerted the British. The consequences of Burr's treachery had a devastating effect on the American war effort because the British were able to use this fortification in Canada as a base for strategic operations throughout the ensuing War for Independence.

Even though large numbers of Americans were slaughtered in the horrible debacle at Quebec, Burr managed to emerge from the carnage as a hero. A buddy from his days at Princeton, also in the ranks of that army at the time, circulated a tale about Burr's "heroics" that made its way to the Continental Congress. Years later, a portrait of the diminutive Burr, entitled "Little Burr," was widely circulated in order to reinforce the suggestion that Burr was a war hero. In that painting, the nineteen-year-old Burr is shown under enemy fire before the walls of Quebec bearing the lifeless body of Montgomery back to his troops. In reality, though, Burr left Montgomery's body on the battlefield after British fire had killed the General.

Refusing to give up on the plan to seize the fort at Quebec, Arnold obtained reinforcements and remained encamped near Quebec during the following winter, but Burr managed to secure an appointment to Washington's staff in New York, so he deserted Arnold and took off for that destination. Arriving in New York with his reputation for heroics established, Burr then assumed his new job copying top-secret military documents. However, before long, General Washington fired him. Distrustful of Burr, it seems that Washington objected to letting him engage in top-secret work. Thereafter, whenever Burr managed to appear in Washington's circles, Washington would always get rid of him.

Successive military promotions allowed Burr to advance his enemy-sponsored mission. In the winter of 1776, when Washington's army was encamped, cold, hungry and ragged, in Valley Forge, Pennsylvania, Burr rendezvoused with British camps in New York, exchanging information and always managing to obtain supplies and clothing. When he would appear at Valley Forge arrayed in fine clothing, to deter suspicion, he would claim that he had just raided a British supply wagon. As he continued to move around the various colonial camps gathering intelligence information for the enemy, he was able to watch the movement of the troops on both sides. To mask his secret intentions, he even supplied information to the Continental army in order to make it possible for them to experience a victory at Harlem Heights in 1776. When his health began to suffer as a result of years of exposure on horseback, he resigned from the military to study law. In 1782, he married the widow of James Prevost, a high-ranking British military officer. Burr's treachery had only just begun.

War has long been a favorite tool of the enemy. The British have typically used it anywhere and anytime a nation begins to express its sovereignty by putting protective tariffs into place in order to develop a manufacturing base. We have previously documented how France, under the reign of Louis XIV, had begun to enjoy a profound prosperity because that king assumed the wise counsel of a famous French minister, Jean-Baptiste Colbert. Colbert had espoused the republican economic philosophy of post Renaissance circles in Europe that included Gottfried Leibniz of Germany, John Milton of England and both Mazarin and Richelieu of France. Through embracing these republican economic principles, France became a greater manufacturing power than Britain. So, to deter her progress and ruin her prosperity, Britain then successfully seduced Louis into waging another war with her and this successfully brought France back under empire control.

Later, under Louis XVI, by again returning to Colbert's protectionist policies, France revived and once again became economically strong and independent. So, in 1786, Swiss empire agent, Jacques Mallet du Pan, new cousin by marriage to Aaron Burr, launched a revival of the free trade propaganda that the empire's lackey, Adam Smith, had promoted in his 1776 volume, The Wealth of Nations. And another member of the other part of Burr's new family, Pierre Prevost, translated this work for wide-scale promotion among the French. Then the enemy began to pressure Louis XVI into signing a treaty with British Prime Minister Pitt that was designed to dismantle French protectionist measures.

At the same time, France was indebted to foreign credit, so international banking houses led by the Swiss refused her any more extensions on her credit. Louis was then faced with the prospects of a collapse of France's domestic economy, so he was forced to sign Pitt's treaty. Mercilessly, the British then moved in, dumped cheap manufactures on

France and cut off her supply of wool from Spain. This brought economic starvation to France.

Over the next few years, as more credit was withdrawn from the French economy, the King of France became further indebted to the forces of empire. Then he was forced to reinstate an old Swiss banker whom he had fired many times in the past. This finance minister, Jacques Necker, then pushed harsh austerity measures on the already suffering masses in France and this destabilized French society. Then he cunningly blamed France's sad plight on the king and queen by claiming that their wasteful spending had caused the demise of the French nation. Insulted, the king then once again fired Necker. But, by this time, British-infiltrated desperate French mobs had been aroused and they roamed the streets clamoring for Necker, saying that he was their only hope. Then these mobs stormed the Bastille and all of this planned anarchy led to the start of the British-orchestrated French Revolution.

Mallet du Pan, Aaron Burr's new kinsman, his dastardly work accomplished, then settled in London where he established spy networks for the British and, through them, maintained contact with his agents in France. From there, he also worked with the British to destroy the alliance France had made with the American colonies during their War for Independence. This is how the cruel forces of the British Empire, through subterfuge, succeeded in pressuring a not-too-bright sovereign French king into destroying his once-free French national economy. Our ensuing story, shall tell about the use of this economic ploy in repeated attempts by British oligarchs to rule through the destruction of sovereign economies.

1775-1786

4

THE COUSINS COLLABORATE

"How often are we forced to charge fortune with partiality towards the unjust."

HENRY CLAY

eanwhile, the Anglo-Swiss spy network that had been at work dismantling the system that had brought prosperity to France was keeping its eye on the British colonies in the New World. These colonies were fighting a war to throw off the British imperial system. Victory by the colonists would free them from the British Empire—free them to legalize the principle of the sovereign nation-state and make their new nation lawfully independent of foreign credit. This would curtail the potential for empire exploitation in the New World. In the British world view, American independence had to be prevented, so British-Swiss secret intelligence dispatched nineteen year-old Albert Gallatin to America to gather intelligence information. Conventional historical accounts have suppressed the details of his subversive political career, but a perusal of the true facts reveal that Gallatin worked at trying to dismantle the United States during the entire length of his long career.

Born in Geneva, Switzerland, in 1761, Gallatin came from a Swiss family with deep connections to the Mallet and Prevost families. These two intermarried families had, for centuries, served as financiers to the feudal nobility in Europe. **Gallatin's mission in America aimed to overthrow all efforts to establish a fiscally-independent republic** in the New World. The enemy viewed both Burr and Gallatin as integral to the success of their covert operations.

Gallatin arrived in Boston in 1780 and anxiously awaited the outcome of the plot by Benedict Arnold to affect the surrender of West Point. A carefully laid out enemy plan, had it succeeded, it would have effectively split the colonies in half making it easier for the British to re-establish control in America. The plan, of course, was ruined when Arnold's British accomplice, Major John André, was caught with secret West Point maps that Aaron Burr is thought to have supplied to him. With the plan foiled, Gallatin left Boston, headed for Canada and ended up hiding out in the northern woods for the duration of the war.

After the British surrender at Yorktown, Gallatin returned to Boston to briefly assume a post his handlers had obtained for him at Harvard University. Then, in 1786, he moved to a 60,000 acre estate in Fayette County, Pennsylvania, where he began working on a covert plan to prevent Pennsylvania from ratifying the new Constitution. Happily, his efforts were defeated when Pennsylvania's state convention ratified the Constitution by a two to one majority. Still he did not want to accept defeat, so he organized Tory opposition in the state and called for another convention. But that, too, proved futile, so he quickly integrated himself into Pennsylvania society and, beginning in 1790, became a Pennsylvania state legislator. In that position, he was very influential in drafting legislative bills favorable to the enemy. He also joined covertly with his cousin, Aaron Burr, to incite future armed insurrections against the new federal government.

As part of his program of support for the centralized federal government he had just organized, Alexander Hamilton suggested a national excise tax on liquor. Pennsylvania had had an excise tax on liquor since 1684, so Hamilton's proposal should have been non-controversial. Gallatin, however, wanted to prevent the development of a flourishing economy, so he sponsored a state legislative resolution to defeat the tax. And he personally vowed to harass anyone in Pennsylvania who became a tax collector.

In 1793, Gallatin's widening influence in Pennsylvania helped him secure an appointment as senator, but, suspicious of him, the Senate effectively introduced a motion to bar him from that body because he did not qualify under the nine years citizenship requirement. Using every moment to enemy advantage, before leaving office, Gallatin introduced a legislative measure intended to forestall Hamilton's economic initiatives by forcing him to submit a time-consuming detailed accounting of treasury operations. Meanwhile, in the Senate, Burr led an abortive fight to retain Gallatin, but it was unsuccessful, so Gallatin returned to Pennsylvania. Coincident with his return, rioting broke out in the western part of the state and in parts of Maryland and South Carolina, too. This Whiskey Rebellion, as it has come to be called, bore a striking similarity to the British-sponsored Jacobin-inspired mob scenes that had occurred five years earlier in Paris. Those riots had led to the French Revolution. Part of this British/Swiss family intelligence affair, they had been fomented by Gallatin's cousin, Jacques Necker, the British imperialist-allied finance minister Louis XVI was forced to rehire after pro-British factions in Europe destroyed France.

The Whiskey Rebellion destroyed life and property as armed mobs roamed the countryside burning homes to the ground. Federal marshalls were defied. The mob hero, Albert Gallatin, made periodic appearances to make token appeals for the restoration of order, but no real peace occurred until President Washington dispatched troops, under the command of Alexander Hamilton, to Pennsylvania, to put down the insurrection. At that time, it was well-known among political circles that Albert Gallatin incited the Whiskey Rebellion and that he was a menace to civil society. For many years afterwards, patriots lamented the fact that he was never shot when the opportunity had presented itself. With Gallatin in mind, an attempt was made to pass a constitutional amendment lengthening the number of years of citizenship required to hold congressional office, but it ended when its sponsor, Thomas Johnson, governor of Maryland, died suspiciously.

In 1795, Gallatin was elected to Congress. There were the usual attempts on the part of decent people to prevent him from taking office on the grounds that the election had occurred during an insurrection, but he made his way to Washington anyway! Incensed by this and tired of the relentless assault upon his economic program, Hamilton soon resigned from his post as treasury secretary, but continued to promote his program from outside formal office.

In Congress, Gallatin continued to work tirelessly at suppressing the development of the national economy. He also worked to downgrade the national military defenses. Senator Burr, on the other hand, never proposed a single bill or opened a debate in Congress during this whole time. He was busy snooping through the records of the State Department, trying to access secret information. It is said that he was trying to get something on Washington, but he never succeeded. With Hamilton, as we shall later see, he was more successful.

Concurrently, in New York, Aaron Burr developed a law practice and acquired a clientele made up of wealthy New York Tories and "white collar" criminal types. Soon he developed a reputation for securing not guilty verdicts by effectively confounding juries. It was during this time that Hamilton began to seriously dislike Burr. During the war, as chief aide to Washington, Hamilton had had opportunities to observe Burr and he'd become suspicious of him. Then, during the difficult process of ratifying the Constitution, Burr made the mistake of suggesting to Hamilton that he organize a coup in order to further his political ambitions. Devoted as he was to the lawful rule of government, Hamilton was horrified. He had spent his entire career working for the lawful establishment of the republic, so, of course, he did not consider coups legitimate. In later years, when Burr was seeking the presidency, Hamilton, in recounting this story to members of Congress, helped prevent Burr's election to that high office.

While Hamilton was busy penning his political masterpiece, *The Federalist Papers,* Burr was busy expanding his Tory clientele and his sphere of influence. As a result, beginning in 1790, he was appointed state attorney general of New York, then land commissioner and finally U.S. Senator. As land commissioner, he took advantage of laws passed by the New York Legislature that had been designed to promote the development of the western frontier by offering financial incentives to people willing to go there to work the land. But, Burr surmounted the law and instead sold public land at cheap prices, and with long-term credit, to wealthy Tories and groups of London financiers whose only intention was to sit on the land, block western expansion, and curtail development.

Eventually, Burr became a powerful New York political boss, and so, he was able to place a huge amount of upstate New York land into the hands of the British and their sympathizers. One of Burr's most notorious clients was a British intelligence agent he knew from his days in the army. His name was Captain Charles Wilkenson. Captured during the War for Independence, Wilkenson had been returned to Britain as part of a prisoner exchange. There he became the land management agent for a group of London financiers who, through Burr, had bought large tracts of land in northwestern New York. When Wilkenson returned to America and became naturalized, he engaged in covert intelligence work. Living on the land he managed for his London financiers—land that adjoined the still British-occupied forts of Oswego and Niagara—he set up an Indian courier mail system in order to send sealed British intelligence information down to enemy agents in Philadelphia. Then he got himself elected to the New York Legislature and immediately began to write legislation favorable to British land takeover interests. Burr aided him in this endeavor by circulating bribes from his large British land-holding client companies and he worked feverishly on behalf of British secret intelligence to prosecute anyone standing in the way of this land takeover scheme. As we shall see, Burr would later inaugurate other schemes aimed at facilitating British plans for re-colonization in the Americas.

1780-1794

5

THE GENIUS POLITICAL ECONOMIST

In describing the relationship between Jefferson and Madison, John Quincy Adams once said: "The mutual influence of those two mighty minds on each other is a phenomenon like the invisible and mysterious movements of the magnet in the physical world."

Statesmanship defines the life of Alexander Hamilton. With next to no training in politics, for the length of his illustrious career, Hamilton furthered the cause of freedom by continuously out-smarting the British every time they moved to subvert U.S. constitutional government. He did this more consistently than any other person of his time. The U.S. Constitution is Hamilton's legacy to the American people.

Hamilton was born on the West Indies island of Nevis in 1755. Fatherless at an early age, his mother personally took charge of his early education. When he showed signs of genius, his minister, too, took an early interest in him. By age twelve, he was managing a local store for an absentee American owner, one of many who conducted a bustling trade in the West Indies at that time. Then, at age fifteen, Hamilton wrote an account in a local newspaper, of a serious storm that had befallen the islands and it captured the attention of the whole town. As a result, a group of local people got together and sponsored an education for him in New York. Then, after two years of study at King's College, in New York, Hamilton became engaged locally with the people in a fight with King George III over the issue of "taxation without representation." He did this first by writing pamphlets and making speeches. Then, later he became a commissioned officer in the Continental army.

It was in Brooklyn, after the British army had laid a horrible defeat on American troops, that Hamilton, with his leadership initiative, captured the attention of General George Washington. Soon Washington appointed him as his aide-de-camp. So, at age twenty-one, Hamilton began a career writing for the Commanding General that would not stop until after Washington retired as president.

After several years serving as Washington's aide-de-camp, Hamilton became frustrated by his inability to get the Continental Congress to address the urgent needs of the army, so he sought release from his post. But, Washington highly valued Hamilton's services, so he refused to let him go. Hamilton then resigned. He wanted to become a fighting general. Later, knowing that Hamilton would ably fulfill that post, too, if given an opportunity, Washington put him in charge of a battalion at Yorktown. Quickly, Hamilton began drilling his men in full view of the British, yet they did not attack, so, in a nighttime fearless show of leadership, Hamilton led his men in a charge that succeeded in breaching the British defenses. Hamilton would demonstrate such heroics for the rest of his life. When he ascertained a righteous principle, he embraced it and never looked back.

At the end of the war, Washington returned to private life and would have been happy to have remained there, but not so with Hamilton. He had a mission to complete. During the war, he had been reading and researching, with the intention of formulating a plan for the permanent defeat of the enemy banking oligarchy in London, should there be a victory. The government that Hamilton envisioned would not go into debt to private bankers. It would issue its own credit based on its sovereign independence. This plan called for first permanently uniting the states.

As an able student of history, Hamilton knew that the loose affiliation of states that had united for the defeat of the enemy during the war needed to afterwards be formalized into a strong federal union, so that historical mistakes from the past could be averted. Loose affiliations like the Greek city-states, for example, had defeated the powerful Persian Empire when they had temporarily united, but because they failed to maintain that union, they were later crushed during the Peloponnesian War, never to be prosperous again. Hamilton urgently wanted to constitutionally sanction a formal union of the colonies in order to permanently maintain an American victory.

In 1783, John Adams and Ben Franklin were both away in Europe, so Hamilton stepped forward to lead the Continental Congress. He also collaborated with both John Jay and James Madison and personally wrote over half of eighty-five sophisticated essays justifying the formation of a strong centralized government. They were collected in a volume called *The Federalist Papers*. So persuasive were its arguments, that *The Federalist Papers* secured the ratification of the U.S. Constitution in 1787.

When Washington was inaugurated president in 1789, Hamilton became his choice for treasury secretary. At the request of Congress, Hamilton then published his first *Report on the Public Credit,* in order to tackle the issue of funding the public debt that had accrued from the war. The revolution had not only been funded by European banks, but it had also been funded through private donations made by wealthy army officers, some of whom had spent their entire fortunes on the purchase of supplies for their combat units. The states had also borrowed to fund the war and the promissory notes they had issued needed to be paid. **Hamilton wanted the federal government to assume both the foreign debt and the debts of the states through the legal issue of government credit.** He also **wanted it to independently fund industrial development through the same kind of credit, so that the usurious European bankers would never become involved in future U.S. affairs.** Under this plan, over time, he maintained, a prosperous government-sponsored economy would blossom. With its accrued prosperity, the new nation would then easily be able to pay off its debt. At the same time, it would develop a reputation for fiscal sovereignty. Towards that end, he proposed that old bonds be redeemed at face value and new higher-yielding U. S. bonds be issued for use as collateral for new loans. With Hamilton's insistence that a reasonably-sized public debt would be a "powerful cement of our union," Congress endorsed the plan to pay off the foreign debt, but refused to assume the debts of the states.

Before drafting his *Report on the Public Credit,* Hamilton had conferred with James Madison because he had been a key contributor to *The Federalist Papers.* So, Hamilton fully expected Madison to support his plan, but, Madison had also been in correspondence with Thomas Jefferson, who was in Paris from 1784 serving as foreign minister. There, Jefferson had come under the sway of radical enemy-inspired Jacobins and they had gained a grip over his mind. He had also given assurances to European bond holders that it would be safe for them to buy up old U.S. bonds, so, he began writing to Madison expressing doubts about Hamilton's plans to issue new government bonds based on the credit of the United States. Madison then opened congressional debate on the subject and, by his persuasive arguments, convinced the House to vote down Hamilton's plan for the federal assumption of state debt.

The major disagreement between Hamilton and Madison revolved around the fact that many soldiers had already sold their state bonds to speculators at rates below market value, giving speculators the opportunity to profit. Madison said that this was unfair, but Hamilton insisted that they had assumed a risk, and, therefore, they were entitled to profit from that risk. Hamilton was surprised by what he considered to be Madison's petty view of the matter because Madison was an accomplished scholar who had already concurred with Hamilton, when he had argued in *The Federalist Papers,* that "the end justifies the means." Hamilton couldn't, therefore, understand why Madison did not embrace assumption as the means for the establishment of a strong federal union.

The matter was not resolved until Jefferson returned to the U.S. to become secretary of state. The story, according to Jefferson, went something like this: Jefferson lived on the same street as Hamilton in New York City and, while walking down that street one day, he bumped into Hamilton. Because Hamilton looked distraught, Jefferson inquired into the reason for his distress and, after hearing Hamilton's side of the assumption argument, he invited Hamilton to join with him and Madison for dinner at his house. At that dinner, a compromise was forged that allowed for the passage of Hamilton's assumption bill in exchange for an agreement to locate the new U.S. capital on the banks of the Potomac in Virginia, a decision that pleased both Madison and Jefferson. As a result of this compromise, Congress narrowly passed the assumption bill and forged the beginning of a profound new prosperity.

Hamilton followed the passage of his successful assumption bill with a *Second Report on the Public Credit*, in December, 1789. It called for the establishment of a national bank, owned in part by the federal government, but, after a bill for its establishment was submitted to the House, Madison let loose a loud cry of objection to it, claiming that the bank was unconstitutional. There were no specific powers, he said, in the Constitution that allowed the government to form corporations and the bank was a corporation. A great debate then arose with Madison opposing the bill and Hamilton defending it. Then, on February 8, 1791, the bill passed. Jefferson and Attorney General Edmond Randolph then joined with Madison and they went straight to President Washington to urge that he veto it. But, Hamilton worked through the night, penning an argument for Washington's consideration, and, after the President read it, he quickly signed the bill. He had concurred with Hamilton's argument that the "manifest design and scope of the Constitution is to vest in Congress all the powers requisite to the effectual administration of the finances of the United States."

Disagreements between Hamilton and Jefferson continued to grow. With the death of old Ben Franklin in 1790, Jefferson seemed to have lost his original focus—a focus that had been very helpful in forging the Declaration of Independence. So, Jefferson went off on a track that played right into the enemy's hands by insisting that the country would be better off if it remained an agrarian nation. The enemy then quickly capitalized on Jefferson's new politics to inaugurate secret intelligence plans aimed at returning the new nation to its former colonial status.

In 1791, Washington went on a popular tour of the South to bolster the new Union. His administration was popular in large part due to the success of Hamilton's economic program. Spirits were high and so was credit. Hamilton was running the customs service and overseeing the revenue from tariffs. A system of protective tariffs had been put into place as a result of Hamilton's 1789 *Report on Manufactures.* In that report, he had insisted that the U. S. would never become a strong nation unless it developed its manufacturing capacity. And it would never develop that capacity unless the unrestricted flow of British goods into American ports was regulated. After the revolution, Britain had continued to enjoy a profitable trade with the U.S., while the U. S. had no market for her goods in Britain. At the first Congress, regulations on trade were discussed. After weeks of debate, a tariff schedule was designed for the purpose of running the government and paying off the national debt. It was Hamilton who largely guided the United States into this protective policy.

Hamilton was successful by any standards, but he did not rest. On the nation's behalf, when the capital was relocated to Philadelphia, in 1790, Hamilton moved there while his wife and family went to Albany for the summer. Meanwhile, enemy-agent Burr was determined to destroy Hamilton's nationalist agenda, so he sought a way to set Hamilton's career up for destruction. Having shrewdly assessed that Hamilton had a weakness for women, while Hamilton was away from his wife in Philadelphia, Burr sent his client, Maria Reynolds, to Hamilton's door one evening with a lying story of impoverishment. Touched by her story, Hamilton quickly drafted a personal check to her boarding house for payment of her back rent. Then he began an adulterous relationship with her that eventually erupted in a scandal. Burr had also involved Maria's already divorced husband in the scheme and he was an inveterate criminal, so he then blackmailed Hamilton. Not realizing that the man was actually divorced from his wife. Hamilton then agreed to pay him money—hush money, as it would be called today—in order to keep the scandal a secret. Then, when the man was later accused of stealing public funds, he implicated Hamilton in his scheme. Hamilton was then called for questioning before a private congressional board. In that interrogation, Hamilton admitted his adultery, but steadfastly denied any involvement in stealing public funds. Even though Hamilton eventually rebounded from the scandal, he remained concerned about his tarnished reputation. Without an honorable reputation, he knew that it would be difficult for him to promote his noble cause.

Hamilton served as treasury secretary until 1795, when he resigned to return to the practice of law in order to meet the pressing expenses of a growing family. He remained as an advisor to Washington, though, and even helped write his Farewell Address in 1797. Hamilton's financial policies had helped create the means for many to speculate and grow wealthy, but he never engaged in such practices himself. The pursuit of money held little appeal for him because he was, at heart, a true statesman and, as such, he considered it a conflict of interest for a public servant to make money from the public policies he worked to create.

Meanwhile, Jefferson launched a whispering campaign against Hamilton in order to bolster his own political career, so Hamilton came to view Jefferson as a demagogue who would say anything to gain votes. In the face of continued slander and innuendo, Hamilton plodded along, continuing to speak, both personally and publicly, for his principles—hoping, by his masterful arguments, to bring others to his point of view. But, the enemy was largely in control of public opinion, so they repeatedly caste Hamilton as a villain in the aristocratic tradition. As a result, Hamilton grew to hate public opinion. A working man from the start, Hamilton was no aristocrat. He was the representative of the true American, the new man—the man whose very opportunity he had helped to create by making government the agency of the people.

Hamilton continued to write for Washington and remained a leading member of the waning Federalist Party. He also engaged in charity work and became an intense abolitionist. Then, when John Adams became president, Jefferson became vice-president and his popularity began to rise. All the while, Hamilton had to persistently defend his character amidst continued attack. Many still suspected that he had stolen money from the treasury, so, in an attempt to completely vindicate himself, he decided to publish the scandalous letters he had exchanged with Maria Reynolds, exposing the details of their affair in the hope of squelching the lies his detractors were fabricating about him. Meanwhile Jefferson and Madison watched Hamilton's actions with horror. They did not understand how he could jeopardize his chances to become president with what they considered to be such self-destructive actions. During this whole time, Washington remained Hamilton's staunch supporter. He even sent Hamilton a beautiful silver bowl as a gift and accompanied it with a tender note of affection, expressing his respect for him and never mentioning the scandal.

Ever the patriot, in 1798, Hamilton was commissioned a major general in the army when war with France threatened the new nation. Napoleon had invaded Egypt and Syria and Hamilton couldn't help but wonder if he was contemplating an invasion of America, too. When President Adams declared his intent to not only make peace with France, but to also down-size the army, Hamilton was shocked.

Then, when Hamilton learned that Adams had been behind a recent round of attacks upon his character, he wrote a fifty page pamphlet deriding his actions at the Continental Congress. Washington died in 1799. In the role of fatherly protector, had he still been alive, he would probably have cautioned Hamilton about publishing the pamphlet and this might have stopped him. But, Washington was dead and Hamilton was feeling his loss, so, without Washington's calming presence, Hamilton became erratic. Meanwhile, in their attempt to defeat the republic, the enemy had become determined to promote Burr for president in the election of 1800. In the next chapter, we shall see what happened to that plan.

1775-1800

ALEXANDER HAMILTON
GENIUS AMERICAN STATESMAN AND FOUNDER OF THE
AMERICAN SYSTEM OF POLITICAL ECONOMY

In recognition of the working supremacy of natural law in the lives of human beings, Hamilton once said: "The sacred rights of mankind are not to be rummaged for among old parchments and musty records. They are written, as with a sunbeam, in the whole volume of human nature, by the hand of Divinity itself, and can never be erased or obscured by mortal power."

6

THE LEGACY OF
TAMMANY HALL

Speaking of Aaron Bur, Hamilton once said: "...This man has no principle, public or private... [H]is sole spring of action is an inordinate ambition as an individual...There is no means too atrocious [for him] to implement [and] no engagement that can be made with him can be depended upon."

As a U.S. Congressman, Albert Gallatin continued to try to legislatively defeat the interests of the new nation he had covertly been dispatched to destroy. In their developed opposition to a strong central government, both Jefferson and Madison then became impressed with Gallatin's efforts to downsize the government through a policy of spending austerity. So, with his eye on the presidential election of 1876, Jefferson asked Gallatin to draw up an elaborate study in order to "prove" that the U.S. debt was growing at an alarming rate. In the upcoming election, Gallatin then used these studies to promote a Jeffersonian campaign of wide-scale reduction in the size of the military. But, even with Gallatin's vigorous promotion of this campaign, the Jeffersonians were defeated in the 1796 election that made John Adams president. Madison's affiliation with the mistrusted Gallatin had, by then, become so obvious that his opponents accused him of being in league with Gallatin, so Madison resigned from Congress.

In 1799, Gallatin's cousin, Aaron Burr, powerful New York political boss, asked the state of New York for a charter that would permit him to organize the Manhattan Company. The city of New York, he said, needed fresh water in order to prevent the spread of water-borne diseases. On this basis, he succeeded in obtaining his charter. But, in forging this charter, he had other clandestine schemes in mind, so, he subtly included a clause in the contract that permitted "surplus capital to be employed in any way not inconsistent with the law." Thus, he created a way to use the investments his campaign for clean water had garnered to establish the Manhattan Bank. Over the years, he then used the Manhattan Bank to fund subversive political projects.

Burr's scam was eventually exposed, and so his reputation for crooked dealings grew. As a result, in 1799, he lost the election for New York state legislator in his home district. But, as the presidential election of 1800 drew near, Burr's cousin, Albert Gallatin, from his position as minority leader in the U.S. Congress, began to promote him for president.

Thomas Jefferson probably never knew the true nature of the relationship between Burr and Gallatin and their subversive intent to destroy the United States, but Alexander Hamilton knew that Burr posed a terrible threat to his country While Burr's election-rigging apparatus was busy running New York politics and Gallatin was busy exerting his influence in Pennsylvania, those who were supportive of Hamilton's program for constitutionally-sponsored industrial advance stayed silent. So, in 1799, Hamilton rose up to single-handedly fight the New England slave-trading merchant families who were backing Burr for president. He did this by writing letters to all leading Federalists. He also spoke, both publicly and privately, of the danger Burr posed to the U.S. experiment in fiscal freedom. He knew that Burr was striving for absolute power on behalf of the enemy and he fought him with all the energy he could muster. As a brave lone voice of protest, he stunned the nation with his passionate intensity. Fortunately, when the too-close-to-call presidential election of 1800 went to the House of Representatives to be decided, Hamilton, with his considerable influence in Congress, was able to mobilize the lingering nationalist faction there and Burr was defeated. This was fortuitous for the new nation, because had Burr been elected president, he might have, early on, succeeded in returning the country to the British. The silence of the Hamiltonians, however, continued after Jefferson became president, appointed Gallatin secretary of the treasury, and then proceeded to listen to his enemy council.

Aaron Burr would murder Alexander Hamilton in 1804, not, as some historical documentation insists, over a petty personal insult that Hamilton delivered to Burr. He murdered him because Hamilton had not only single-handedly defeated the enemy's plan to make Burr president, but he also defeated Burr's subsequent attempt to become governor of New York. Here is the background to what happened: Burr had established a sophisticated election-rigging apparatus in New York City that later became known as Tammany Hall. Originally founded in 1786 as a fraternal organization called the Tammany Society of New York, it soon evolved into a political machine that successfully established and promoted the politics of a new political party opposed to the pro-nationalist Federalist platform of Alexander Hamilton. There had, for a while, been treasonous ongoing enemy opposition to the nation-building efforts of Hamilton and Washington, but Burr's political machine organized these efforts and cunningly spread enemy propaganda, so that the masses were deceived into voting against their own interests. In the process, a new political party emerged that, over time, assumed several different names—Republicans,

Democratic-Republicans, and finally it was referred to as the Democratic Party. We have already spoken of Jefferson's inadvertent involvement in the formation of this new party.

Unfortunately, the Federalist Party, which had been the only party during the Washington-Adams years, had also changed. The enemy had infiltrated its ranks to seduce the New England merchant class into conspiring with the enemy. They, too, then began to work at bringing the nationalist platform down. In defense of his government plan, Alexander Hamilton then assumed personal responsibility for educating the public, but, he had to fight a constant uphill battle against Burr, who was organizing for the enemy. Hamilton knew that the future of his country was at stake. He disliked Jefferson because he had returned home from France preaching an acquired fear of centralized government and this had undermined the principles Hamilton had so thoughtfully and passionately embraced. Hamilton did not understand Jefferson's acquired confusion. He did know, however, that Jefferson would not sell out like Burr and plot to overturn the government, so in the election of 1800, Hamilton supported Jefferson for president.

In that election, there were three candidates—the incumbent John Adams, Jefferson and Burr, but no one garnered a majority of the electoral votes, so the election went to the House of Representatives to be decided. Jefferson and Burr had tied for the highest number of votes and many key Federalists were going to go with Burr out of an aversion they felt for Jefferson, but Hamilton unceasingly labored to convince them to vote for Jefferson by effectively speaking about the defective character of Burr. As a result, Hamilton out-maneuvered Burr in his bid for the presidency and secured the election of Jefferson after the House had cast thirty-six ballots.

Thomas Jefferson was sworn in as president in 1801 and Aaron Burr became vice president, but distrustful of Burr, Jefferson immediately isolated him. Seemingly unaware of the ongoing treasonous collaboration between Burr and Gallatin, however, Jefferson appointed Albert Gallatin secretary of the treasury and proceeded to take his advice seriously, and so, Gallatin set the new priorities for Jefferson's administration. Principle among them was debt reduction. Designed to contract the economy, create hardships, and promote disinformation, this treasonous program soon weakened the nation's defenses by putting an end to military spending. Spending on infrastructure stopped, too. As ship building was discontinued and docks, yards and fortifications were allowed to fall into disrepair, the enemy rejoiced. They wanted the United States to be weak—economically and militarily—because they were still unofficially committed to regaining "the Colonies" through their free trade policy.

Before he became vice-president, Burr was New York state attorney general. In that post, he had surrounded himself with British intelligence strategists and military officers. As a private attorney, he also worked for British special interests by aiding those seeking to curtail U.S. western development by buying up western land. Then, in 1804, Burr again sought to capture the presidency, but under the watchful eye of Hamilton, he failed again, so Jefferson was elected to a second term. Burr then sought the support of the enemy-infiltrated Federalist Party and, with their covert backing, ran as an independent candidate for governor of New York. But in this election, Hamilton again spoke out against Burr, making it clear that Burr was involved in Tory plans to menace the republic.

He also characterized him as a dangerous man who could not be trusted with the reins of government. Angered by Hamilton's incessant and effective opposition to every political move he made, Burr then knew that he would never be elected to high political office as long as Hamilton was alive, so he challenged Hamilton to a duel with the intention of murdering him.

Hamilton had lost his favorite son, Phillip in a duel in 1801 when Phillip had stepped forward to defend his father's honor and this loss had devastated the family. Hamilton's daughter even had a nervous breakdown over it—a breakdown from which she never recovered. So Hamilton at first tried to mitigate the situation by making a feigned apology to Burr, but testy exchanges between the two men continued until a duel was arranged. In that duel, Hamilton was shot dead when his gun is said to have misfired. In the spirit of a fallen hero, the public mourned the death of Hamilton at a huge funeral in New York City, while Burr escaped as a wanted man. Burr had finally succeeding in silencing the great American patriot, Alexander Hamilton. By ending the life of Hamilton, however, he had also ended his own political career, so, on behalf of the enemy, he took on a bigger challenge. Read on to learn more about it.

1795-1804

7

THE WESTERN CONSPIRACY

"Great souls care little for small morals."

Aaron Burr

As we have seen, the early establishment of the new United States was fraught with difficulties. Despite this, though, President George Washington did get the nation off to a good start by sanctioning the economic policies of Alexander Hamilton. He also strengthened the nation's military defenses, built forts and lighthouses all over the country, and forged the beginning of a coast guard.

From as far back as the earliest settlement in Massachusetts, that colony harbored loyalists who sympathized with the Crown, but, as time went on, they became more numerous. So Cotton Mather sent the young Ben Franklin to Philadelphia, in 1723, to coordinate patriot resistance from that city. A revolution later ensued, but even after her defeat in that war, Britain was still committed to warring against her former subjects, so she characteristically aligned herself on both sides of the U.S. political landscape. On one side, the tight-knit Boston Brahmin Tories, unable to change the politics of the high Federalists aligned with Hamilton, then began to officially organize with the intention of conspiring with the enemy. Judge John Lowell, the early acknowledged leader of these pro-British forces, had retreated from public view when the revolution broke out only to re-emerge in 1782, to help organize British covert operations. Many other leading Tories had either fought on behalf of the British during the war or had fled the country to also later return to serve British interests.

Publicly they attacked Jefferson's new democracy, but, at the same time, they secretly began to covertly hijack that new political party, too. As a result, these Tories eventually came to dominate both the Federalist Party of Alexander Hamilton and the Jeffersonian Party. By infiltrating both parties from the top down, they planned to destroy the founding platform of government-sponsored industrialization that Hamilton had so thoughtfully forged. Under the premise that southern slaveholders were dominating the government and deliberately averting their commercial interests, they then organized as the Essex Junto and quickly swung into action with the intention of forging a separate northern confederacy dedicated to serving British interests. Besides Judge John Lowell, this northern Tory cabal included Senator George Cabot, former U.S. Secretary of State Timothy Pickering, merchant Steven Higginson, Massachusetts Supreme Court Justice, Theophilus Parsons, Aaron Burr's brother-in-law, Tapping Reeve of Connecticut and Judge Lowell's son, John "the Rebel" Lowell.

In December of 1803, Timothy Pickering wrote a letter to Richard Peters calling for a separation of the northern U.S. states from the slaveholding southern states. The British province of Canada was to be included in the proposed northern confederacy. This early conspiracy did not oppose slavery. They suggested only that plantation interests be separated from northern shipping interests. All along, the purposeful intent of the scheme included the creation of a separate southern plantation colony controlled by the British. Slavery, after all, served British commerce and, aligned with the British, these conspirators never intended to interfere in that commerce.

In January, 1804, Pickering also wrote to George Cabot, the head of the Lowell/ Cabot/ Higginson inter-married family gang. In that letter, he admitted that he did not believe in the "practicality of a long-continued union." During that same year, Pickering and others had enlisted Burr to run for governor of New York, so that they would have a British agent in the seat of government in New York when their proposed northern confederacy materialized. Only the efforts of Hamilton defeated that enemy plan.

At the same time that Burr was running for governor of New York, he wrote British ambassador to the U.S., Anthony Merry, a letter in which he offered to help the Queen of England forge a separation of the western U.S. from the established eastern seaboard. So, Merry, in turn, wrote the Queen a letter informing her of this offer. Based on ideas already formulated in the British Workman Memorandum, Burr then began laying plans for his Western Conspiracy.

The Workman Memorandum surfaced in 1800. Cloaked in the garb of an attack upon the Spanish colonies in the Americas, its author, James Workman proposed a scheme for reviving the life of Britain's trade empire. Except for a brief pause in the 1780s, Britain had been fighting a quarter-century long war with France for the purpose of deterring her development. But, by 1790, the French national reformer, Lazare Carnot, had risen to a position of influence in France and he once more rescued her economy. Then, he turned French fighting forces upon Europe with the intention of dismantling the old European feudalistic trade barriers that the empire had systematically imposed in order to serve her trade interests.

Workman submitted an outline of this plan to Henry Dundas, British Minister of War, who delighted in it suggestions and speedily had the memorandum approved. Then he dispatched Workman to South Carolina to publish a report for consideration by those in the Jefferson administration who might be enticed to help with his plan to "liberate the Spanish colonies." The Workman document was also printed in the *Charleston Courier,* where it was probably spotted by Burr's daughter, who lived in that city, and she undoubtedly told her father of it.

As part of this plan, the Workman Memorandum proposed attacks upon both Florida and the newly acquired Louisiana Territory. Louisiana was an immense tropical area of almost one million square miles and it contained the strategic port of New Orleans—-a port that the British coveted. Overjoyed by the opportunity that the Workman project presented, Burr then began to organize a mercenary army with the intention of seizing both U.S. western territory and Mexico in order to forge this British-aligned southern empire in the New World. When it arrived in New Orleans, Burr's mercenary army was to be backed up by British naval convoys sent west.

With the defeat of the Essex Junto plan to have Burr elected governor of New York, to aid the enemy's persistent plan to recapture their old colonies, Treasury Secretary Gallatin then counseled Jefferson to appoint enemy agents to key posts in the Louisiana Territory. These appointees then joined with other pro-British forces that Burr had already installed there. James Workman went there, too, and had himself appointed as a judge of New Orleans County. Edward Livingston, from New York, was appointed district attorney. From their posts in Louisiana, both Workman and Livingston intended to organize a Mexican Association that would wait for the arrival of Burr's mercenary army. In New Orleans, that army would join with the Mexican Association to raise the Mexican standard there. With the aid of British convoys sent west, a huge British-controlled Louisiana-Mexico "buffer" state on the southern border of the United States would then be established as a center for the expansion of the planned British-controlled tropical plantation system.

Andrew Jackson, the future President of the United States, who would be elected to that high office through the efforts of Burr's New York political machine, was aiding Burr and his mercenary army by supplying them with boats. But, in 1806, Burr's expedition was foiled because Joseph Hamilton Daveiss, district attorney from Kentucky, wrote to President Jefferson about the plot and called for him to investigate the matter. Then, James Wilkenson, Commanding General of the United States Army and a Mexican Association operative, panicked, turned against Burr, and had Burr, along with several co-conspirators, arrested. Edward Livingston, who had been installed as grand master of the Louisiana Masonic Lodge then managed to have himself and most of the conspirators exonerated. Burr was tried for this crime, but was acquitted due to insufficient evidence. Andrew Jackson, too, managed to evade charges because he had also warned authorities of Burr's plot.

Though acquitted of any crime, Burr was hated. Mobs tried to lynch him and several states wanted to prosecute him for treason, so he made his way to New York in disguise. There he received cash advances from John Astor, and fled to the British safe-haven of Nova Scotia. In Nova Scotia, he was greeted by his nephew-by-marriage, Sir George

Prevost, who gave him letters of recommendation and a warm send-off to Britain. While exiled in Britain, Burr kept a diary of his life there among the British elite. That diary chronicles a life of debauchery and opium use. Although suppressed for nearly a century, it stands today as a testimony to the British aristocratic life-style of his time. It also stands in stark contrast to the diary of the statesman, John Quincy Adams. In later chapters, we shall examine the distinguished career of John Quincy Adams

1793-1807

8

THE WAR HAWKS

"A nation can survive its fools, and even the ambitious. But it cannot survive treason from within. An
enemy at the gate is less formidable, for he is known
and carries his banner openly. But the traitor moves
against those within the gate freely,...his sly whis-
pers heard in the very halls of government itself... he
speaks in accents familiar to his victims and he wears
their face and their arguments."

Marcus Tullius Cicero,
Roman philosopher and statesman, 106 B.C.-43 B.C.

John Quincy Adams knew of the Essex Junto conspiracy to dismantle the United States. In fact, it was his father who had actually dubbed that cabal of conspirators the Essex Junto. In 1804, Quincy Adams asked President Jefferson for an urgent confidential meeting. Here is what he told the President: New England traitors, members of his own defunct Federalist Party, were organizing to bring about a secession of the New England States from the Union. A group of leading merchant and banking families had recently organized into an association, the Essex Junto, and they were working with British secret intelligence to effect this separation. While ostensibly appearing to be motivated by opposition to the President's recent Embargo Act, which prohibited U.S. vessels from trade with Britain, they had really become determined to have a British colony in America.

Nearly all of the family members of the Essex Junto were born north of Boston in Essex County, Massachusetts. These families had a complete devotion to Britain, its aristocratic life-style and the bountiful wealth its system of colonial exploitation had created. In alliance with British secret intelligence, they had become complicit with British efforts to effect a separation of their section from the rest of the country. These secessionists were loosely connected to Tammany Hall, the political machine that Aaron Burr had organized in New York City and they wished to make New York the eventual center for the secession. They had the backing of powerful financier families in London, Venice and Geneva. In 1800, they had met with near success in promoting Burr for president, but, as we have seen, the single-handed efforts of Alexander Hamilton prevented this from happening. In the winter of 1803-1804, after Burr's failure to capture the presidency, they secretly formulated a plan to promote him for governor of New York, but Hamilton foiled that, too. When John Quincy Adams decided to alert Jefferson to these new developments in New England, powerful new nationalist sentiments were about to be revived.

By 1809, the Whigs had grown tired of the rampant British-inspired austerity of the Jefferson administration, so Henry Clay recruited new young men and also some Revolutionary War veterans to run for Congress. As speaker of the House of Representatives, he then summoned Congress to put an end, once and for all, to British terrorism on the seas by calling for war with Britain.

Madison had been newly elected as president, but his administration was seriously infiltrated by the enemy. In fact, Treasury Secretary Albert Gallatin, held so much power over Madison that he virtually controlled his presidency and he continued to call for government austerity. But Clay had had enough of austerity, so he called upon the newly formed Whig-dominated Congress to rebuild the nation's military defenses. Then he brought political pressure to bear on Madison to comply with Congress and declare war. But, even though he knew of the Essex Junto's affiliation with British secret intelligence, Madison wavered. So, to nudge him into declaring war, Clay told him that if he did not get behind the "War Hawks," as Clay and his associates were called, they would look for a new candidate for president in the next election. Clay's pressure proved to be enough to get Madison to act, so war against Britain was declared in 1812.

We have previously noted that Aaron Burr fled to Britain after his involvement in the Western Conspiracy was exposed. There he circulated among British intelligence circles and befriended Jeremy Bentham, the darling of Lord Shelburne. Shelburne had given Bentham an apartment at his Bowood estate, so that he could pen a treatise that would promote the radical British propaganda that successfully established the British philosophy of liberalism. The popularity of Bentham's writings helped place him in the center of the newly-formed British foreign office. This philosophy, created on behalf of the empire, rejected any distinction between man and the beasts. Rather, it suggested that man's only motivation in life was rooted in the avoidance of pain and the seeking of pleasure. The Christian notion that man can achieve immortality through selflessly devoting himself to helping elevate the condition of man upon the planet had been intentionally attacked.

After his stint in Britain, Burr, still focused upon destroying the U.S., traveled widely throughout Europe. Finally he arrived in Paris. There among secret intelligence circles, he suggested that France drive the U.S. into a war with Britain, so that France, with Burr's help, could seize Canada, Florida, Cuba and Mexico. When this diplomacy failed, he returned to Boston in disguise just as the U.S. war with Britain was about to break out. Directly, he proceeded to Harvard University, then a hotbed of political insurrection, and went straight to its president to secure funds from Harvard's treasury. Armed with this financing, he then returned to New York. Still under indictment in several states for the murder of Alexander Hamilton, he had his daughter petition the help of both Gallatin and Dolley Madison and they secured his release from these indictments. From the time he returned to the United States, on behalf of the British, Burr arduously worked at getting a British puppet in the presidency. His chosen candidate was Andrew Jackson, a man who had ably demonstrated his commitment to the enemy during the days of his collaboration with Burr in the Western Conspiracy.

In 1807, under the guise of a war being waged against Napoleon, but really as an incentive for war with the U.S, Britain's Privy Council ordered U.S. ships to cease trading with France or any of her colonies. The British navy then began to impress American sailors into her service under the pretense that American ships were violating this order. The British navy had long functioned as an instrument of piracy. More than half of its sailors were foreigners who had been captured at sea. The British were also accustomed to using press gangs to drag men off her streets at home to quarter them on British ships where they were forced to live like animals and work at plundering the ships of other nations. By 1812 the British had kidnapped thousands of American sailors, so this eventually sparked a war with the U.S.

The first six months of that war with Britain went badly. Enemy espionage in the United States was very well-organized, and so, on several occasions, the British were alerted of American military plans. And, of course, with Burr's Boston agent and personal physician, Dr. William Eustis, appointed as secretary of war, he could and did reject plans to curb the enemy. Even more horrifying, however, was the fact that bond brokers in Boston, in league with the British in Canada, sold high-yielding British war bonds to "Americans" in many cities and this lent financial support to the enemy. But the treason did not stop there. From New England, the Essex Junto aided the British by supplying them with food and war materials. And, whenever they could, they tried to block the recruitment of American troops and prevent the purchase of U.S. war bonds. It wasn't until the U.S. Treasury was nearly bankrupt, that pressure was brought to bear upon Gallatin to do something about all this treason, but all he did was make underhanded deals with his British-allied banking contacts.

Meanwhile, the Essex Junto continued to plot and, in 1814, they began calling for a convention to be held in Hartford, Connecticut. At this Hartford Convention, they intended to formulate their grievances into a more formal policy of regional difference. But before this convention could be convened, another American patriot rose to the defense of his country. His name was Matthew Carey and his impact on the early nation was immense. Originally an Irish patriot, he fled to Paris, in 1779, to enter into a close collaboration with Benjamin Franklin who was organizing American counterintelligence efforts there during the American War for Independence. From Paris, Carey immigrated to Philadelphia to join the American secret intelligence network created by Franklin. A brilliant economist, he also engaged with Franklin in many scientific and technological projects.

In 1814, just as the Hartford Convention was about to convene, Carey made a last ditch attempt to save the Union, by publishing *The Olive Branch,* an earnest bi-partisan pitch designed to circumvent differences in both parties by making an appeal for the restoration of national solidarity. In the process, he exposed the traitorous motives of the Hartford Convention. This exposure curtailed the convention, and so the New England conspirators retreated to secrecy. They would not renew their treasonous public efforts at disunion until the 1830s when the nullification movement arose in South Carolina. **Their persistent plotting was not the result of petty regional differences, as traditional history claims, but, was part of a trans-Atlantic enemy conspiracy orchestrated to prevent the success of the American experiment in financial sovereignty.** We have already mentioned some of the early correspondences between northern pro-British traitors that document early efforts to break up the Union.

After the defeat of the British in the War of 1812 or the Second War for Independence, as it was called back then, the War Hawks began pushing for a revival of the economic principles of Alexander Hamilton which had been abandoned under the twelve-year "reign" of Albert Gallatin as secretary of the treasury. In the years leading up to the war, U.S. trade with Britain had been so adversely affected, that many goods had to be manufactured at home. A dramatic prosperity resulted. Then, after the war, tariffs were lowered and the people quickly began to suffer again. The Whigs then began to promote a new campaign of anti-imperialism. A new push for government-sponsored infrastructure projects was also revived. The common people were widely supportive of these projects. From retirement, Jefferson even gave his support to the program. After the war, the British tried to dump cheap goods on the country—even going so far as to incur losses—but by then both North and South had had a taste of a protected economy, so the whole country began to unite under a revived protectionist agenda.

Then Henry Clay of Kentucky, John C. Calhoun and William Lowndes, both of South Carolina, all fought for the re-chartering of the second Bank of the United States which, under the tutelage of Albert Gallatin, had been closed in 1811. Five years later, before he left office, President Madison then presided over its re-chartering. Mathew Carey also wrote tirelessly about the American System of Political Economy in order to educate the public. He also directly attacked British free trade propaganda when the enemy purposely revived Adam Smith's 1776 volume, <u>Wealth of Nations</u> in an attempt to internationally promote free trade after the war.

President James Monroe supported protective tariff legislation. He also authorized the military to design canals and railroads. Iron forges were also built in both the South and in the West. With this new push for industrialization, even the South's psychological investment in the plantation system was abandoned. Then, the Missouri Compromise of 1820 was passed in order to restrict the spread of slavery westward. With all the prosperity that industrialization was about to forge, the plantation system was poised to die out.

When the Bank of the United States was re-chartered in 1816, the nationalist, Nicholas Biddle, was appointed as its president and he aided American nationalism. Through a ruling by the Supreme Court, the government also took express control of interstate commerce, thus preventing any monopoly in shipping. Then, the Marquis de Lafayette returned to the United States for a triumphal two-year tour to set the mood for the election of the patriotic president, John Quincy Adams, in 1824. As president, Quincy Adams continued to embrace the nationalist vision for the South—a vision of progressive buildup of that regional economy. Under his sponsorship, the first U.S. railroad was chartered in South Carolina.

While he was president, John Quincy-Adams spoke to the American people about their pacifist heritage and established in their minds the fact that the United States had been organized under a mandate to scientifically advance her culture. He also said that she had a duty to spread her system throughout the world, so he began planning for the export of the American system to South America. Toward that end, he sent U.S. emissaries to an organized fraternal meeting of American republics, called the Congress of Panama.

Unfortunately, at the same time, British agents in the U.S. were busy organizing for the election of an enemy puppet-president and they succeeded in getting Andrew Jackson elected in 1828. With his election, nationalism then experienced a defeat. Had it survived, the U.S. might have early on succeeded in exporting its prosperity to South America. Instead, though, a string of British-style treasonous presidents followed, and they successfully promoted the enemy's agenda by abandoning protectionism. After they re-established free trade as U.S. policy, slavery then became, not only the leading feature of the U.S. economy, but the center of British world trade. Then, with the Congress dominated by slave-owner politicians, the South's prospects for industrialization vanished and the notion of eliminating slavery was abandoned altogether. Not until Lincoln became president, in 1861, did protectionism and constitutional government again revive.

1804-1828

9

A GREAT DIPLOMAT FORMULATES THE MONROE DOCTRINE

"America does not go abroad in search of
monsters to destroy."

JOHN QUINCY ADAMS,
FROM A FOURTH OF JULY SPEECH GIVEN IN 1821

John Quincy Adams, with Henry Clay, among others, had negotiated a satisfactory peace treaty in Ghent at the conclusion of the War of 1812. With exceptional skill, as chief negotiator, Quincy Adams out-maneuvered the British in their attempt to cut off parts of New England from the rest of the country. He also prevented the realization of their plan to shut down U.S. western expansion by an attempt to extend the border of Canada down to the Ohio River.

Following the peace, Philadelphia publisher and ally of Henry Clay, Matthew Carey, wrote about the need for technology development and westward expansion and this helped spark a new fervor of nationalism at home. Then, the nationalist, James Monroe, was elected president and he embraced tariff protection. As Monroe's secretary of state, John Quincy Adams then delivered a Fourth of July address that was meant to prepare the public for the Monroe Doctrine about to be released. In that speech, he asked the rhetorical question: "What has America done for the benefit of mankind? Then he proceeded to answer his question by saying: "With the same voice that spoke herself into existence as a nation....America, in the assembly of nations, since her admission among them, has invariably... held forth...the hand of honest friendship, of equal freedom, of generous reciprocity." Then, after reciting the Declaration of Independence in full, he called that document "the world's first declaration of legitimate civil government—the cornerstone of a new fabric, destined to cover the surface of the globe." In a stroke, he said, it "demolished the lawfulness of all governments founded upon conquest and swept away the rubbish of accumulated centuries of servitude."

When traitorous New England Federalists criticized his speech by calling it tasteless, John Quincy Adams wrote a letter to his friend, Edward Everett, and proudly proclaimed that, in that speech, he had demonstrated that the system of colonial establishments could never fulfill the great object of civil society. He also said that he looked forward to the liberation of South America and the downfall of the empire's hold in India. Boldly, he then proclaimed that colonial establishments were "mighty engines of wrong and that in the process of social improvement, it would be the duty of the human family to abolish them."

John Quincy Adams, as we shall see, had a classic education that included diplomatic travel that began when he was only a child. While accompanying his father and others on missions to Europe, he had the opportunity to mingle with Ben Franklin. His early diplomatic education spanned decades and was so thorough that, over the years, it was impossible for him to fall for British schemes aimed at subverting the United States.

During the whole month of November, in 1823, Monroe's cabinet was occupied with discussions of American foreign policy. In Europe, the prevailing imperialist powers had entered into a "holy alliance" designed to stamp out all European efforts to substitute republican government for the imperialist system and they were considering extending their tyranny to South America. In order to give imperialism a badly needed push there, both Spain and France had proposed this European alliance in order that Spain might recapture her lost American colonies and thereby "adjust" the affairs of the newly emerged republics of South America. Shrewdly, in order to entice the U.S. into an alliance with her, Britain then opposed this scheme by insisting that Spain could never recover her lost colonies.

Monroe consulted with both of the former presidents, Jefferson and Madison, about this situation and they urged the formation of the alliance with Britain. But the aware Quincy Adams dissented and, as a lone voice of protest, convinced Monroe not to align himself with the long-standing enemy of the U.S. He did not trust her. As he colorfully said, he did not favor "coming in as a cock boat in the wake of the British man of war." He knew that forming an alliance with Britain would mean stepping into a trap. He also knew that an alliance was unnecessary because Britain would continue to overtly oppose European intervention in South America anyway and Spain and France would take no action without her.

John Quincy Adams had come down just as hard on America's long-standing friend, Russia, when, in 1821, Tsar Peter the Great sent vessels to the Pacific Northwest coast and then warned all other vessels not to come within one hundred miles of any part of the coast north of the fifty-first parallel. The Tsar declared that Russia had a right to that area based on the fact that she had sent a few settlers there in the eighteenth century. But,

Secretary of State Adams quickly took a stand and announced that the U.S. would contest the "right" of Russia to any territory established in North America. American continents, he said, were no longer "subjects for any new colonial establishments." The remainder of both American continents, he said, "must, henceforth, be left to the management of American hands."

With all his acquired diplomatic prowess, when John Quincy Adams became president in 1825, he continued to passionately speak to his people about their heritage. Seven years of revolution, he said, had freed the people of the United States to declare a rebirth of the civilized world. By embracing the principles sanctioned in her Constitution, the U.S. was destined to forge an elevation in the moral standards of man. This would result, he said, in peaceful world coexistence. It would also render conquest by war obsolete and destroy indentured servitude.

As we shall see, beginning in the 1830s, threatened by the moral strength of John Quincy Adams, the enemy retaliated by launching a covert scheme to divide the country over the issue of slavery. All but a few leaders were deceived. South Carolina would be the nexus for the establishment of British southern operations. That colony had been established on a much different footing than the Massachusetts Bay Colony, the colony that had given rise to John Quincy Adams, Ben Franklin and other far-sighted patriots. In following chapters, we shall learn more about the genius American nationalist, John Quincy Adams.

1821-1830

10

AMERICA PLANS
FOR A CANAL

"The day will come when we shall see Erie water
flowing into the Hudson."

DeWitt Clinton,
when he was elected Governor of New York in 1817

As we have seen, in order to advance industrial development on the American
continent, Franklin wanted to build a system of canals. From as early as 1724,
he had been promoting the construction of a canal in New York to connect the
Hudson River with Lake Erie. But American colonists became engaged in a political
battle with George III for their sovereign rights as free Englishmen, so Franklin postponed
the promotion of this project and instead focused on building canals in England.

The initial impetus for building the New York canal can be traced to a Scottish-born
emigrant to Philadelphia. His name was Cadwallader Colden and he had been active in
London nationalist circles during the early part of the eighteenth century. There, during
the reign of Queen Anne, he had made contact with Franklin and other members of the
broader republican circles in Europe and he became a key collaborator with Franklin for
scientific advance.

In 1754, Franklin attended a scientific meeting of Colden's New York Albany
Congress. That congress had been organized to bolster the world's latest scientific advances
because false science was making a great headway in Europe. Armed with the latest scientific knowledge, after the conference, Franklin returned to England to spear-head the

beginning of the industrial revolution there. So, we might say that plans for canal-building in America actually pre-dated those in England, even though England's canals were
built first. We have already documented the rise of England's canals in an earlier chapter.

Thought on the actual construction of the Erie Canal can be traced back to the days of
the Revolutionary War. In 1777, General James Clinton and General Israel Putnam sent
a message to George Washington, who was encamped at Valley Forge, about the construction of a proposed fort on the bluffs over-hanging the Hudson River at West Point. In
1778, after the fort had been constructed, Washington made a visit to West Point where
a newly formed engineering school was operating.

People knew, for a long time, that it was cheaper and easier to move freight by water
than by land. So, after the revolution, a private company engaged in building small canals
around the falls in the James River in Virginia, another along the Connecticut River in
Massachusetts and others in Pennsylvania. Washington then traveled to New York to
join Elkanah Watson for an expedition to the Hudson River area where a survey for the
best route for a much larger New York canal was underway. After publishing the findings of this survey in a pamphlet, Watson then went into business with Philip Schuyler
to privately finance and build this canal. Eventually, however, they ran out of money. So,
in 1794, DeWitt Clinton, head of the New York State Board of Regents, petitioned the
New York State Legislature for funding and obtained it. The company then continued to
build the canal. DeWitt Clinton was sure that it would make New York City the greatest
city in America.

Meanwhile, by organizing the enemy anti-Federalist vote, Aaron Burr and his solidly
entrenched New York political machine engaged in a long protracted fight to sabotage all
efforts at canal-building in the state of New York. Then, when Thomas Jefferson became
president in 1800, he appointed enemy-agent, Albert Gallatin, secretary of the treasury
and Gallatin orchestrated a contraction of the federal budget. Over the years, Gallatin's
long tenure as treasury secretary created government austerity, so Hamilton's national policy of extending federal credit for infrastructure projects was largely abandoned. The Bank
of the U.S. was also closed. The country was demoralized.

In 1812, with war with Britain underway, canal-building was put on hold. Then,
after the war, the state of New York found itself ill-equipped to fund the canal. So, in
1814, when the New York Legislature convened, Martin Van Buren's New York City
political machine, the Bucktails, zeroed in on the state's small post-war budget and used
it as an excuse to get the legislature to reverse its position on canal-funding. Van Buren
labeled the canal the "Ditch of Iniquity."

Efforts to build the canal dragged on for years. But, still determined to build the
canal, DeWitt Clinton then organized canal "mass meetings" throughout the state to
encourage the development of a plan for the state of New York to finance the construction
of the canal. Then, in 1817, despite opposition by the Bucktail machine, with popular
backing for state-sponsorship of the Erie Canal project, DeWitt Clinton was overwhelmingly elected governor of New York. The legislature then once again passed a bill to fund
the Erie Canal. From his upstate machine, The Albany Regency, Van Buren then publicly
began to support the project while his Bucktails still opposed it in New York City.

The construction of the Erie Canal was a staggering project. It posed a huge expensive technological challenge—a challenge probably as great as the 1960s challenge to put a man on the moon. Prior to the Erie Canal, the longest canal ever built was only 26 miles long. The Erie Canal was 363 miles long. Aside from its length, there were other challenges to be met—challenges like negotiating the 555 foot descent from Lake Erie to the river below. That required the installation of eighty-three regular locks. And then at Buffalo, the challenge to mount a 75 foot high escarpment at Niagara Falls had to be met. In order to complete the project, Governor Clinton repeatedly petitioned the state legislature for millions upon millions of dollars.

There were other problems, too. Laborers were dying from diseases like malaria, ague and typhoid—diseases that science had not yet eradicated. Then a crisis arose when deposits of pumice stone could not be located anywhere in the area. Pumice stone was used to make hydraulic cement. It was found in abundance in Europe, but could not be imported due to the high cost of shipping. So an expedition was mounted to explore local out-lying regions in hopes of locating deposits, but none were to be found anywhere. Then, a construction contractor, in a remote upstate New York town, notified canal builders of a substance found in his area that could be used as a substitute for pumice. It was a powdered form of limestone. Instead of diluting in water, it solidified and worked beautifully. Enthusiasm mounted.

When, in 1820, anthracite coal was discovered in Pennsylvania, it began to be mined in abundance, so plans for more canals were forged in order to make it possible for coal to be transported from Pennsylvania into New Jersey and New York. By 1823, talk of another canal linking the Erie Canal with the Ohio River was frequently spoken of. Then, in 1823, when President Monroe appointed Nicholas Biddle president of the re-chartered Bank of the United States, the federal government began funding canals. Industrial independence was anticipated!

The Erie Canal was finally completed in 1825. By altering the natural geography of the route to the West, it provided an efficient way for inland western settlers to ship their products eastward. In 1824, as a part of his triumphal visit to the U.S., General Lafayette made a visit to the Buffalo locks. There laborers gave him a limestone salute. This kicked off a celebratory mood. Then in 1826, there was a huge national celebration as the very first ship made its way from Lake Erie all the way to the harbor in New York. Governor Clinton rode the whole route. Cannonades echoed throughout the Mohawk Valley. President John Quincy Adams waited for the ship in New York harbor where he had assembled a delegation composed of General Lafayette and the four former living U.S. Presidents—Adams, Jefferson, Madison and Monroe. Everyone was jubilant!

In ensuing years, the Erie Canal triggered the development of other businesses and this greatly enhanced the U.S. economy. Revenue from the canal alone filled the coffers of the New York State Treasury with one million dollars a year, so the canal was paid for in just a few years. The success of the canal project became a living testament to the effectiveness of the American system of government-sponsored credit. American patriots were optimistic. But, ever-committed to keeping the U.S. backward, the enemy viewed all of this inland development as a great setback to their imperialist plans. From before the election of John Quincy Adams in 1824, they had become focused on finding a pro-British presidential candidate who could replace Munroe and end the Era of Good Feeling. But, in 1824, their candidate, Andrew Jackson, lost a too-close-to-call election when Congress had to decide the outcome of that election and they chose the untiring nationalist, John Quincy Adams. He shall be the subject of the following two chapters.

1724-1826

11

OLD MAN ELOQUENT

"Colonial establishments are incompatible with the
essential character of our institutions...Great
colonial establishments are engines of wrong, and
in the progress of social improvement it will be the
duty of the American family to abolish them."

JOHN QUINCY ADAMS,
FROM A FOURTH OF JULY SPEECH GIVEN IN 1821

John Quincy Adams, son of Massachusetts, was a man who deeply understood the significance of the fight for independence his fledgling young country had made once during the War for Independence and then again during the War of 1812. Like Ben Franklin, the elder son of Massachusetts, John Quincy Adams was steeped in the republican tradition of the independent nation-state. During the course of its long history, the Massachusetts Bay Colony had preserved that tradition despite relentless pressure by the British Crown to give up the independence their charter had secured for them. Quincy Adams knew that the American republic had been established as a bulwark against imperial colonialism and through the length of his extensive political career, he fought the enemy by upholding its constitutionally-sanctioned principles.

The son of Abigail Adams and John Adams, the second President of the United States, John Quincy Adams had been a child prodigy. At age nine, he had learned of the Declaration of Independence from letters his father had written to his mother from the Continental Congress. Groomed to be a foreign diplomat from his youth, at great peril, he had accompanied his father on a diplomatic mission abroad before the peace treaty ending the War for Independence had even been negotiated. During this time, his father first suggested to him that he start the diary he was to keep for the rest of his life. At the age of fourteen, serving as Francis Dana's secretary, he accompanied him on a mission to St. Petersburg, Russia, in order to obtain that country's support for the newly emerging United States. There he worked as a French/English translator.

Upon the completion of this extensive travel, he returned home to enter Harvard College and, in 1787, after two years of study, he was graduated Phi Beta Kappa. He then apprenticed as a lawyer for two years, was admitted to the bar, and began the practice of law in Boston. But, like his father before him, he wanted to use his training in the law to establish a political career, so he began to write political pamphlets. His written defense of President George Washington's administration caught the attention of the President, and so he appointed him minister to the Netherlands. Then, in 1796, he was appointed minister to Portugal. At Washington's urging, in 1797, when his father became president, he received an appointment as minister to Prussia. In that post, he was instrumental in forging trade agreements with that country. Upon completion of this diplomatic mission, with a resume like no other young man of his day, at age twenty-one, he returned to the United States to begin serving Massachusetts in that state's Senate and General Court. Later, he served his country as United States senator and then president. After he was defeated in his bid for a second term as president, he ran for a seat in the House of Representatives and was elected. There, during seventeen happy years of service to his country, his colleagues dubbed him "Old Man Eloquent."

During Jefferson's administration, John Quincy Adams was serving as U.S. senator from Massachusetts. Massachusetts Federalists had appointed him to that post even though they knew he was not a party man. In the Senate he then proceeded to support both Jefferson's Louisiana Purchase and his Embargo Act, and so he became unpopular with the renegade Massachusetts Federalists who had placed him in office. Selfishly focused solely on accumulating wealth through foreign trade, they then removed him from the Senate in 1808. This did not, however, change our hero or deter him from continuing to follow his principles. Duty to country was the hallmark of his political life. Completely motivated by it, he acted without political concern saying: "Always vote for principle, though you may vote alone...you may cherish the sweetest reflection that your vote is never lost."

After his forced removal from the Senate, President Madison revived the diplomatic career of Quincy Adams by appointing him minister to Russia in 1809. There, he developed a formal relationship with Tsar Alexander I and made him an ally of the United States by persuading the Tsar to allow American ships to trade in Russian ports. From that post, in 1812, he reported home about the invasion of Russia by Napoleon and kept President Madison accurately informed about that war. In 1814, Madison appointed him a member of the American team that negotiated the Peace of Ghent after the conclusion of the War of 1812. At that conference, through shrewd awareness of the enemy's agenda, he was instrumental in forging a diplomatic victory for the United States.

Then, in 1817, President Monroe appointed him secretary of state. He served in that capacity until 1825 and compiled a record of great accomplishment by fixing the territorial boundaries of the U.S. Not only did he establish a permanent border with Canada that extended all the way to the Rocky Mountains, but he also negotiated U.S. fishing rights off the coast of Canada. It was, however, when he negotiated the 1819 Adams-Onis Treaty, that John Quincy Adams presided over what he considered to be his proudest accomplishment. That treaty transferred the territory of Florida from Spain to the U.S. and fixed the boundary of the southwestern United States at the Sabine River in Texas. It also removed Spanish claims to the Oregon Territory and prevented any future Russian claims in that same region. As U.S. Secretary of State, Quincy Adams also implemented a formal policy for U.S. recognition of the emerging republics of South America. With this background of able service to his country, he emerged as an out-standing candidate for president in 1824.

Through tariff protection, President Monroe had initiated a profound period of U.S. prosperity that was later to be dubbed "The Era of Good Feeling." When he became president, John Quincy Adams continued Monroe's high-tariff policies, and he also began a program of technology development through sanctioning the construction of inland waterways. With this policy, he revived the policies of the great French emperor, Charlemagne, who had, one thousand-years earlier, moved to defeat the forces of empire in a similar way

During his presidency, John Quincy Adams had to contend with a Congress that was largely infiltrated by enemy sympathizers and this made it very difficult for him to realize his progressive nationalist agenda. Then, in 1828, Quincy Adams was denied a second term when Andrew Jackson, the poorly qualified British puppet, was elected president. From as far back as the days of Jackson's involvement in Burr's Western Conspiracy, Burr had been planning to promote Andrew Jackson for president. On behalf of the enemy, Burr's corrupt political protégé, Martin Van Buren, had worked out the details of Jackson's first presidential campaign in 1824. Following the loss of this first bid for president, Jackson was embittered, so he resigned from the Senate to devote himself to constantly bedeviling the Quincy Adams administration.

This is the story of Jackson's 1824 defeat: Besides Quincy Adams and Jackson, three other candidates had chosen to run in the 1824 election—Secretary of the Treasury William H. Crawford, Secretary of War John C. Calhoun, and Speaker of the House Henry Clay. When Crawford succumbed to a debilitating stroke, four candidates remained— Adams, Jackson, Calhoun and Clay. Putting personal ambition aside, Clay, a Whig like Adams, then shrewdly ran on a separate ticket in order to take votes away from Jackson. This strengthened the Adams ticket and made the election so close that no one obtained a majority of the electoral votes. So the election went to the House of Representatives to be decided from among the three highest-scoring candidates. Clay came in last, so he was eliminated, but, popular in the House, he succeeded in using his influence to get John Quincy Adams, a nationalist just like himself, elected on the first House ballot. Jackson had garnered a plurality of the popular vote, so he had fully expected to emerge as president. He was furious when he lost. Clay viewed the election of Adams as a sort of coup for the nationalists.

President Adams then quickly appointed the very competent Clay as his secretary of state. Enraged, Jackson then cried out that it was a "corrupt bargain" and resigned from the Senate. Then, for the next four years, he worked with the political machine of Martin Van Buren and swore that he would be elected president in 1828. All the while, from outside the Senate, he continued to make claims of a "corrupt bargain" between

Adams and Clay. This accusation over-shadowed the whole four years of the John Quincy Adams administration because there were numerous Jackson supporters in both houses of Congress and they wouldn't let it fade from the public mind. Actually, though, it was a false accusation because, Adams, like his predecessor, James Monroe, appointed men to posts in his administration based on qualifications alone. And, because he was respectful of opposing views, he never removed anyone from office except for incompetence.

Quickly, John Quincy Adams had Secretary of State Henry Clay, make selective trade reciprocity agreements with many nations in South America. Quincy Adams intended to befriend these new republics and support them in their struggle to free themselves from empire. This founding pacifist policy had been the policy of George Washington, the first president and hero of John Quincy Adams. He also appointed Joel Poinsett as first U.S. ambassador to Mexico. There, Poinsett made the acquaintance of patriotic Mexican nationalists and spoke to them about how they could free themselves from the ancient feudal system the empire had imposed upon them. He even proposed an informal alliance with the U.S. and a railway from the U.S., through Santa Fe, right down to Mexico City. When the British heard of this proposal, they became enraged, branded Poinsett a meddler and succeeded in running him out of Mexico.

In his first State of the Union Address as president, the far-sighted John Quincy Adams pledged his administration to the advance of science and technology by proposing to build a national astronomical observatory. He called observatories "the lighthouses of the sky." At that time, Russia had the most advanced observatory in the world and Quincy Adams wanted to maintain the same kind of scientific progress in America. He lost his fight for an observatory, but did succeed in advancing the industrialization of the United States by putting the army corps of engineers to work planning for wide-scale railroad development. The Baltimore and Ohio Railroad became the first private railroad company to be financed by the government. West Point graduate, Joseph Gardner Smith presided over the work of the engineers. The President's friends, governors, William Seward and Edward Everett, both then obtained state funding for railroads in their perspective states of New York and Massachusetts. Nicholas Biddle, head of the Bank of the United States, marketed and sold bonds to private corporations in order to advance the country's economic progress.

President Adams then began his inland development program by completing the construction of the Erie Canal. Quickly, it was connected to Lake Michigan and the Ohio River. Then the whole grid was also extended to Indiana, Illinois and the Mississippi River. Cadwallader Colden presided over that whole project. This canal system made New York City a huge commercial center. It also helped Abraham Lincoln, then an Illinois legislator, and his friends create the city of Chicago. The birth of the canal system and the subsequent spread of railroads, initiated a profound U.S. industrialization because it spurred the growth of iron and coal-mining industries. American manufacturing also soared.

In 1827, President Adams originated a bill for a naval expedition to the South Seas and Antarctica. It passed the House, but was defeated in the Senate. He also called for the creation of the Smithsonian Institute as a base for science in America. In tribute to the pioneering insight of John Quincy Adams, when future President John F. Kennedy launched his space program over a century later, he dedicated it to John Quincy Adams. He also made him the subject of the first chapter in his book, <u>Profiles in Courage</u>.

Together with Secretary of State Henry Clay, President Adams studied Spain's position in the Americas and made Alexander Everett his ambassador to Spain. He also recruited the American author, Washington Irving, to write a biography of Columbus. Irving also wrote works on Islam and the great Muslim heritage in Spain.

John Quincy Adams was a man of visionary intellect and great patriotism who pursued progress with unbounded zeal. His learning was so extensive and thorough that during the length of his long political career, he readily surpassed all his contemporaries in knowledge and understanding. Sadly, though, during his presidency, the Congress was widely infiltrated by the enemy, so support for his progressive platform was minimal. After he was defeated by Andrew Jackson in his second bid for president, John Quincy Adams became a congressman in order to continue to promote American progress. To divert the nation's attention away from the U.S. founding progressive mission, enemy operatives then began to fuel disagreements between North and South. So John Quincy Adams thrust himself into the role of out-spoken slave abolitionist by deciding to read before Congress all the many petitions he received on the subject of slavery. In the next chapter, we shall see what happened when, with great moral courage, he not only spoke out against slavery, but also defended free speech.

1808-1827

12

THE POST PRESIDENTIAL YEARS OF JOHN QUINCY ADAMS

"Stop the music of John Quincy Adams."

THOMAS W. GILMER,
SPOKEN IN THE HOUSE OF REPRESENTATIVES, 1842

With his background as a premier intellectual, veteran diplomat, and former president, when John Quincy Adams entered the House of Representatives in 1831, he overshadowed his colleagues in ability and prestige. Historical records of congressional proceedings mention his name more often than any other member of Congress. Those records show that he took part in discussions of nearly all questions that arose in the House. Eventually, he became the self-appointed spokesperson for the abolition of slavery.

In order to forge a union of the states after the War for Independence was won, the founders of the republic had agreed to allow slavery to continue in the South because, in no other way, could they convince all the states to unite. Just as the founders before him, John Quincy Adams considered slavery to be a moral atrocity completely out of line with the principles in the Declaration of Independence. For all his life, he had privately opposed it, characterizing it as "a deep seated disease preying on the vitals of the Union." From as far back as the 1820s, when Missouri had applied for admission to the Union as a slave state, he began to crystallize his thoughts upon the issue. One day, he reasoned, civil war would be inevitable, but the Union needed to first grow strong. Then war, when it came, would cause a temporary dissolution of the Union, but, following victory by the superior Union forces, a re-organization, under terms of complete emancipation for the slave, would follow. So, for the time being, he reasoned, the admission of Missouri as a slave state would temporarily placate the South and time would strengthen the Union. So, like Henry Clay, John Quincy Adams did not oppose the admission of Missouri as a slave state and he gave no public expression on the subject of abolition until after he served as president. Then, in the 1830s, as British secret intelligence orchestrated, not only the beginning of the abolition movement, but also the nullification movement in the South, the anti-slavery impulse suddenly began to stir in the North. **It was not a sudden random stirring, as it appeared, but part of a long-range British-manipulated scheme to divide the Union through planned civil war.**

Religious fervor initially supplied an impetus to the abolition movement when, in 1831, a group of Quakers from Pennsylvania sought the services of the high profile congressman, John Quincy Adams, and asked him to present a petition on the abolition of slavery to the Congress. That petition asked Congress to abolish both slavery and the domestic slave trade in the District of Columbia because Congress had sole jurisdiction over that area. Believing in the right of citizens to petition Congress—a right secured by the first amendment—Quincy Adams agreed to read their petition. Over time, he received more and more petitions on the subject, and so he ardently read them all. Eventually, this led to a committed one man crusade against slavery.

Manipulated opposition to abolition quickly intensified in the South. Fearful of the eloquence of Adams, southern supporters of slavery then tried to "gag" him. With polished parliamentary skill, however, Adams often out-maneuvered his opposition and continued to regularly read the petitions. As a result, he began to receive death threats. When an official gag rule was put in place to silence him altogether, he was threatened with censure and expulsion from the House. His diary documents the fact that he often heard southern congressmen express the opinion that it would be better if he were dead. Unafraid, though, he continued to oppose the southern-dominated House until, in 1844, the gag rule was repealed and the right of petition was restored.

In 1841, the freed slave, Frederick Douglass, speaking about slavery before packed audiences, recalled many instances when John Quincy Adams had eloquently presented these petitions to the House. While still a slave, he had obtained copies of them to read to other slaves. While serving dinner, Negro waiters, he said, often heard their masters cursing abolitionists. Those slaveholders had imagined that their slaves were too ignorant to understand what was going on, but, just hearing of the Quincy Adams speeches had given them hope that they might one day be free.

In 1841, John Quincy Adams enhanced his reputation for moral courage when he argued before the Supreme Court for the release of recently imprisoned captured black slaves. Here is what happened: In 1839, a Portuguese pirate slave trader, the *Tecora,* purchased a cargo of slaves kidnapped in Nigeria on the western coast of Africa and transported them to Havana, Cuba, in the hold of their ship. There they were sold on the open market even though trade in slaves had been prohibited, from as far back as 1817, by treaties signed between Spain and the countries of Britain, Portugal and the Netherlands. The King of Spain had even signed an ordinance declaring that every African slave imported into a Spanish colony in violation of a treaty should be declared free upon entering a Spanish port.

In Havana, the fifty-two African captives were then purchased by two Cubans and they loaded them onto the coastal schooner, the *Armistad,* under cover of darkness, for transport to various locations. Three days into the voyage, the slaves freed themselves from their neck irons by breaking the padlock to their common chain. Then they procured knives and killed the schooner's captain by splitting his skull open with a machete. They fell upon the cook and killed him, too, but kept the Cubans, who had purchased them, alive because they anticipated needing their help in finding their way back to Africa. The Cubans duly set the compass east as demanded, but during the night they veered the compass slightly north, slowly changing course and heading for the United States. In waters off the coast of New York, the U.S. Coast Guard eventually spotted the ship and, under the pretense of suspected piracy, seized the vessel and had the Negroes imprisoned.

News of the captured "slaves" spread quickly as they were taken into custody and held for trial. John Quincy Adams intently followed newspaper coverage of the trial that took place in New Haven, Connecticut. The Spanish minister to the U.S. demanded the release of the prisoners, but the court ignored his demands. Anxious to turn the captives over to Spain, and eager to challenge court rulings, if necessary, President Van Buren cautiously awaited the results of the trial. A committed supporter of the British plantation system, for political reasons, he wanted to speedily settle this issue.

The captives found themselves imprisoned in the New Haven county jail without any friends and unable to speak the language of their captors. Soon, however, abolitionists befriended them and found a translator who proceeded to teach them English and, as they learned the language, they started making heart-felt appeals for release.

The attorney for the slaves argued that the captives had the "natural right" to be free and that they had only been acting in self-defense when they broke their fetters and killed their captors. The U.S. government though took the position that the slaves needed to be returned to their owners under the terms of the out-dated Pinckney Treaty, but the ruling judge denied that request saying that the district court had to decide if the slaves were property or not. The district court then, in turn, ruled that they had to be returned to Africa. Surprised by this decision, the government then appealed this ruling to the Supreme Court.

Even though his son urged him to avoid involvement in the trial, Quincy Adams decided to write a letter to one of the defending attorneys for the captives. The press then got a copy of it and printed it in many New England newspapers. With compassion, the Adams letter described the suffering that the Africans were enduring and stressed the fact that the captives were acting in self-defense when they tried to free themselves from illegal seizure. His letter also made it clear to the defense attorneys that he could be called upon to help defend the captives.

So in February of 1841, John Quincy Adams argued the case of the captives before the Supreme Court, citing international treaty provisions that had made it illegal for Africans to be illegally seized, transported from their homeland, and sold into bondage. The slave trade had been branded as piracy, in 1808, when the United States outlawed it. A similar prohibition soon followed in Britain. The countries of Portugal, the Netherlands and Spain then made similar international agreements. The release of the captives, however, was finally sealed when John Quincy Adams made a heart-rending appeal to the southern-dominated Supreme Court by citing the inalienable right of all men to freedom under natural law. After hearing Adams' emotionally powerful argument, Justice Story wrote to his wife describing it as "extraordinary for its power, for its bitter sarcasm, and its dealing with topics far beyond the records and points of discussion." By a combination of reason, eloquence and fearless moral courage, John Quincy Adams had freed the African captives of the *Armistad.*

1831-1841

JOHN QUINCY ADAMS
SIXTH PRESIDENT OF THE UNITED STATES,
RENOWNED SCHOLAR, FOREIGN DIPLOMAT,
U.S. SENATOR, SECRETARY OF STATE, AND U.S.
CONGRESSMAN

*"Man was not made for himself alone. No, he was made
for his country, by the obligations of the social contract;
he was made for his species, by the Christian duty of
universal charity; he was made for all ages past, by the
sentiment of reverence for his forefathers; and he was
made for all future times, by the impulse of affection for
his progeny."*

*Excerpt from an 1802 speech given by John Quincy
Adams, commemorating the landing of the Pilgrims in
Plymouth, Massachusetts*

13

THE GREAT COMPROMISER

"Give us a protective tariff and we shall have the greatest country on earth."

ABRAHAM LINCOLN

As we have seen, Alexander Hamilton's ideas were critical to the establishment of the United States republic. Without the sweeping political changes that he initiated, it is doubtful that the Union would ever have been maintained. Hamilton knew that nothing in the organization of the Articles of Confederation would make the Union successful as long as a federation of "free and independent states" remained. Like the countries of Europe, they would fight over duties, loans and land. And, with their individual standing armies, they would be poised to fight one another if they felt intimidated.

Hamilton had written several scholarly papers that urged the U.S to build a broad manufacturing base at home. Toward this end, he promoted a protective tariff program that President George Washington whole-heartedly sanctioned during his presidency. Protective tariffs, they knew, would allow the new fledgling nation to develop its economy and compete on the world market. Without protection, the country would be forever relegated to the status of a backward nation because the British Empire would be able to dump cheap manufactures on the country and prevent the growth of a home manufacturing base. In the eyes of all nationalists, the U.S. had to emerge from the British system of free trade and show the way for the rest of the world. This had been her established founding mission!

Opposed to this progress from the start, over the years, the British Empire relentlessly engaged in covert operations designed to subvert this plan for U.S. fiscal independence. From the start, the enemy did such a great job subverting Hamilton's tariff protection that ups and downs in the economy readily became the norm in America. During this time, and for the length of his forty-year career as a U.S. statesman, the brilliant and forceful Henry Clay was the untiring advocate of the nationalist policies of protection established by Hamilton. Clay was uniquely fitted for leadership. A statesman by intuition, he also had the instincts of a politician. With this rare combination of talent, he often established public policy before anyone else realized the issues.

From the day he entered the House of Representatives in 1811, at age thirty-four, Clay's unique talents were evident. He was, therefore, quickly chosen speaker of the House, despite the fact that long-standing congressmen of recognized ability could also have ably filled that post. Clay was continuously re-elected as speaker for the entire length of the time he served in the House. Along with John C. Calhoun and John Quincy Adams, he also became an early leader of the Whig Party which flourished until he died in 1852. Then, after the Whig Party became divided, Abraham Lincoln helped revive it as the Republican Party. Lincoln had expressed admiration for Henry Clay, referring to him as "my beau ideal of a statesman."

Even though the British Empire was relentlessly committed to diverting the attention of the American public away from the issue of protective tariffs, throughout the entire nineteenth century, Clay helped make the congressional fight over protectionism the chief political issue in American life. Traditional historical accounts never emphasize this, **yet the issue defines American freedom.** All nationalists knew that the choice was simple—protectionism and the survival of the grand U.S. mission or free trade and the subjugation of the U.S. to enslavement by the forces of empire. Without protective tariffs, U.S. goods could not compete with the inexpensive slave labor goods the enemy produced. With a choice between cheap low-cost foreign imports or expensive American goods, Americans were tempted to purchase cheap foreign goods and let American manufacturing suffer. But, with the enactment of protective tariffs, prices equalized and then there was no choice. Americans chose to help their own economy flourish.

Early on, under the protective system, statesmen, from both North and South, were largely united by their support for protective tariffs. It wasn't until much later—as profits from the sale of cotton increased dramatically—that southern plantation owners became aligned with the enemy. Then they began to oppose tariffs. As a monopoly in the trade of cotton was forged, southern representatives then relentlessly began to fight for the expansion of slavery to the new territories. During the thirty year period of constant congressional debate over the expansion of slavery, Henry Clay kept the Union together by sponsoring tariff compromise between North and South.

During this same time, a small faction of enemy-directed government agents were also manipulating impoverished southern laborers into crying out for free trade by encouraging them to believe that their inferior economy had been created by northern manufacturers. This helped drive a wedge between North and South. All the while, it was really the enemy-sponsored plantation system that was responsible for the plight of southern laborers. To keep this system in place, southern congressman continually opposed protective tariffs.

From the nation's earlier beginning, southern representatives to the Constitutional Convention had managed to establish a legal three-fifths slave representation in Congress even though slaves had no rights. This helped create a majority southern representation in Congress. In the Senate, this domination was especially evident as long as southern slave-holding states remained as numerous as northern states because just a simple partisan Senate gridlock could defeat congressional legislation. Clay worked against these odds to establish successive compromises. When, however, free U.S. territory began to expand, southern control in Congress was threatened, so the enemy seductively began a mounted attack against Clay's compromises in an attempt to gain territorial control. When this proved difficult, the South was manipulated into pushing for secession.

The average southerner had no idea that the American system was the solution to their economic inferiority. But, Henry Clay knew the truth, so he made economic progress one of the goals of his spirited congressional work. Clay knew that if the South could come to realize the benefits of government-sponsored progress, it would develop a taste for it and this would break the hold that the imperialists enjoyed over their minds. Southern industrial diversification would result.

During the War of 1812, to finance the war, duties had been raised one-hundred percent. A huge prosperity resulted. Then after the peace with Britain was secured, duties were dramatically lowered by the tariff law of 1816. Clay refused to vote for this bill and warned of its dire consequences. When his warning proved to be on target, he perused the results of the lowered duties and commented: "We behold general distress pervading the whole country; unthreshed crops of grain perishing in our barns for want of a market; an alarming diminution of the circulating medium [money], universal complaint of the want of employment; and consequent reduction in the wages of labor. To add to these evils, there is, above all, a low and depressed state of the value of almost every description of property in the nation, which has, on average, sunk not less than fifty per cent within a few years."

The situation was so dire that people began making payments with IOUs. Soon they clamored for relief. To all of this, Clay duly announced that "our complete independence will only be consummated after the policy of protection is recognized and adopted."

But Congress was stubborn, so no relief came until 1824. Then a new high-tariff law was passed and relief was immediate! Passage of this new law was largely the work of Clay. In defense of enemy-aligned commercial class interests in Massachusetts, Daniel Webster though, argued against the bill calling the notion of protectionism obsolete. James Buchanan of Pennsylvania, however, remained Clay's staunch ally because Pennsylvania was a manufacturing state. In those early days, protectionism was a regional issue rather than a party issue.

This new bill favorably advanced the general welfare, so during the Quincy Adams administration, the nation prospered. In celebration of the passage of this bill, Clay said: The greatest want of a civilized society is a market for the sale and exchange of the surplus of the labor of its members. This may exist at home or abroad or both, but it must exist somewhere if society is to prosper; and whenever it does exist, it should be competent to the absorption of the entire surplus of production. It is most desirable that there should be both a home and a foreign market. But with respect to the superiority, I cannot entertain a doubt. The home market is first in order and paramount in importance. The object of the bill under consideration is to create a home market, and to lay the foundations of a genuine American policy. The creation of a home market is not only necessary to procure our necessary wants. If we cannot sell, we cannot buy. The sole object of the tariff is to tax the produce of foreign industry with a view to promoting American industry." The effects of Clay's legislation were immediate and the United States began to prosper as he had predicted.

By 1828, protectionism had become so popular that duties were raised even higher. Even Daniel Webster voted for the new bill. But, in 1832, President Andrew Jackson began pushing for a revision in the protective tariff and he achieved it. Earlier, he had been a tariff supporter, but by 1832, he had come under the influence of enemy-agent, Martin Van Buren, who encouraged Jackson to push for a universally low tariff. The passage of Jackson's low tariff bill proved so disastrous to the economy that it was later referred to as the Tariff of Abominations. Clay warned that it would prove calamitous. Astutely, he said that Jackson's bill had been nothing more than free trade and that free trade was just a return to the British colonial system. If adopted, he said, it would lead to re-colonization of the states and bring the nation once again under the dominion of Britain. John Quincy Adams agreed with Clay. He said, "Under the system of protective policy, the nation has risen from a depth of weakness, imbecility, and distress to an eminence of prosperity unexampled in the annals of the world."

South Carolina, a state covertly occupied by the enemy, then pushed for duties to be set even lower. She did not get her wish, though, so she proceeded to pass an Ordinance of Nullification, proclaiming that tariff duties were unconstitutional and that Jackson's tariff would be voided in South Carolina. And she further stipulated that, if the government tried to enforce the tariff law by calling out the army or navy, she would secede. Jackson signed the bill legalizing the Tariff of Abomination, but at the same time made it clear that if South Carolina tried to secede, he would militarily enforce the law if he had to. So, for the time being, South Carolina abandoned the idea of nullification.

South Carolina continued to maintain her states' rights claim, so, ever despairing, Clay introduced a new refined bill to keep the peace with South Carolina. He knew it would be disastrous to the economy, but, committed to maintaining the Union, he saw no other way to placate South Carolina. The new bill called for initially maintaining a protective tariff, but gradually reducing the duties. Four New England states voted against it. New Jersey, Delaware, Missouri, and Ohio also voted against it. The new compromise calmed the South, but was otherwise harsh on the economy. It helped bring on the great financial crisis of 1837. Then, once again, gloomy times similar to those of pre-1823 emerged. Henry Clay had not abandoned his creed, so he was again vindicated. This time, he hoped the people would not only again clamor for relief, but also learn something about tariff protection.

Just as he had hoped, the people soon made the connection between their distress and low tariff duties and they promptly threw all those elected officials responsible for the passage of the compromise legislation out of office. Then, in 1840, as a result of all the suffering that the depression had created, General William Henry Harrison was elected president on a promise to bring back protective tariffs. Clay then redressed the issue, and so protective tariffs were again set to be quickly implemented. But then President Harrison suddenly died, so Vice President John Tyler became president. While serving under Harrison, Tyler had hidden his free trade allegiance, but once he became president, he gave support to the domestic enemy, and vetoed the protective tariff law. The House submitted the tariff legislation to him twice, but, both times, he vetoed it. When the House tried to override the veto by mustering up the required 2/3 majority, he tried to interfere in House protocol, so John Quincy Adams called for his impeachment, but the House merely censored him.

Clay's protective bills had a history of working so well and so quickly that Clay ran for president in 1844 against James Polk. But Polk waged a dirty tricks campaign in which he portrayed himself as a "better protectionist than Clay," so he narrowly won the election. He then appointed the free-trader, Robert J. Walker, of Mississippi, as treasury secretary, and Walker proceeded to assail the protective tariff. Walker also wrote a report accusing American manufacturers of being enemy conspirators. In Britain, his free trade report received high praise. In fact, the British government was so pleased with it that they actually printed up copies for circulation. Then, as Walker directed the repeal of the Whig tariff law, many congressmen became so incensed that even Democrats like Daniel Webster and Simon Cameron of Pennsylvania, allied themselves with the Whigs.

During this period, Polk engaged the country in an unpopular British-designed war with Mexico, but the Congress eventually condemned Polk's policies, so the Democratic congressional majority was exchanged for a Whig majority. Then, in 1848, the self-styled Whig, Zachary Taylor was elected president. By that time, protectionism had become so popular that even the state of Pennsylvania, which had consistently voted democratic from the days of Jefferson, voted for Taylor based in his commitment to protectionism. As we shall see, as president, Taylor surprised the enemy with his uncompromising commitment to strengthening the Union, so the enemy had him poisoned.

Then, as enemy operatives effectively dismantled Clay's Compromise of 1820, he returned to the Senate from retirement to forge the Compromise of 1850. Nothing, however, could stop the enemy's relentless plans to spread slavery to all parts of the Union. During the presidential election of 1852 that enemy set the stage for an embroiled North/South fight over this issue. Then, with the nation's attention deterred from the subject of tariffs, protectionism was abandoned. By 1857, a tariff was enacted that set the duties lower than it had been during any period since 1816. Some Republicans, like William Seward of New York opposed the bill, but the attention of the country had been so effectively captured by the embroiled North/South fight over slavery that there was no real objection to it. The results of the tariff of 1857 were so disastrous that the country suffered another panic with ensuing depression. The newly-organized Republican Party then began to attack the free trade policies of the Democrats. The stage had also been set for the masterful leadership of Lincoln. In later chapters, we shall see what his genius had in store for the nation.

1816-1860

HENRY CLAY
EMINENT AMERICAN STATESMAN, U.S.
CONGRESSMAN, SPEAKER OF THE HOUSE, U.S.
SENATOR, AND SECRETARY OF STATE

As a testament to the universal nature of the United States Constitution that he loved so well, Henry Clay once said: "The Constitution of the United States was made not merely for the generation that then existed, but for posterity, unlimited, undefined, endless, perpetual posterity."

14

OPERATION
SOUTH CAROLINA

"If we trace back any great civil convulsion, we will
find its source originating in some quarter equally
unsuspected and obscure."

EDWIN DELEON, FATHER OF THE YOUNG AMERICA MOVEMENT

A s we have seen, the enemy responded to the strength of the John Quincy Adams
presidency with a covert divide and conquer scheme aimed at destroying the Union
over the issue of slavery. All but a few wise leaders were deceived as British secret
service then managed a behind-the-scenes popular uprising centered in South Carolina.
There they armed that state for a trained rehearsal in civil war many years before it actually
broke out in 1861. Matthew Carey was one of a few aware Americans who warned of this
British plot by writing a series of pamphlets in the late 1830s. In them, he called for all
patriots to engage with him in a war against what he called "the British secret service in
their South Carolina disunion project."

It was in 1660 that Britain first established a colonial settlement in South Carolina.
John Locke, their liberal spokesperson, helped write its constitution. As a major stock-
holder in the Royal African Company, he then presided over the importation of thousands
of slaves into the colony where they were sold to aristocratic settlers. Disgusted with the
situation, John Oglethorpe eventually founded a settlement in Georgia where slavery was
outlawed in 1732. But, by 1750, the empire had succeeded in crushing him, so slavery
became the norm in the South.

To truly realize the covert nature of British intelligence operations in South Carolina, one must understand some of the strategic political details involved in the establishment of that colony. When, in 1687, Elias Prioleau and his family arrived in South Carolina with a group of family refugee followers, the social and political life of that colony began to be dominated by Tory families with a long history of allegiance to empire. Under the name of Priuli, this family had, for seven centuries, ruled among the upper nobility in the slave kingdom of Venice. With unbridled tyranny, the elite of Venice had enslaved the captives of the perpetual wars they waged in Europe. They even sold the children of these captives to Muslim chieftains for their use as slaves. Then, when Venetian financiers moved their financial center to Holland and then England between 1550 and 1660 and took over the maritime merchant economies of those two countries, they brought the idea of trafficking in slaves with them. It was during this time that the Prioleau branch of the Priuli family in France and Switzerland became engaged as Venetian intelligence agents.

When the wealthy Elias Prioleau arrived in Charleston, South Carolina, in 1687, he organized the pre-existent French and Swiss Huguenot society into an official congregation and became their pastor and community leader. Later, as more immigrants arrived, congregational membership swelled and "blue-blood" oligarchs ruled the community.

Later, the De Saussure family would arrive to join the Prioleaus. As members of the Geneva Council of 200, they had served beside the Gallatins and du Pans as European espionage agents of empire. With a British royal grant of land, Henri de Saussure, of Lausanne, Switzerland, moved to South Carolina in 1730. There, his son, Daniel, became a rich merchant and his other son, Henry William de Saussure, became the leader of the South Carolina Federalist Party and chief justice of the state. His son, in turn, became grand master of the Scottish Rite of Freemasons in South Carolina. After establishing themselves in South Carolina, the De Saussure family always maintained close contact with British-Swiss intelligence agents in Europe, especially British Prime Minister, Lord Palmerston. Palmerston directed British-inspired U.S. secession strategy right down through the time of the Civil War.

Throughout his long political career, Henry Clay was aware that the British were promoting a spirit of divisiveness between North and South, so he constantly compromised with the South in order to give the North time to grow strong. All the while, the well-organized enemy continually conspired to promote free trade in order to weaken the North. They did not want the public to make the connection between protective tariffs and prosperity. In 1822, in order to distract the people from the issue of tariff law, they conspired to launch a feigned South Carolina "slave" revolt and it succeeded in creating a state of diversionary mass hysteria. They accomplished this by first inciting a wild gathering of some thirty-odd slaves. Then, after the unruly crowd had damaged property, Daniel Vesey was accused of trying to forge a slave revolt. Quickly, he was then tried and executed. In an atmosphere of fear and paranoia, the African Church was then burned down and armed guards were placed in the city of Charleston to prevent further "uprisings."

Afterwards, in an attempt to further confuse the people, enemy agent and South Carolina College president, Thomas Cooper, made an anti-tariff speech that blamed the state of chronic southern depression on northern manufacturers. Then he wrote a widely circulated anti-tariff pamphlet. Copies of the pamphlet were even given to Essex Junto members in New England.

Following Cooper's speech, Robert J. Turnbull also enhanced this anti-tariff propaganda by publishing a pamphlet called, *The Crisis, or Essays on the Usurpation of the Federal Government.* In his State of the Union Address to Congress in 1828, patriotic President John Quincy Adams counterattacked *The Crisis* and raised the disunion project to a place of national attention.

In the wake of the Cooper-Turnbull initiative, Samuel Prioleau actively organized statewide tariff opposition forces in South Carolina. Then, when the pro-British John Hamilton became Governor of South Carolina in 1830, he began arming militants for war.

With British secret intelligence forces in place, in 1832, the South Carolina legislature called a convention to declare U.S. protective tariffs null and void. American patriot, Matthew Carey, watched with horror. He knew that British secret intelligence was behind this nullification movement, but, try as he would, he could not once again rally the forces of nationalism to action as he had done in 1814 with *The Olive Branch*. His warnings about impending civil war were also ignored.

Meanwhile, back in New York, Aaron Burr organized his network of traitors—-Gallatin, Astor and the Boston Brahmin families—and they utilized anti-tariff sentiment in South Carolina to nationally promote British free trade by arranging for William Cullen Bryant to become editor of the enemy-aligned *New York Post*. In that newspaper, Bryant then reprinted everything Thomas Cooper wrote on South Carolina disunion. In 1831, Cooper's colleague, Theodore Sedgwick, also helped organize a national free trade convention, in Philadelphia, in order to lend the stamp of respectability to all the pro-British sedition that had been penned in South Carolina. That convention appointed Albert Gallatin chairman of a committee organized to lobby Congress for the repeal of the tariff and it was successful. There would be later attempts to restore the American System of Credit and high tariffs, but, not until the presidency of Abraham Lincoln would that system truly revive. Then, after Lincoln's murder, Henry C. Carey, son of Mathew Carey and former economic adviser to Lincoln, would be responsible for the revival of a grand prosperous post-Civil War economy. That story will be the subject of a series of later chapters.

1687-1830

15

WILD MAN FROM TENNESSEE

"Government is a trust and the officers of the
government are trustees. And both the trust and
the trustees are created for the benefit of the people."

HENRY CLAY

Popular versions of history have placed Andrew Jackson among the ranks of the greatest American presidents. In reality, though, he was little more than an ignorant opportunist who was manipulated by forces he didn't understand. Let's dig into his background and let the facts of his life speak for themselves. Raised on the Tennessee frontier, Jackson got his legal start there collecting debts for the wealthy land owners, slave traders and speculators who were all his early clients. Naturally strong, he was not afraid to fight, so he garnered a reputation for courage. Often, though, he lost his temper and flew into wild rages. Habitually, he would then call for a duel. He killed many men this way. As a general, under the auspices of military law, he hung soldiers without compunction. All kinds of men inhabited the Tennessee frontier from before the turn of the nineteenth century. Some were pioneer patriots like Daniel Boone and John Sevier, Tennessee's first governor. They worked to promote orderly frontier government. But, there were others who did not view Tennessee as a permanent part of the United States. Nor did they want that to change. They were there for opportunity. The ignorant under-educated Andrew Jackson was one of these people.

In 1789, Jackson made the acquaintance of Andre Fagot, a Spanish army officer and intelligence agent working to bring American western settlements under Spanish control. Intrigued by Fagot's mission, Jackson wrote a letter to district militia leader, Daniel Smith, a fellow opportunist, advising him of Spain's desire to gain the support of unhappy frontier Americans willing to revolt and side with Spain. Then, with Smith, Jackson organized the support of a rebel Tennessee frontier group and delivered a letter to Miro, the Spanish military governor. In that letter, he apprised Miro of his group's intention to approach the legislature of North Carolina, Tennessee's mother state, to solicit an act of separation from that state. For his work promoting Spanish interests on the Tennessee frontier, Miro gave Andrew Jackson a tract of valuable waterfront land on the Mississippi River. In true enemy-style, Jackson then proceeded to create a slave plantation on that land.

Treason continued on the frontier as the Tennessee legislature sent William Blount to the U.S. Senate. Within one year of this appointment, however, he was expelled from that body for leading a plot to recruit both American settlers and Indian tribes in a British-sponsored plot to seize the Gulf Coast from Spain. Blount's supporters then designated Jackson as Blount's replacement in the Senate.

Both Blount and Jackson were working closely with Aaron Burr who was, early on, a U.S. Senator. And, as we have previously mentioned, Burr was tirelessly working with the British to promote a separation of the western frontier from the United States. When the U.S. purchased the Louisiana Territory from France in 1803, Burr's agent, Edward Livingston, former New York mayor, moved to Louisiana and, with James Workman, formed the Mexican Association of New Orleans. As we have learned, the avowed aim of that association was the British seizure of Louisiana and the conquest of Mexico.

In May, 1805, while he was a fugitive from justice for the murder of Alexander Hamilton, Burr met with Jackson at Jackson's Nashville plantation, the *Hermitage.* There they discussed the Mexican Association and Jackson, a major general in the Tennessee militia, was enticed to help with the plan by recruiting mercenaries for Burr's private army. Burr would also later pay Jackson to secure the boats that would enable him to transport his small army down the Ohio and Mississippi Rivers to rendezvous with the British navy off the coast of New Orleans. There the Mexican Association's plan for the conquest of Mexico was to be completed.

However, before the plan could be launched, Jackson heard a circulating rumor about Burr's plot to divide the Union. Alarmed that his cover might have been compromised, he then publicly refuted the claim and immediately circulated another story implicating General James Wilkenson as the sponsor of the plan. Wilkenson had also been aiding Burr in his plan, but, when the plot became public, to protect himself, Wilkenson wrote to President Jefferson and exposed the scheme. Jefferson then immediately issued a proc-lamation that warned of the conspiracy and urged all patriotic Americans to report any information they might have about it. The government later seized Burr's boats. When Burr heard that the government had confiscated his boats, he again went to the *Hermitage* to confer with Jackson. Then Jackson sent for his nephew and instructed him to accompany Burr to New Orleans. There, Burr donned a disguise and tried to flee to Spanish territory, but, instead, he was captured and arrested for treason.

When Burr's trial convened, Jackson was called as a key witness. Under oath, Jackson then proceeded to lie about his relationship with Burr and the details of Burr's plot, maintaining that Wilkenson, not Burr, was the true perpetrator of the crime. During a break in the trial, he went out in the streets to stir up some mob sentiment against President Jefferson, complaining loudly that Jefferson was a bully and a coward, incapable of handling his official duties as president. He said that Jefferson lacked the courage to stand up to British aggression on the high seas, and so, instead, he harassed Burr, an innocent American. This Jackson-sponsored anti-Jefferson rhetoric made Jackson popular among the Tory political forces in the South. At the same time that Jackson was publicly denouncing Jefferson, he secretly joined a British-backed organization known as the Quids. That organization had first tried to secure Jefferson's aid in treasonous attempts at disunion, but when Jefferson made his pro-Union position clear, they denounced him.

Due to insufficient evidence at his trial, Burr was acquitted of treason, but, today there is irrefutable evidence that he was guilty. A letter penned to the Queen of England, by the then British ambassador to the U.S., Anthony Merry, acknowledges his receipt of a letter from Burr. In that letter, Burr offered to help the Queen secure a secession of the western part of the U.S. from the eastern seaboard. At the time of Burr's trial, this letter was either unavailable or was not allowed as evidence. Had Burr's letter to Merry been presented at his trail, Burr, undoubtedly, would have been found guilty of treason and sent to the gallows.

Burr lived in Britain until 1812 when he returned to the U.S. to resume the practice law in New York. He also then began to arduously promote Andrew Jackson for president. Jackson had won a sweeping victory over the British in a brief battle fought in New Orleans in 1815, so he received notoriety as a conquering general. This notoriety helped make him popular with the people. Jackson lost his first bid for the presidency in 1824, but was successfully elected in 1828. Generally accepted to be the originator of the spoils system in government, upon election, Jackson proceeded to put all of his crony friends into government positions of influence and opportunity. This made the corrupt bargain charges he had hurled at John Quincy Adams four years earlier seem ridiculous. He appointed Burr-ally, Samuel Swartwout, to the lucrative post of collector of the Port of New York, but, charged with embezzlement, Swartwout was soon driven out of that office.

Jackson also appointed the pro-British agent, Edward Livingston, for one term as secretary of state. That same year, Livingston was also installed as the grand high priest of the Scottish Rite of Freemasonry. In response to this, John Quincy Adams wrote his famous *Letter on the Subject of Masonry* and exposed the conflict of interest inherent in holding the two posts. Masonic membership required swearing an oath of secrecy to the order and that oath, he said, was incompatible with the trust required to hold public office. With this exposure, John Quincy Adams was trying to break the back of British secret intelligence because it was partly through this secret Masonic agency that British intelligence operated. There was another order of Masons that Ben Franklin had, many years earlier, established—the Free and Accepted Order of Masons. They sought to further American nationalism. The enemy has, over the years, tried to confuse these two organizations. And they have even cited Franklin's involvement with the patriotic Masons as a reason to place him in the enemy camp!

Jackson's election to the presidency was largely the result of the efforts of the "Little Magician," Martin Van Buren, powerful political boss of New York. Threatened by the election victory of John Quincy Adams in 1824, and determined to abort the American industrialization it was posed to unleash, Van Buren had quickly and cunningly planned to deceive the American public in the following presidential election by manipulating unaware mobs of German and Irish immigrants into voting for Jackson. They were largely responsible for Jackson's election as president in 1828.

After Jackson's successful election, Van Buren further weakened the nationalists by manipulating John C. Calhoun into joining the southern nullifiers, a group that had organized to oppose protective tariffs. This is how it happened: Van Buren resurrected an old letter that Calhoun had written in which he denounced Jackson's conduct as a general. Then he showed the letter to Jackson and, when Jackson read the letter, he flew into one of his mad fits of rage and denounced Calhoun. Then he withdrew his support for Calhoun. With the loss of this support, in order to continue to nurture his desire to become president, Calhoun then began to consider defecting to the side of the nullifiers.

At the same time, Van Buren began to circulate fictitious tales about the damage done to the South by "northern-inspired" tariff laws. And this caused southern groups to further pressure Calhoun into siding with them in the growing disunion project centered in Calhoun's native state of South Carolina. In order to be able to continue to nurture his political ambition, Calhoun then capitulated and joined the disunionists. This was a great blow to the nationalists because Calhoun had been one of their out-spoken advocates. He had even helped found the *Patriot*, a political magazine organized for the express purpose of limiting Van Buren's power by stripping the New York legislature of its ability to determine election vote count in the state of New York.

In the growing national crisis, Jackson actually opposed nullification by threatening South Carolina with armed invasion if that state refused to sanction federal laws. In fact, his hatred for Calhoun actually caused him to delight in opposing it. But, devoid of any real dedication to the American system, at the same time, he rolled back tariff protection, leaving the nation economically defenseless. Then, for decades, southern opinion was so manipulated that the common people were never allowed to realize that tariff law was the great friend to all—the great equalizer of the American economy. Ensuing chapters of this book will continue to document the sad story of the political manipulation of public opinion in the years prior to the Civil War.

1789-1832

16

THE WILD MAN DESTROYS
THE NATIONAL BANK

"The banking powers are more despotic than a
monarchy, more insolent than autocracy, more
selfish than bureaucracy. They denounce as public
enemies all who question their methods and throw
light upon its crimes."

ABRAHAM LINCOLN

As we have seen, the election of Andrew Jackson to the presidency in 1828 was the culmination of years of promotional work by the "Little Magician," Martin Van Buren and his Albany Regency. Some historians have long suspected that Martin Van Buren was the illegitimate son of Aaron Burr, the first political boss of New York. When Van Buren was just eighteen, Burr had plucked him from obscurity to initiate him into politics. Then, in 1801, Burr's political aide, William P. Van Ness, brought Van Buren into his law office and trained him as an attorney. Later still, he was brought into the Tammany Hall political machine that Burr had created in New York City. Well-suited to politics, Van Buren quickly rose to power in New York State. We have already documented the fact that he initially used his power to oppose the construction of the Erie Canal in New York. Then after its success was assured, he switched sides, so he could install himself in a position of influence over its lucrative revenue.

By 1821, Van Buren was a U.S. Senator and his Albany Regency had become very powerful. Judges, newspapers, banks, and social and political institutions all across New

York were controlled by his New York State political machine. It chose all candidates for public office in the state of New York—from the highest to the most menial. The Regency was powerfully aligned with Wall Street and did everything it could to promote its interests. Through its control of the Democratic Party, Van Buren's machine effectively manipulated American public opinion for years.

As chief spokesman for this newly-created "democracy," Senator Martin Van Buren attacked President Monroe. A pre-eminent statesman, President Monroe believed in appointing the best men he could find to political office. These appointments crossed party lines and, once appointed, no one was ever dismissed from office for holding an opposing opinion. To him, America was a free place where competent political appointees could hold their own opinions even if they were different from those of the president! For all of his high statesmanship, Van Buren accused President Monroe of stifling democracy. Van Buren's brand of democracy aimed at advancing the power of the empire in America.

In March of 1822, Van Buren made the first of a series of trips to the South to form alliances with leaders of the plantation aristocracy in Virginia. In 1823, he made a visit to William H. Crawford of Georgia, a states-rights anti-nationalist, to suggest that he run for president in the upcoming election. In that same year, he also secured a powerful alliance with states-rights radical, Thomas Ritchie of Richmond, Virginia. This alliance established the beginning of the Albany-Richmond Junto, a political organization aimed at overturning the technological and industrial advances that Monroe's Era of Good Feeling had initiated. A letter written by Ritchie to the son-in-law of President Monroe survives today and documents Van Buren's motives. In that letter, Ritchie actually says that the members of the new junto "give and receive hope from each other, and confidently expect to govern this nation." In 1827, Van Buren also wrote to Ritchie touting the political alliance he had forged "between the planters of the South and the plain Republicans of the North." The plain Republicans of the North that he referred to were the members of the City of London/Wall Street-allied banking cartel. In this same letter, he also referred to the fact that the Monroe administration had tried to weaken this alliance. Monroe's nationalist policies were also challenging the hold that slavery held in the South. And, of course, no southern British-loving aristocrat could tolerate the notion that the slave system might be weakened because that might curtail their lucrative profits in cotton. We have already mentioned that the exploitation of Andrew Jackson's fame as a military general in the War of 1812 was part of a years-long promotional scheme directed at making him president.

It is ironic that from as far back as 1817, in his first inaugural address to the nation, President James Monroe spoke to his fellow Americans about the danger posed by populist demagogues. The people, he said, needed to become aware of the forces that were at work manipulating public opinion. Under control by these forces, he said, "the people themselves become the willing instruments of their own debasement and ruin." Unfortunately, that enemy-created manipulated mob elected Andrew Jackson president in 1828. Shrewdly, Jackson's handlers had sold him to everyone! To northerners, they presented him as a nationalist, but to southerners, he was a states-rights candidate. It was demagoguery at its best!

Under Jackson, Martin Van Buren was appointed secretary of state. From that position, he counseled Jackson to veto the transportation projects that John Quincy Adams had submitted to Congress for approval. During Jackson's second term, Van Buren then counseled Jackson to dismantle the Bank of the United States, the chief instrument of American national resistance to the British Empire and the City of London bankers. It had promoted the sovereignty of the U.S. government. Jackson planned to run U.S. finances through the states, a scheme, you will recall, that Hamilton had objected to years earlier. That plan had been tried and conclusively proven disastrous after the renewal of the first bank charter failed in 1811. When President Madison witnessed the results of that first take-down, he had a Damascus Road-type conversion, so he changed sides and presided over the renewal of the bank charter in 1817.

The second charter was due to be renewed in 1836. In anticipation of the upcoming fight he knew Jackson was planning, in 1832, Henry Clay called for an early vote on its renewal, but Jackson refused to take up the matter. He preferred to continue to work on the minds of the people in order to create confusion. But, Speaker of the House Henry Clay pushed back, and so Congress voted to renew the bank charter. Jackson vetoed it. In response to this veto, Clay boldly spoke out, claiming that the issue of the legitimacy of the National Bank had already been settled once in 1817 when a "tribunal of the greatest American minds" had debated it.

Jackson was obsessed with dismantling the Bank of the United States. Many in his cabinet advised him to just let its charter expire in 1836, but he would not listen to them. Instead, he sent his secretary of the treasury to Nicholas Biddle, the bank's president, with a notice that the U.S. government planned to withdraw six million dollars in order to pay off an old loan. In order to divert a financial disaster, Biddle then pleaded for a delay, but was given only four months to make up for the shortfall that this withdrawal would create. The confused Jackson then, of course, insisted that the bank was insolvent. In his paranoia, he also insisted that the bank was the tool of his enemies Clay and Calhoun.

One-fifth of the deposits in the Bank of the United States belonged to the people. Mindful of this, two successive treasury secretaries would not remove the government deposits from the bank as Jackson directed. When, however, Jackson appointed Roger B. Taney to that post, he removed them without compunction. Taney put the National Bank's deposits into the Union Bank of Baltimore where he was chief counsel and co-owner. From Congress, former President John Quincy Adams, remarked: "Resolved that the thanks of the House be given to Roger B. Taney, Secretary of the Treasury, for his pure and disinterested patriotism in transferring the use of the public funds from the Bank of the United States, where they were profitable to the people, to the Union Bank of Baltimore where they were profitable to himself." Jackson's forces tried to suppress Adams's statement, but he printed it up at his own expense and circulated 50,000 copies to the public. A copy is in the Library of Congress rare book collection today.

Soon after the removal of the deposits, Clay brought a resolution before the Senate for the censure of the president, insisting that he had violated the Constitution by removing two successive treasury secretaries when they would not comply with his order. When this measure passed, Jackson was typically infuriated. Later when his actions were cited as the cause for the deterioration of the economy, Jackson denounced the complaint by insisting that the bank was waging a vendetta against him, while others insisted that Jackson himself was organizing a vendetta against Nicholas Biddle for having opposed his election. When businessmen appealed to him for relief, the crazed Jackson told them to go to the "monster" for relief. And, later, when others insisted that he was not listening to the people, he maintained that, under great peril, he had protected them and that they were with him in all that he did.

The Bank of the United States was an institution of protection for the American people. By issuing currency, monitoring bank reserves, and issuing low-interest credit, it had created independence from the predatory practices of the world banking cartel centered in London. Some historians falsely proclaim that that bank was the enemy of the people and that Andrew Jackson was the people's hero because he dismantled it. This is not true. Jackson was no hero. He was a deluded puppet of enemy-installed agents in his own country.

After Congress had issued a second charter for the Bank of the United States in 1817, Nicholas Biddle became the bank's president. Biddle was a former diplomatic aid and an outstanding Greek scholar who came from a Philadelphia family of republicans who had been members of Franklin's Philadelphia junto. Biddle had campaigned hard for the re-establishment of the Bank of the United States. The old charter had expired in 1811 as a result of pro-British intrigue and demoralization inaugurated by Albert Gallatin when he was secretary of the treasury under both Jefferson and Madison. Biddle had insisted that without a national bank, the American people were at the mercy of British Empire financiers who were relentlessly trying to re-infiltrate American life.

While Biddle was president of the Bank of the United States, the bank had helped finance both canal and railroad construction. As we have seen, this opened the West up to settlement and created a U.S. coal industry. When London/Wall Street bankers tried to interfere with American industrial progress by manipulating the costs of construction commodities, Biddle would regularly intervene to counter-act this manipulative speculation. Steady progress ensued!

After Jackson vetoed the bill to renew the charter of the Bank of the U.S. in 1836, and ordered the removal of government deposits from that bank, in tandem, the Bank of England also called in loans and withdrew its investments from the bank. Gold then went flooding into England. With the amount of gold in circulation reduced, under the advice of his handlers, Jackson then issued an order known as the Specie Circular. It prohibited settlers from purchasing public lands with anything but gold or silver. All of this immediately reduced credit and resulted in a dramatic depression called the Panic of 1837. From as early as 1833, the private banking oligarchs in London and on Wall Street had been calling for the establishment of a U.S. "government" repository for federal funds under their control, similar to today's Federal Reserve Bank. In response to this, Nicholas Biddle wrote that Jackson's war against the U.S. Bank was "a mere contest between Mr. Van Buren's government bank and the present institution—between a faro bank and a national one." Mr. Biddle was far-sighted and wise, don't you think?

1821-1837

17

TRAIL OF TEARS

"Say to the chiefs and warriors that I am their friend...
but they must, by removing from the limits of the
states of Mississippi and Alabama and by settling in
the lands that I offer them, put it in my power to be
such...There, beyond the limits of any state, in possession of land of their own, which they shall possess
as long as grass grows or water runs, I will protect
them and be their father."

ANDREW JACKSON
TO THE CHOCTAW AND CHEROKEE INDIANS

From the early days of white settlement on the North American continent, the
relationship between Native American Indians and white settlers was a precarious
one. Many famous Americans—men like Ben Franklin, Thomas Jefferson, William
Penn and, later, John Quincy Adams, wanted to peacefully assimilate the Indian into the
white culture. These moral men, and others like them, espoused a platform of Indian
acceptance because they believed in the dignity of every living soul. Determined to forge
progress on the continent, they wanted the Indian to have a share in it.

Before the white man ever arrived in the Americas, the Indians had enjoyed a high
civilization on both continents, but it had collapsed. They then retreated to a nomadic
existence. In the early years of white settlement, the British armed the Indians with guns
in exchange for furs. Then they further demoralized them and incited them to war against
the colonists.

After victory in the War for Independence was won and the U.S. was established as a republic, its first president, George Washington, and his secretary of war, Henry Knox, publicly maintained that, as the first occupants of the land, the Indians had a right to possess it. In 1791 Washington's secretary of state, Thomas Jefferson, maintained that Indians living within state boundaries "should not be interfered with, and that the government should remove white settlers who tried to encroach on them." In 1793, Congress even allocated funds for the education and vocational training of the Indians.

There were others, however—members of the plantation aristocracy—who did not espouse this moral philosophy, so they challenged early treaties that the U.S. had made with the Indians in order to strengthen the rights of the plantation interests in Georgia and elsewhere. On their behalf, and in his own interests, Andrew Jackson then waged many fights to dispossess the Indians of their native lands.

After the War for Independence, a land surveyor from North Carolina, John Donelson, managed to "acquire" 20,000 acres of Tennessee land from the Chicksaw Indians, a tribe that had aided the republic in its fight for independence. Then, in the year 1795 alone, his son-in-law, Andrew Jackson, made twenty-two trips out of Nashville to make land deals. This marked the start of a life-long career of service to southern plantation aristocrats that made Andrew Jackson the greatest foe the Indian ever had.

After garnering a reputation for courage in the War of 1812, Jackson waged a fight with the Creek Indians at Horseshoe Bend and killed 900 members of that tribe. Then, in 1819, he turned his sights on the Spanish colony of Florida and attacked the Seminole Indians, burning villages and capturing forts, until he "persuaded" the Spanish to sell Florida under terms favorable to American land speculators. Then, until 1824, Jackson presided over ensuing land grabs that stole huge amounts of land from the Indians of the Southeast.

By 1830, the Indians had, in large numbers, given up their nomadic ways in favor of a more settled existence. The Cherokees, Creeks, Choctaws, Chicasaws and Seminoles, in particular, tried so hard to live in harmony with their white neighbors that whites began referring to them as the Five Civilized Tribes.

From as far back as 1802, federal law had given Congress sole authority to negotiate with the Indians. But, in 1829, when he became president, Jackson ignored these long-standing laws and instead began to support illegal state legislation drawn up by plantation interests in the South.

Then as president, Jackson launched his most appalling attack upon the Indians—an attack against the Cherokee Nation. Here is the background to that story: After the War for Independence, the Cherokees had signed a peace treaty with the U.S. that made them an independent people. Then, in 1791, in another solemn treaty, the U.S. government forged an alliance with the Cherokees and recognized their right to a substantial portion of land in northeastern Georgia. The Cherokees then settled down on this land to live in the style of the white man—raising cattle, and growing cotton. They also welcomed missionaries, built schools and churches and created legislation that regulated the purchase and sale of property.

Then, under Jefferson's presidential leadership, the United States government forged a friendship with the Cherokees and Sequoyah, their chief, invented a written language.

Thousands of Cherokees learned it. Then, in 1828, they ordered a printing press and started a newspaper, the *Cherokee Phoenix*. It was printed in both Cherokee and English. With this cultural advance, the Cherokees began to threaten the ruling plantation elite of Georgia who were vying for their land. So, in 1828, the Georgia Legislature took jurisdiction over Cherokee land and began taxing the Cherokees. All the while, the legally-formed Cherokee constitution had made that nation exempt from Georgia state taxes.

Then the enemy puppet-president, Andrew Jackson, in the face of increasing southern opposition to federal protection of the autonomous Cherokee Nation, ignored the guarantees of the federal government and, in 1830, submitted a bill to Congress that legislated for the removal of the Cherokees to land west of the Mississippi River. Henry Clay objected and Congressman Davy Crockett bitterly opposed the bill.

In order to get the bill through the Congress, Jackson had shrewdly made it voluntary, reasoning that the cruel state laws put into place in Georgia would give the Cherokees no other choice but to comply. But still some Cherokees refused to move. And, in their newspaper, they printed an appeal to the U.S. government, citing the friendship that they had forged with President Jefferson and the encouragement he had given them during the period when they were transitioning to a farming life. They also recognized the aid that missionaries had given them when they came to help them establish schools. Then they reviewed the inspiring letters their beloved white friend, Thomas Jefferson, had sent them.

In a desperate plea to Jackson, the Cherokees then asked him to honor the memory of Jefferson who, they maintained, had never said that, when they reached a high level of achievement in government, in the arts, and in the sciences, all that they had achieved would be forfeited by forced adherence to criminal state laws sanctioning land theft. Jackson ignored their appeal for mercy and, instead stepped up his Indian removal policies.

Unhappy with what they viewed as their forced removal, in 1831, the Cherokees turned to the courts for protection. They brought three cases to the Supreme Court, and, in all but the first case, the Court declared that laws directed against the Cherokee Nation were unconstitutional. President Jackson then defied the Supreme Court rulings and made it clear that he would tolerate no independent nation within the United States. When the Court took no action against him, he stepped up his Indian removal.

In 1837, when Martin Van Buren became president, he continued Jackson's policies. In 1838, he ordered Major General Winfield Scott to move the Cherokees west by force. Crowded into stockades, seventeen thousand Cherokees were moved along what has come to be known as the Trail of Tears. As they moved westward they began to die. Some went by wagon, but many had to march alongside by foot. By the time they reached the Mississippi River, it was wintertime. It is estimated that about four thousand Cherokees died on that march—mostly from pneumonia. With the removal complete, Van Buren proudly proclaimed the "success" of the project to Congress by saying: "The measures authorized by Congress at its last session have had the happiest effects."

1791-1838

18

THE PANIC OF 1837

Referring to the election of 1836, in his diary,
John Quincy Adams made the following comment:
"The remarkable character of this election is that all
the candidates are at most third-rate men whose
pretensions rest not on high attainments or upon
eminent services, but upon intrigue and
political speculation."

With his popularity at an all-time high, Jackson left office in 1837 just as the repercussions from the destruction of the National Bank were worsening. As the center of attention at the inauguration of his successor and political handler, Martin Van Buren, despite the horror created by his take-down of the National Bank, Old Hickory made a dramatic exit from Washington amid popular cheering and praise. It was the people's last chance to acknowledge their misplaced allegiance to the populist demagogue. Within months of his exit, the banking Panic of 1837 broke loose in all it fury causing the worst depression the young nation had ever experienced. The suffering it unleashed caused many of Jackson's supporters to wonder in hindsight about the legitimacy of his assault upon the Bank of the United States.

By springtime, as the New Orleans cotton brokerage house, Herman Briggs & Co. failed, Wall Street began to reel. Like the toppling of a house of cards, the collapse of other banking houses swiftly followed. Bankruptcy sales soon became commonplace and real estate values plummeted. The immense fortunes that had accrued with the rampant land speculation that followed the withdrawal of government funds from the Bank of the U.S. also disappeared. With rumors of widespread bank insolvency spreading, the common people, who had placed their savings in newly established savings banks, lined up to withdraw their meager funds. As New York banks suspended payment in specie, unruly crowds assembled, so city militias had to be called out to maintain a semblance of civil order. With all this suffering in the cities, the cost of food stayed high, so farmers remained quite prosperous.

Merchants were despondent. Quickly they turned to Nicholas Biddle for counsel and he urged an immediate re-chartering of the Bank of the United States. Like most nationalists, Biddle had foreseen the crash. Parties of disgruntled merchants then organized to meet with President Van Buren to try to affect this re-chartering. They also insisted that he rescind the Specie Circular, an executive order decree that Jackson had issued when the sudden collapse began. That order stipulated that public lands could only be purchased with gold.

After Bank of the United States funds were placed in state banks under private control, bankers began the practice of extending risky loans for land purchases. Without the proper government oversight, a speculative frenzy then ensued. And, to make matters worse, after the bubble began to collapse, New York banks began to demand that loans be paid back in specie. All of this made the enemy-orchestrated crisis more severe.

Merchants also wanted Van Buren to initiate a return to protective tariffs. But, enemy agent that he was, Van Buren, of course, refused any real help. Instead, he called a special session of Congress and, in addressing it, stubbornly maintained that the nation's financial woes should rightly be attributed to the Bank of the United States. That Bank, he said, had been responsible for fostering "rapid growth among all classes, and especially in our great commercial towns, of luxurious habits founded too often on merely fancied wealth, detrimental alike to the industry, the resources, and the morals of the people." By choosing to deny the truth, he angered many of his Whig opponents who knew that the crisis had really been caused by the monetary speculation that ensued following the dismantling of the National Bank.

In true enemy style, Van Buren then proposed the passage of a bankruptcy bill to create a private enemy-controlled central bank for the dispersal of public funds. He also authorized the short-term issue of paper currency to alleviate the constriction of credit. The Whigs knew that this was not enough, so they violently attacked his deceptive plan and continued to argue for the re-chartering of the Bank of the United States, so that bankruptcy reorganization could be conducted. Van Buren's bill passed the Senate, but the House continued to wrangle over it, so the special session of Congress adjourned without supplying any relief at all. The working class then continued to suffer under high prices.

During the Twenty-fifth Congress, in his 1837 annual address, President Van Buren proudly proclaimed a recovery. But, in his diary, John Quincy Adams astutely disagreed, referring to Van Buren's address as Jackson's message of 1832 "covered with a new coat of varnish." When his optimistic predictions proved to be unfounded, Van Buren became very unpopular.

Soup kitchens and bread lines like the ones organized in 1819 were then established to relieve the suffering of the newly-made poor. Then, in the spring of 1838, Congress repealed the Specie Circular—the Jackson law that had required payment in hard money for the sale of public lands. Enthusiasm then began to mount and stocks began to rise.

Despite the depression, in 1839, the country celebrated the fiftieth anniversary of Washington's presidential inauguration. The Whigs used this occasion as an opportunity to bemoan the loss of the old Federalist spirit that had launched the republic off on a sure footing. That same year, the Democrats elected James Polk as governor of Tennessee. Having already served as speaker of the House of Representatives, the enemy was grooming him to become president.

To test for a possible Whig nomination for president himself, in 1840, Henry Clay then engaged in a popular political tour of Saratoga, N.Y. Arriving with a band and a mile and one-half long parade of carriages and wagons, he was warmly received by the people.

Afterwards, he traveled to New York City and appeared in a parade down Broadway. There, the crowds gave him the same hero-like welcome. But Daniel Webster, who had deep ties with the enemy, had just returned home from a summer-long visit to Britain. In true enemy style, upon his return, he conspired to block Clay's nomination by agitating the many staunch abolitionists, from among the ranks of the Whigs, to oppose Clay on the grounds that, even though he was a nationalist, he owned slaves. So, instead, amid great fanfare, at the Whig party convention in Philadelphia, William Henry Harrison was nominated for president even though he was not of the same caliber as Clay. Like others before him, Harrison had capitalized on his career as a military general to emerge as a presidential contender. This was the second time he had been nominated for president and he ran once again with the enigmatic John Tyler. In a campaign of unprecedented slogans, Harrison swept the election with a nostalgic appeal for a return to the "good old times." In the next chapter, we shall see how the enemy-aligned "accidental president," John Tyler, in the wake of Harrison's mysterious death, canceled the nationalist program Harrison had quickly put into place. This allowed the enemy to once more control the White House.

1837-1840

19

CALEB CUSHING

"Free trade results in giving our money, our
manufactures, and our markets to other nations."

WILLIAM MCKINLEY, 1892

Conventional historical accounts of the life of Caleb Cushing conveniently fail to acknowledge his role as principle enemy-aligned U.S. government official during the 1840s and 1850s. In that role, he worked tirelessly at subverting the U.S. Constitution by sabotaging American system economic policies. He also helped unleash war with Mexico, promoted terror and bloodshed in Kansas, and, years in advance of the Civil War, helped coordinate the buildup of a Confederate army in the United States.

Commissioned as a pro-British agent by Essex Junto publicist, John "The Rebel" Lowell, Cushing became a master of political manipulation and intrigue. He was deeply imperialistic. A cousin of John Perkins Cushing, the richest American opium dealer of the nineteenth century, he developed a masterful ability to misrepresent facts. The slave "abolitionist," William Lloyd Garrison was his political protégé. Cushing began indoctrinating the young Garrison in disunion rhetoric when he met him at the *Newburyport Herald,* that town's radical anti-U.S tabloid. There, in 1822, Garrison had been apprenticed as a type-setter and Cushing was writing editorials on behalf of the Essex Junto. Cushing then guided the ambitious Garrison into political writing and groomed him to be the out-spoken northern spokesperson for radical abolition. By the 1850s, as secession loomed close, Garrison then threw all caution to the wind by displaying his anti-Union stand and boldly announcing "there can be no union between us." Before he met Cushing, devoid of any sympathy for the slave, Garrison had been an ardent supporter of colonization. Years earlier, in Philadelphia, Ben Franklin had organized authentic patriotic opposition to slavery. The members of this group were not radical revolutionists like Garrison. They were nationalists who wanted to defeat slavery through an American program of industrialization.

Garrison came from a multi-generational Tory family. His grandfather had left Massachusetts, sometime before 1764, to live in New Brunswick, Canada. In 1776, when the people of his village signed a declaration siding with the American colonists against British tyranny, Joseph Garrison was among a small number of villagers who opposed this declaration. Then, when William Lloyd Garrison's father left Canada for Newburyport, Masssachusetts, in 1805, he did so only by first giving his parents assurances that he was not defecting to the side of the patriots. When William Lloyd Garrison was just a small boy, his alcoholic father deserted the family, so his mother sought the patronage of wealthy Essex county families and eventually became the nurse to the daughter of Timothy Pickering, one of the organizers of the Hartford Convention. Garrison grew up admiring Timothy Pickering, and with the help of Pickering's local Tory friends, he became apprenticed at the *Newburyport Herald* while he was just a young man. In 1831, with the support of wealthy New England Tories, Garrison furthered the enemy cause by founding the *Liberator*. We will speak more about this newspaper's founding insurrectionist platform in subsequent chapters.

Over the years, Cushing and Garrison appeared to be extreme political opposites. Garrison was the leader of the northern Tory abolitionist faction, while Cushing became the main northern strategist and spokesperson for the slave plantation system. In secret, though, they were both politically allied to British Empire interests in America. The British operation has always routinely used this kind of divide and conquer scheme to establish its influence in the world. Their agents often rally around opposing sides of intentionally created conflict and appear to be hated enemies, but this is just a ploy. It takes awareness to stay on top of these constant enemy-developed charades.

After Cushing's failed 1826 bid for election to Congress from Essex County, Massachusetts, Garrison began to write articles promoting agent Cushing as a Henry Clay-style Whig, but, despite efforts to cloak him in the garb of nationalism, the public largely viewed Cushing as a leftish anti-union candidate and they distrusted him. Still, Garrison tried to garner respectability for Cushing by writing an anti-free trade pamphlet for him. At Cushing's behest, he also wrote a presidential campaign biography about William Henry Harrison. In reality, though, neither Garrison nor Cushing had anything in common with Harrison or his protective tariff platform.

In 1840, in the wake of serious economic depression following the banking panic of 1837, Harrison was elected president. As a devoted protectionist, he immediately submitted new tariff legislation to Congress. But despite the fact that he appeared to be robust and healthy at the time he took office, within one month, he was dead. No official autopsy was performed. Today, we are suspicious because, by 1840, the enemy had largely penetrated state medical associations and, with their accrued influence, they became emboldened—perhaps emboldened enough to sanction the president's death by poisoning. The president's attending physician, Frederick May, could have done the job. Trained at Harvard by Dr John Warren, the pro-Tory brother of Joseph Warren, the American revolutionary hero of the Battle of Bunker Hill, Frederick May had many Tory affiliations. The enemy routinely assassinates nationalists when they rise up to promote the American system, so it is not unreasonable, in this instance, to suspect murder.

By the time Vice President Tyler was inaugurated as president, Congress had already begun to implement the deceased president Harrison's policies by passing a bill designed to re-establish the Bank of the United States. Quite unexpectedly, Tyler then vetoed the bill and effectively displayed his allegiance with the enemy—an allegiance he had previously kept very well hidden. Henry Clay was outraged by the veto and nearly the whole Harrison-appointed cabinet resigned over it. Daniel Webster was the only cabinet member who did not resign—probably because he was financially indebted to Cushing. In his whole lifetime, Webster never repaid any of the loans Cushing made to him.

The House tried to mister up the two-thirds majority required to pass the bill vetoed by Tyler, but they failed. Incensed by the presidential veto of the bank bill, Henry Clay spoke out in Congress, saying, "There is a rumor abroad that a cabal exists—a new sort of kitchen cabinet, whose object is the dissolution of the Whig Party, the dispersion of Congress without accomplishing any of the great purposes of the extra session, and a total change in the whole face of our political affairs." Despite Clay's caution, the presidential veto was sustained and, sadly, the United States never again had a national bank under public control.

Emboldened by the political success of the enemy, Caleb Cushing then threw all caution to the wind and stood up to display his hidden support for Tyler. His sudden "conversion" to the side of the "accidental president" then made him even more unpopular with Congress. Three times, Tyler nominated him for secretary of the treasury, but the House would not approve his nomination. Subsequently, under the recommendation of Daniel Webster, Cushing was nominated for the chairmanship of the House Foreign Relations Committee. The great nationalist statesman, John Quincy Adams had also been vying for this position, but Congress ratified Cushing's nomination for the post. Adams, of course, was an American pacifist, not an imperialist like Cushing. Dedicated to the American founding vision, in that position, he would have promoted world peace. Cushing, as we shall see, stirred up trouble.

Cushing then became an intimate adviser to the president and constantly worked to organize support for his pro-British agenda. Then, to help coordinate the enemy's plans to divide the Union, he proceeded to plan for future southern insurrection by arranging to place his life-long Newburyport friend, Albert Pike, in a position of political power in the state of Arkansas. There, Pike rose to a high position in the Scottish Rite of Freemasonry, an arm of British secret intelligence. From that position, for man years, he covertly worked at southern disunion. Letters survive today in the Library of Congress that prove Cushing's patronage of Pike.

As chairman of the House Foreign Relations Committee, Cushing then proceeded to influence U.S. foreign policy. As we have seen, when John Quincy Adams was president, he aspired to create peaceful cooperation among all the newly emerging republics in South America. Cushing, on the other hand, did all he could to sabotage a planned Panama Peace Conference by creating a U.S. leadership void. This effectively destroyed the potential for a strong alliance of independent nation-states in the Western Hemisphere. Later, under the "leadership" of a string of enemy puppet-presidents, Latin America was further alienated.

During this same period, the emperor of China, incensed by the widespread addiction of his people to opium, tried to stand up to the criminally oppressive British Empire by halting the flood of opium into his country. This trade had fabulously enriched British merchant families and their associated Boston Brahmin counterparts. The Cushings of Boston had become wealthy from their participation in this illegal trade.

In response to this Chinese attempt to halt the import of opium into their country, the British dispatched an expeditionary force from India to Canton to fight a brief war with the Chinese. The Chinese forces—forces that had been decimated by ten years of opium addiction—were easily defeated   The emperor then had to sign a terrible treaty that required the Chinese to make restitution to the British for all the opium that had been burned during the war. And, as part of a British free trade agreement, the Chinese were also forced to cede the island of Hong Kong to the British. Cushing happily reported this economic rape of China to President Tyler and suggested to him that in the wake of this British "success," a U.S. agent might also be dispatched to that country to "secure" American trading rights there. Three days later, Tyler sent a letter to Congress requesting an appropriation for this mission. He also pushed for Cushing's appointment as first minister to China. Congress approved both requests.

In true British military style, before leaving on his mission to China, Cushing had himself outfitted in an ostentatious blue major general's uniform replete with embroidery and a white plume. Then, when he arrived in China, in 1843, he presented a letter from President Tyler to representatives of the emperor. This letter, written by Daniel Webster, introduced Cushing as "Count" Caleb Cushing, minister of peace, wise and learned man of his country. Then along with the letter, Cushing sent the emperor's representatives off with a personal message that "suggested" that the emperor make a treaty with Cushing, so that "the peace would not be disturbed."

When the emperor displayed no desire to make another "peace" treaty, Cushing began to intimidate him by sending a frigate up Canton Bay to fire a few threatening rounds. Still continuing to experience rejection, Cushing then mobilized a whole American squadron and sent it on up the river, too. Sufficiently intimidated, the emperor then signed the desired treaty. Among other things, it included a stipulation that allowed both the Americans and the British to enjoy reciprocity benefits for any future trade "favors" obtained in China by either country.

Upon hearing that Tyler was pushing for the annexation of Texas to the Union, despite the Senate's rejection of this proposal, on his return from China, in 1844, Cushing, in his own style, set about to promote this annexation. As the ship bringing him home from China approached America, he disembarked on the west coast of Mexico. From there he proceeded to the interior of that country by horseback. His intention was to travel the Mexican countryside and acquire knowledge of the Mexican character and habits. Cushing was delighted when his findings indicated that Mexico would easily be defeated should the United States go forward with British-inspired plans for a war with that country. Armed with this information, in 1845, he returned home to formulate these findings in a report.

Even though the Mexican government had stated in 1843, that it would consider the U.S. annexation of the republic of Texas to be a declaration of war on Mexico, covert preparation for an enemy-inspired war with Mexico continued. The American people had demonstrated their opposition to such a war, but that made no difference to Tyler or the next British-installed president. James K. Polk. Like his predecessor, Polk, too, was determined to provoke war with Mexico.

1822-1845

20

THE EMPIRE
PUSHES OPIUM

"If the trade is ever legalized, it will cease to be
profitable...The more difficulties that attend it, the
better for you and us."

A STATEMENT ON OPIUM TRADE
BY THE DIRECTORS OF JARDINE-MATHESON

The cultivation of opium reaches far back into history. No remnants of any wild varieties of opium exist today. The ancient Sumerians cultivated opium for medicinal purposes and, over time, knowledge of the drug's narcotic properties spread throughout the Mediterranean. Pipes designed for smoking opium found on the island of Crete can be dated to as early as 1100 BC. Around 400 A.D., the Arabs brought opium to China via their ancient trade road and around 700 A.D., the Chinese first began producing opium for medicinal use.

The history of the British Empire's forced addiction of the Chinese people to opium began when the Portuguese brought the first European-traded opium to China. Opium trade, however, remained marginal until the advent of the empire-inspired royal-chartered European mercantile companies. Then, by 1659, as the Dutch and the English began to prevail over trade in the Far East, opium became second in trade only to spices.

In 1715, when the British East India Company opened up its first Far Eastern office in Canton, China, officers of the company began to marginally trade there in the drug.

Then, in 1757, the British won military victories in Bengal, India, and that province became a Crown colony, so the British began to widely cultivate opium there.

By 1750, opium was being deliberately pushed on native peoples who had been enslaved on empire plantations. Then, in the early 1770s, by surpassing all competition, the British Empire became the leading supplier of opium to the Chinese. Contemptuous of Westerners and referring to them as "white devils", however, there was precious little that the Chinese wanted to buy from the British, but the British coveted many Chinese items for trade—items like porcelin, silk and especially tea, So, in order to establish a balance of trade and stop the flow of silver out of the British treasury, in 1787, British Secretary of State, Henry Dundas, proposed that the amount of opium shipped to China be stepped up. As the Chinese became increasingly addicted to opium, silver then flowed back into the British coffers.

From before the American Revolution, a significant number of select enemy-aligned New England families had been allied with the trading empire—initially in the profitable East Indies slave trade. Then, in anticipation of the outbreak of the 1776-1783 American Revolution, many British loyalists fled the colonies. Prominent among these loyalists, were three members of the Perkins family of Boston. One of them—Thomas Handasyd Perkins, made a fortune trading in slaves. His early trade ledgers also show the names of Cabot and Forbes as his early trading partners. But, Caribbean slave revolts, and then a prohibition by U.S. law that banned the slave trade altogether, forced Perkins out of that business. Then, coincident with the above-mentioned 1787 Dundas plan for the expansion of empire trade in opium, the Massachusetts law that banned the return of British loyalists to that former colony was repealed, so, Thomas H. Perkins returned to Boston. Then, in 1789, he sailed to China with Elias Derby of Salem to engage in the opium trade. After a profitable stint in China, T.H. Perkins then returned to Boston to organize J. & T. H. Perkins and Company, his own opium-trading company.

Meanwhile, cousin George Perkins, one of the three above-mentioned Perkins family members who had fled the colonies as loyalists at the start of the American Revolution, had been busy setting himself up as a merchant in Smyrna, Turkey, where opium was grown in abundance. By the time that J. & T. H. Perkins and Company was established, Smyrna had become an American port of call, so the Perkins brothers had access to a supply of opium that made their business independent of British-controlled Indian opium. This established the Perkins family as leading American traders in that drug.

Perkins & Company became an extended family affair when other families—like Cabot, Sturgis, Forbes and Cushing married in to the Perkins clan. Favored by his uncle, the second-generation, sixteen year-old John Perkins Cushing, later sailed to China to run the family business and, under his management, company revenues increased so dramatically that a portion of the Perkins family business was then transferred to Russell & Company of Connecticut. By 1829, Russell & Company had absorbed the entire Perkins company trade, so it emerged as the third largest opium-smuggling company in the world.

From as early as 1818, due to the growing unpopularity of the opium trade among members of the British Parliament, Jardine-Matheson was engaged, under the guise of an independent trading company, to run opium to China on behalf of the empire. Then, after Russell & Company grew to be its near equal competitor, the two companies, informally associated as the "Combination," expanded their trade routes up and down the China coast. In typical empire fashion, they also worked together to maximize profits by fixing opium prices. Like the Perkins Company, Russell & Company was also a family affair whose connections extended beyond the company to banks and other fronts. American opium dealers always worked side-by-side with the British in the tiny Canton area where foreigners were domiciled in China.

While the Bank of the United States supplied the early credit for U.S. infrastructure improvements and the growth of domestic enterprise, the Tory China trade was financed almost entirely by the empire-aligned Baring Brothers Bank in London. Ralph Bennett Forbes, member of the Perkins clan, had not only developed a relationship with that bank, but he also enjoyed a trade relationship with the Chinese merchant, Houqua. These powerful relationships helped forge the success of the illegal Perkins family drug trade. It also provided the British with an early opening into the affairs of the young United States. It was, in fact, the empire-financed opium traffickers who paid for the free trade propaganda that eventually succeeded in closing the Bank of the United States in 1836, further consolidating the empire's control over the young United States.

Following the dismantling of the Bank of the United States, a speculative crash created the Panic of 1837 and specie became scarce. Acting as agent for the Rothschilds, August Belmont then went to the United States to buy up securities as well as debts and property. George Peabody, an old China trader himself, then settled in London and brought Junius Morgan into the empire's banking sphere of influence. In 1841, Robert B. Forbes went to London with his uncle, T. H. Perkins, to confer with the Barings and the Rothschilds. All these Anglo-American relationships helped strengthen the London/Wall Street allied banking oligarchy.

In the heyday of its blossoming wealth from trade in opium, the Perkins syndicate became the ruling class of both Salem and Newburyport in Essex County, Massachusetts. In Salem, they formed the East India Society and held an annual Salem gala where members paraded through the streets in Chinese costume, subtly celebrating the source of their wealth. Many of the members of the extended Perkins syndicate lived in neighboring Newburyport and from there they established the Essex Junto, an organization that figured predominantly in the many treasonous operations that led to the American Civil War. After its early formation, that junto assumed control of Harvard College. As a student at Harvard, Caleb Cushing, cousin to the wealthy John Perkins Cushing, ingratiated himself into Harvard circles where the powerful enemy-aligned Judge Lowell noticed his ambition and rewarded him with a prominent role in Essex Junto operations. From that initiation, he developed a career of devotion to the intended enemy breakup of the United States.

Like their Perkins family counterparts associated with Harvard College, the Russell family was steeped in Yale College tradition. In 1833, the graduating class of Yale, operating under the Skull & Bones pirate emblem, established the Skull & Bones Society to secretly promote covert enemy operations. The impetus for the establishment of that society largely resulted from the dwindling number of memberships in Masonic organizations that the American patriot, John Quincy Adams, had created with his anti-Masonic writings. In those prolific writings, Quincy Adams had asserted that secret society membership was incompatible with holding public office because taking an oath of secrecy violated the public trust required of elected officials.

Covert empire operations always seek to create banking and trade monopolies. Monopolies are, in fact, a hallmark of empire operations. At secret meetings, long-range plans are set. Terrorism and prolonged warfare are tools used to by the enemy to implement their strategies. This book seeks to expose the history of behind-the-scenes enemy planning in order to promote awareness because only an aware ever-vigilant nation-state electorate can permanently defeat the enemy.

1689-1840

21

THE MACHINE CRUSHES CLAY

"I'd rather be right than be President."

HENRY CLAY

While a student at the University of North Carolina, James K. Polk skillfully mastered the art of oratory. Then, in 1824, at the age of twenty-nine, he was elected to the House of Representatives where he served for fourteen years. There he became a pronounced follower of Andrew Jackson and delighted in joining with Jackson in unreasonably opposing the John Quincy Adams administration. Loyalty to Jackson advanced Polk's political career. As chairman of the Ways and Means Committee during Jackson's presidency, Polk supported the removal of government deposits from the Bank of the United States. Then, when he became speaker of the House, he was charged with mounting an inquiry into Samuel Swartwout's conduct as collector of customs for the port of New York, but, because of his reputation for the most vindictive kind of partisanship, the House would not allow him to name the investigating committee. Polk later ran for governor of Tennessee and served one term, but unpopular with the people, he was later defeated in bids for re-election. With this background, in 1844, he was snatched up by the New York political machine and promoted for president.

In that election, Polk waged a particularly dirty campaign against the Whig Party candidate, the nationalist, Henry Clay. Clay was a patriot schooled in the tradition of the founders of the republic and he would have made a monumental president. The British knew this, so, in their strategy to defeat Clay, they poured large amounts of money into Polk's campaign.

During the election of 1844, as part of their platform, the Whig Party then issued a pamphlet proving that the British were financing the campaign of James K. Polk for the purpose of subverting protective tariffs. In this pamphlet, the Whigs asked the rhetorical question: "Shall British gold buy what British valor could not conquer?" Then they actually documented the transfer of $400,000 into Polk's election campaign. This was a huge amount of money back then—the equivalent of hundreds of millions of today's dollars.

Polk's dirty tricks campaign had powerful support from the New York political machine which controlled the Democratic Party. Van Buren had been defeated for re-election to the presidency in 1840 by the Whig candidate, William Henry Harrison, but despite this, in 1844, the Democrats initially sought to again promote him for president. So Clay, fully anticipating that Van Buren would be his opponent, eagerly sought the presidential nomination of the Whig Party in order to promote his nationalist agenda— re-enactment of the National Bank, protective tariffs, internal improvements and the distribution and sale of public lands. With the campaign revolving around these issues, Clay knew he would have an advantage over Van Buren.

From his youth, as we have learned, Van Buren had been trained to manage the New York political apparatus that Aaron Burr had established on behalf of the enemy. That political machine controlled the Democratic Party. In his role as enemy political operative, Van Buren became an expert in misrepresenting himself on behalf of that enemy. He had even cultivated a friendship with Clay in order to disguise his plan to manipulate the issues of the 1844 campaign. Clay could not have known the extent of Van Buren's treachery.

Even though the Democratic Party initially wanted to again nominate him for president, Van Buren shrewdly determined to instead have Polk nominated as the Democratic Party candidate in order to make the annexation of Texas the major issue of the campaign. To do this, he publically opposed the annexation himself in order to reduce his own popularity among Democrats. Polk was then nominated as the party's compromise candidate.

Clay had earlier that year been nominated amid great fanfare at the Whig party convention in Baltimore and he had begun his campaign with great extravaganzas— parades and banners, badges, pennants, and streamers. He was exuberant. It looked like his chance to become president had finally come. He looked forward to promoting U.S. nationalism in the upcoming campaign. As a dedicated statesman, he had made the preservation and strengthening of the Union the mission of his entire political life.

Then, when the Democrats changed the focus of the presidential campaign and zeroed in on the annexation of Texas, Clay shrewdly perceived the enemy "divide and conquer" agenda behind this move, so he wrote an article for the *National Intelligencier,* attacking the idea of annexation, calling it "perfectly idle and ridiculous, if not dishonorable." He also declared it tantamount to declaring war with Mexico. He knew that a war with Mexico was exactly what the British wanted.

Knowing that the Whig Party had been factionalized by the infiltration of abolitionists who preferred Clay to Polk, in the midst of the campaign, Van Buren then organized for the promotion of a third party candidate, James Birney, from among the ranks of the abolitionists in order to take votes away from Clay. When the third party candidate emerged and threatened to split the Whig Party vote, Clay was understandably disappointed.

Sensing a shift in the momentum of the campaign, with an eye to gathering votes, Clay then modified his position on the annexation of Texas and, in the process, alienated many northern Whigs. The Democrats then mercilessly attacked Clay's character, calling him both vindictive and immoral, so Clay began to tirelessly write in his own defense. All the while, Polk, under the tutelage of Van Buren, stayed cool and quiet and let both Clay and his challenger struggle and write ceaselessly. All the while, with war on his mind, Polk kept promoting the issue of Texas annexation with an eye to the whole reason for his campaign—the inauguration of a future British-designed war with Mexico. He also lied and claimed that he was a greater protectionist than Clay.

When election day rolled around, in order to help engineer Polk's election, Louisiana's political boss, John Slidell, transplanted trained operative from New York, promoted voting fraud by personally arranging for the transport of huge numbers of Polk voters up and down the Mississippi River by steamboat. All along the way, that steamboat stopped at every parish to let this crowd vote multiple times. But it was the weight of the influence of the New York political machine that sealed the defeat of Clay by narrowly swinging the election in favor of Polk even though Polk had largely been recognized as inexperienced.

The election of 1844 was conducted with intense energy. Clay had many friends and admirers and their love for him as immense. That love, however, could not prevail against the organized efforts of the enemy and their ally, Martin Van Buren. The enemy's duped stooge, Andrew Jackson, also worked from retirement at the *Hermitage* to elect Polk. Triumphant over Polk's election, the old warrior then died seven months later happy that he had had a final chance to satisfy his old hatred for Clay.

In Congress, three days before Polk's inauguration, enemy agent, Robert J. Walker, from Mississippi, helped orchestrate the passage of Tyler's bill for the annexation of Texas. In regular contact with Tyler during the campaign, Polk had successfully cleared a path for the promotion of the upcoming British-planned war with Mexico.

1825-1844

22

POLK'S WAR

"The world has nothing to fear from military ambition
in our government."

JAMES POLK

As we have seen, Polk began his duplicitous 1844 campaign for the presidency on a Whig-style platform by calling himself a better protectionist than Clay. All the while, his campaign of service to the empire aimed at annexing Texas in order to strengthen the hand of the British-sponsored plantation aristocracy in the South. The British wanted to promote the expansion of the slave system to Texas and beyond, in order to realize the establishment of their planned tropical colony in the New World. The founders of the republic, you will recall, had wanted to eradicate slavery, but, unable to secure ratification of the Constitution by any other means, they agreed to grandfather the slave system under the condition that it would remain within the bounds of the existing South. Committed to promoting the expansion of the slave plantation system, once he became president, Polk immediately focused in on inaugurating war with Mexico in order to seize land from that country. War had been, and still is today, the chief means by which the empire realizes its geopolitical goals.

Polk won the 1844 election by the narrowest of margins. Without the influence of Van Buren's New York political machine and the Democratic Party's dirty tricks campaign, he would have been defeated by Henry Clay and his masterful statesmanship. Before Polk even assumed office, and just as Caleb Cushing was returning to Washington with his own plans for war with Mexico formulated, Tyler engineered a resolution for the annexation of Texas. Congress quickly acted upon the resolution. Then, as soon as he took office, Polk sent agent Slidell to Mexico, as another Cushing-style peace "commissioner," to try to negotiate for the annexation of Texas, but he was turned away. Mexico had already stated that it would consider the U.S. annexation of Texas a declaration of war, but that made no difference to the expansionist-minded Polk.

Before actually declaring war with Mexico, Polk also tried to use the threat of impending war to negotiate with Mexico for the purchase of California. Americans held millions of dollars in claims against Mexico for the illegal seizure of property and the Mexican government had no money, so Polk shrewdly tried to entice the Mexicans into giving up California as settlement for their debts, but this plan failed.

After the Mexican refusal to negotiate with Polk for the purchase of California, Polk sent a message to Congress recommending war. Knowing that such a request would elicit huge opposition from the North, as an incentive for war, Polk lied to Congress by claiming that the Mexican army had crossed over onto U.S. territory, fired upon U.S. troops commanded by Zachary Taylor, and "spilled blood" there. Not knowing that this was a lie, Congress then voted to allocate money for supplies and the war began in earnest.

Many of Polk's supporters largely suspected that he was waging a war of aggression against Mexico and many citizens questioned the legitimacy of the war. The Whig press also relentlessly criticized Polk and denounced his war as one that had been imposed upon Mexico by a president who was controlled by slave-owning imperialists who had put him into office by unscrupulous means. Abraham Lincoln was then a congressman from Illinois and he suspected that Polk was lying. So, calling Polk a "bewildered, confounded and miserably perplexed man," he challenged him to prove that the Mexicans had been the first to shed blood as claimed. When this challenge went unmet, Lincoln launched a government investigation into the matter. Because of its emphasis on the exact spot where blood was shed, Lincoln's investigation became known as the "Spot" Resolution. The facts ascertained from this formal inquiry confirmed that Polk had been lying. The Mexicans had not actually crossed over into U.S. territory to start a war.

Polk's proclivity for dirty double-dealing extended to his own military leaders, too. Concerned that both Generals Zachary Taylor and Winfield Scott would speedily conclude the war and then capitalize on victory to emerge as heroes and challenge his presidency, in prosecuting the war, Polk routinely procrastinated. Then, when he did act, he sent orders that made no sense. So, both Scott and Taylor, in particular, made their own field decisions. As a result, the war was, indeed, speedily concluded. Both Taylor and Scott were then lauded as heroes, just as Polk had feared. Unhappy with the early conclusion to the war, Polk then refused to commend their bravery.

Even though historians have recently been disposed to give Polk high marks as a president because of all the territory he amassed for the U.S., a diary he left behind, when studied, reveals that Polk was an unscrupulous character who routinely used threats and bribery to realize his goals. Even his staunch supporter and confident, Thomas Hart Benton, of Missouri, in characterizing Polk, called many of his military decisions "infinitely silly." A true patriot would undoubtedly have described them in stronger terms.

Compare these years, if you will, with the moral stand that the American patriot, Abraham Lincoln embraced during the Civil War years. Having to contend with ambitious generals, Lincoln held firm to his decision to preserve the Union under trying circumstances. While the British promoted the enemy occupation of Mexico during the war, Lincoln aided the resistance forces of the Mexican patriot, Benito Juarez, supplying them with arms and munitions. He even ordered Grant to make the Union army ready for a possible invasion of Mexico, if necessary. With his determination to defend the Union, Lincoln remained true to his nation's founding mission. In the process, he also helped strengthen nationalist forces in Mexico, so, after the Civil War victory, Napoleon III pulled his troops out of the region. Then Maximillian was executed and Juarez was restored to power. With his noble actions, Lincoln succeeded in neutralizing all the bitterness Polk had created among Mexicans.

Later, out of admiration for Lincoln, the great nineteenth century president of Columbia, Rafael Nunez, was inspired to emulate Lincoln by enacting protective trade policies that kicked the free-trading British out of his country. He also wrote a U.S.-style constitution for Columbia. After Lincoln's murder, President Grant continued to have cordial relations with Columbia. He sent the Civil War counterintelligence expert, General Stephen Hurlbut, there to negotiate for a canal through present-day Panama which, at the time, was part of Columbia. That canal was designed to be of mutual benefit to both American nations, so the British conspired to prevent it. Plans for a canal in Panama were not secured until Teddy Roosevelt became president and then, under his administration, the canal was built to suit British imperial interests. In later chapters, we shall explore the workings of the enemy during those years.

1844-1863

23

YOUNG AMERICA

"Whenever I hear anyone arguing for slavery, I feel a
strong impulse to see it tried on him personally."

ABRAHAM LINCOLN

Against the backdrop of the war just fought with Mexico, Edwin DeLeon, student
of Thomas Cooper, gave a speech at South Carolina College that launched the
organization of Young America, a British enemy-inspired political movement
aimed at promoting civil war in America. Giuseppe Mazzini had already organized
similar movements in Europe. Their aim was the same—the overthrow of nationalist
governments through insurrection. In the Americas, the specific goal would be the
breakup of the United States, the conquest of Latin America, and the conversion of the
Americas into a huge slave plantation system.

At the same time that they were promoting slavery in the South through the establishment of the Young America movement, the British were also promoting abolition, a
counter-movement, purportedly dedicated to emancipating the slave. Through support
of both of these hate-driven opposing groups, they were aiming to divide the people and
foment civil war. Then, by winning that war on behalf of the Confederacy, they hoped to
re-enslave America.

The leader of the abolitionist counter-movement was William Lloyd Garrison.
Trained by Caleb Cushing from as far back as 1831, Garrison started *the Liberator*, an
anti-slavery newspaper. Through that newspaper, he promoted the abolitionist movement
by initially sending free *Liberator* subscriptions to blacks. In its early years, the tabloid
had few white subscribers, but Garrison eventually changed all of that by sending free
subscriptions to southern pro-slavery newspapers, too. After reading his controversial

articles, these southern newspapers then published their own articles and counter-editorials in which they denounced abolition. Then they sent copies to Garrison and he would respond back. In this way, both sides lent notoriety to the slavery issue and strengthened the British divide and conquer agenda.

In 1848, Zachary Taylor, hero of the Mexican War and Whig party candidate, was elected president. He was both a slave-owning southerner and a patriotic pro-Union president who took office at a time of deepening national crisis. You will recall that, under the leadership of the enemy-installed president, James K. Polk, the U.S. had been manipulated into engaging in a war with Mexico, but, Taylor had helped bring that war to a speedy conclusion by commanding his forces in a brief battle there. Then, when he became president, he proceeded to denounce Young America and its relentless plans for the breakup of the Union.

During this same time, the Northern Scottish Rite of Freemasonry had installed a Young America agent in Mississippi in order to create a new front for British-inspired insurrectionist operations. His name was John Anthony Quitman and, from Mississippi, he began to work toward the permanent annexation of Mexico. At the end of the Mexican War he had even presented a formal plan for this to then President Polk.

Zachary Taylor's job as president was complicated by the fact that, as a result of the war victory over Mexico, along with Texas, the U.S. had come into possession of additional territory from Mexico. This raised widespread concern over whether this area would become slave-holding or free. And, to make matters worse, back from Mexico, John Anthony Quitman began to openly advocate for southern secession. To further British geopolitical goals, he even arranged for an invasion of Cuba under the pretense of opposition to "oppressive" Spanish colonial rule. All the while, the Spanish were becoming less oppressive and more tolerant of the idea of freedom. It was the British Empire and her agents in America who were intently committed to the continuation of slavery in the Americas. They also had an investment in the continuation of slavery in Cuba because they wanted to include that fertile island in their planned slave plantation colony.

Tired of all this treason, President Taylor decided to oppose it by sending agents to California and New Mexico to arrange for formal free admission of these states to the Union. Then he took action against Quitman by getting a grand jury in New Orleans to indict him for financing the invasion of Cuba. Meanwhile, Quitman sent a telegram to Washington announcing that he would be personally leading an anti-federal army of several thousand troops from Texas into New Mexico to claim parts of that territory for Texas. The same day that the telegram arrived, President Taylor held a meeting with some southern visitors and announced that "if it becomes necessary I will take command of the army myself to enforce the laws. And ... if you men are taken in rebellion against the Union, I will hang you with less reluctance than I hanged the spies and deserters in Mexico."

By the next day, Taylor had drafted a half-finished message which he left on his desk. In it, he declared that he would never let any part of New Mexico be seized by Texas. That day was Independence Day, July 4, 1850, and so, in the afternoon, President Taylor went to an Independence Day celebration. That evening he suddenly fell ill with vomiting. He died five days later. His death, unofficially attributed to eating too many cherries and drinking cold milk, made him the second recent president to die under suspicious circumstances. Like William Henry Harrison before him, Taylor had assumed office under a national program of tariff protection and a pledge to resume federal construction projects aimed at improving transportation and commerce. Then, after announcing his adamant opposition to the spread of slavery, he suddenly died.

The following year, under indictment for his Cuban conspiracy, Quitman resigned from the office of governor of Mississippi and went to Boston in the company of General Jefferson Davis and others who had all been allied in the Cushing-Quitman operation that had promoted the Mexican War. There they met to begin arranging for the Democratic nomination of the next pro-British president, Franklin Pierce of New Hampshire. They also plotted further anti-Union operations.

Caleb Cushing met the generals in Boston and took them to his home in Newburyport, Massachusetts. (You will recall that Newburyport had been the place where the Essex Junto had been established.) There they held a days-long strategy session planning for the next presidency. Midway through the meeting, they introduced their prospective nominee, Franklin Pierce. Through a full-scale charade of mass manipulation, they planned to make him the surprise nominee at the next Democratic convention. At that convention, they planned to suggest several weak candidates for initial nomination, but none of them would be popular enough to garner the two-thirds majority required to secure the nomination. Then, with everyone beginning to despair of ever finding a nominee, they would create a burst of enthusiasm around Pierce. With momentum building, Pierce would then quickly secure the required two-thirds vote and be nominated. Reality played-out exactly as planned and, in 1852, Franklin Pierce became the Democratic presidential nominee.

The enemy-infiltrated Whig party nominated the patriot, General Winfield Scott, for president, but in the election he was actually defeated by subversive agents in his own party. Among them was Daniel Webster, his bitter opponent. Webster participated in a plan to split the votes of the Whig party by running on a third party platform, so that Pierce could emerge as the front-runner and win the election.

During the campaign, Young America worked hard to elect Pierce. Through mass propaganda efforts, they enticed the huge newly-nationalized immigrant population, mostly made up of Irish and German refugees, to vote for him. Had Scott been elected president, he would have surely fortified the forts in Charleston Harbor and this may have prevented the treasonous arming of the Confederacy. It also might have prevented civil war. But, instead, the election of Pierce ushered in a new phase of planned insurrection. Even though, as a candidate, Pierce had pledged allegiance to the Union, his secret plans were consistent with the platform of Young America. Like treasonous presidents before him, upon entering office, Pierce proceeded to appoint all his crony colleagues to posts in his administration. Caleb Cushing was made attorney general, Jefferson Davis, secretary of war, August Belmont, ambassador to Holland, Edwin DeLeon, U.S. consul in Egypt, and George Sanders, U.S. consul to London. Sanders would later help plan the assassination of Abraham Lincoln.

Once Pierce became president, John Quitman, Northern Scottish Rite of Freemasonry Supreme Council member, again began to unceasingly devote himself to the promotion of an "independent" new government in Cuba. Then, when the Spanish government heard that Quitman was out of jail and planning a new invasion, they quickly moved to counter it with a plan to thwart the Quitman-aligned white plantation aristocracy in Cuba by suppressing the slave trade and freeing the slaves. They then formed a free black militia and disarmed the whites.

The Spanish government later confiscated the *Black Warrior*, an American cargo ship which had suddenly appeared in the harbor at Havana carrying undeclared cargo. And they arrested its traitorous American captain, James D. Bulloch, the notorious British agent and revered uncle of future U.S. President, Teddy Roosevelt. Eager for war, using the seizure of the ship as a pretense, Pierce then quickly called for military action against Cuba. All his Young America friends, too, called for war, but Congress successfully opposed him.

Young America continued to attempt to overthrow the government in Cuba and they promoted a successful mercenary attack upon Nicaragua. Afterwards, the commander of that mercenary force, William Walker, quickly installed himself as that country's dictator. There he re-instituted slavery and prepared to dig a canal across Nicaragua, so the British could further their plans for exploitation in Central America. In 1856, Franklin Pierce officially recognized Walker's dictatorship.

While Quitman was trying to conquer Cuba, the Northern Scottish Rite of Freemasonry worked to advance civil war at home by sending Killian Henry Van Rensselaer from New York to Cincinnati to align the Scottish Rite of Free Masonry with the Knights of the Golden Circle, a military secessionist organization already established there. To arm the future Confederacy and recruit revolutionary insurgents, the Knights dispatched organizers all over the South. General P.T. Beauregard, who would later lead the attack on Fort Sumter and officially start the Civil War, was one such recruit. The Knights of the Golden Circle drilled openly all over the South, even in such prominent cities as Baltimore and Washington. To realize their long-awaited British scheme for the creation of a New World slave plantation colony through planned civil insurrection, they were determined to spread slavery into the U.S. West and on into Latin America. Newspapers in both the U.S and Europe reported upon their operations. By the start of the Civil War, the Knights of the Golden Circle had recruited and armed over 65,000 troops for service in the rebellion. As we shall see, these armed troops made the presidential inauguration of Abraham Lincoln very difficult.

1845-1856

24

BLEEDING KANSAS

"Our progress in degeneracy appears to me to be
pretty rapid. As a nation we began by declaring that
'all men are created equal.' We now practically read it
'all men are created equal except Negroes.' When the
Know- Nothings get in control, it will read 'all men
are created equal except Negroes and foreigners and
Catholics.' When it comes to this, I shall prefer
emigrating to some country where they make no
pretense of loving liberty— to Russia, for instance,
where despotism can be taken pure, and without the
base alloy of hypocrisy."

ABRAHAM LINCOLN,
FROM A LETTER TO HIS FRIEND, JOSHUA SPEED, 1859

The Knights of the Golden Circle, the secret enemy-sponsored militant organization established in Cincinnati, not only armed the South for civil war, but also worked at "convincing" the general population of the inevitability of a North/South conflict. This threatened to destroy the long legacy of North/South compromise that had been secured by Henry Clay. All the while, on the heels of the Compromise of 1850, the enemy's puppet-president, Franklin Pierce, secretly worked with Senator Stephen Douglas to forge the Kansas-Nebraska Act. Henry Clay had returned from retirement in Kentucky to help forge the Compromise of 1850 when agitators for slavery, in the wake of the mysterious death of President Taylor, had succeeded in nullifying his Missouri

Compromise of 1820. The Missouri Compromise had prohibited the establishment of slavery above the line demarcating the southern border of Missouri, except in Missouri itself.

The passage of the Kansas-Nebraska Act, in 1854, divided the Nebraska Territory into the two regions of Kansas and Nebraska and allowed residents to decide locally if slavery was to be permitted in their areas. With the passage of this act, old controversies over slavery were effectively renewed. Douglas then proudly declared that Congress had no constitutional authority to prohibit slavery in any region and the Supreme Court issued the Dred Scott decision to uphold this argument. These actions ignored the original wishes of the nation's founders who had intended for slavery to be eradicated through industrial advance. The Kansas-Nebraska Act so thoroughly shocked Abraham Lincoln that it brought him from the practice of law in Illinois back into politics.

During the winter of 1853-54, in anticipation of the passage of the Kansas-Nebraska Act, enemy-aligned forces in Massachusetts, issued a charter to the Massachusetts Emigrant Aid Company "for the purpose of aiding emigrants to settle the West." It received widespread publicity, and caused pro-slavery proponents in Missouri to organize a society of their own. It was called the Platte County Self-Defensive Association and it vowed to "remove all emigrants who go to Kansas under the auspices of the Northern Emigrant Aid Societies." With the sides clearly defined, border ruffians from Missouri and abolitionists from New England then poured into Kansas to fight one another. It was all part of a major British campaign designed to advance their planned civil war. Widespread carnage resulted. Under the watchful eye of Attorney General Caleb Cushing, thugs determined to spread slavery in the area, then proceeded to destabilize local government by holding all manner of fraudulent elections. Mobs roamed the area burning towns to the ground. Caleb Cushing made no attempt to stop them and President Pierce promptly removed the legitimate governor of the Kansas Territory from office when he tried to faithfully arrest local voting fraud.

In 1856, the northern abolitionist, John Brown, went with four of his sons and three other followers to the cabin of the pro-slavery Kansas leader, James Doyle. In the middle of the night, while his wife cried in horror, Brown dragged Doyle and two of his sons outside. There he shot Doyle and split the skulls of both of his sons. Then he hacked their bodies to pieces and proclaimed victory for the Army of the North. Next, he proceeded to the house of Allen Wilkerson, a pro-slavery local legislator, and dragged his house guest outside, splitting his skull, slashing open his side, and chopping off his hand. Abolitionist newspapers defended the actions of John Brown. Like other assassins, he had been funded in part by the enemy Astor family. They had first begun the financing of assassins back in 1804 when Aaron Burr murdered Alexander Hamilton.

As the violence in Kansas continued, the Boston Brahmin Cabot family, along with stockholders in the Emigrant Aid Society, sent $4,000 worth of rifles into Kansas to aid Brown's work. Among other Boston Brahmins who gave support to John Brown was Thomas Wentworth Higginson of Newburyport. In January, 1857, John Brown met with Higginson in Boston. There he was introduced to William L. Garrison and others in the Essex circle. The Massachusetts State Kansas Committee then made Brown its official agent and one member gave Brown money for the purchase of two hundred revolvers. At this meeting, the Astor family of New York also pledged money for guns.

The Kansas-Nebraska Act defeated all the years of tireless compromise work that Henry Clay had forged during his long years as a statesman. The act pleased New York Senator Seward, leader of the radical wing of the newly established Republican Party who chanted: "To the victor belong the spoils." The prospects of civil war loomed closer. Under enemy direction, Attorney General Caleb Cushing made no attempt to capture John Brown.

In 1857, in an atmosphere of demoralization caused by the enemy free trade policies that were re-enacted following the dismantling of the U.S. National Bank in 1836, James Buchanan was elected president. The United States was then suffering a depression similar to the one that had occurred in 1837. Henry Clay had died in 1852. Had he been still alive, he would have loudly blamed this 1857 demise on the abandonment of tariff protection.

By 1857, British-planned civil war was a near certainty. The war to come was not the result of happenstance, nor was it the work of disorganized angry men. **It was the work of a minority of enemy-agents who worked under British direction. They had duped and confused many of the men who decided to join the ranks of the organized southern army.** The men that history identifies with the southern insurrection were not its organizers. Men like Jefferson Davis and Robert E. Lee were front men used by the enemy.

The Knights of the Golden Circle organized the militant Confederacy while the northern Scottish Rite of Freemasonry organized its political leadership. From the beginning, the Freemasons did their organizing work largely from the North through the efforts of Albert Pike of Newburyport, Massachusetts. But, as war loomed closer, Pike was dispatched to Arkansas to more closely coordinate secession. He and Caleb Cushing, lifelong friends and enemy-agents, had worked feverishly for decades to promote disunion. The Buchanan administration, easily infiltrated by the enemy, was so corrupt that, as war loomed closer, the secessionist Confederate party ran its new government election campaign from the White House. Insurrectionists were armed by the traitors in the Buchanan White House. Attorney General Caleb Cushing presided over the whole operation. There was one thing though that the enemy hadn't foreseen—the strength of the great hero, Lincoln—who was about to become president and single-handedly defeat their plan.

1850-1860

25

HARPER'S FERRY

"I have heard something said about allegiance to the South. I know no South, no North, no East, no West to which I owe any allegiance."

HENRY CLAY

We have seen that the bloody fight in Kansas was largely a fight promoted by radical factions in both the North and the South—men who were serving the interests of empire in the United States—and they were slowly building this British-sponsored regional fight in Kansas into a southern move for secession. Southerners not only wanted popular sovereignty in the new territories recently created, but they also wanted police protection for slave owners who decided to take their "property" into these territories. Southern radical agents like Bob Toombs were among the early southern voices calling for secession. He said it was foolish to seek legislation at such a late stage in the game. Things, he said, had already gone too far!

Southern radicals had formed a powerful cabal in Washington and in 1857 they surrounded the new pro-southern Democratic president, James Buchanan, and held him captive. Howell Cobb had been appointed secretary of the treasury and he was the strong man in Buchanan's cabinet. He owned more than a thousand slaves. Like his political ally, Bob Toombs, Cobb was a British-agent. John Floyd was secretary of war. A former governor of Virginia, he had once been an anti-slavery man, but he had turned southern radical. Jefferson Davis was serving as senator from Mississippi. With Buchanan as president, it seemed that there was no one in Washington who would speak for the Union.

Standing apart from Washington politics, enemy agent William Yancey also boldly championed the cause of secession by organizing The League of United Southerners. He stated that "No national party can save us... no sectional party can do it." Then he called for the organization of Committees of Safety all over the South "to fire the southern heart and instruct the southern mind to give courage to each other." He wanted to precipitate a revolution. In true British fashion, he said that the South needed to copy European ways and split off from the motherland to form a separate country.

Meanwhile, Jefferson Davis was being swept up into something he knew nothing about. He had no idea that enemy extremists on both sides of the fight had been organizing secession for thirty years. He always thought that the conflict would be fairly resolved through the establishment of legally-formulated southern rights, so he went right on making speeches. All the while, a group of abolitionists in Petersboro, N.Y., were outfitting a guerrilla force to invade the Virginia town of Harper's Ferry.

When these abolitionists seized the U.S. arsenal at Harper's Ferry in 1859, sectional strife was far from the minds of the average citizen in Virginia. As rumors of the invasion first began to circulate, Virginians assumed that the dreaded peril of a Negro insurrection was at hand, but by the next day, the true facts had been ascertained. John Brown, the leader of abolitionist mass murder in Kansas, had seized the U.S arsenal in Harper's Ferry. Then he captured some whites and held them hostage, but murdered others. He had also murdered a free black man who was finding his way to work. He and his twenty-one followers tried to arm Negroes for insurrection, but terrified, they refused to fight. While all this was happening, the whole Virginia countryside took up arms and marched upon Brown and his mercenaries, besieging him in the arsenal.

A marine corps, under the leadership of Robert E. Lee, sent by President Buchanan, finally killed all but John Brown and five others. Within thirty-six hours, Brown's attempt to create a Negro insurrection had ended, but the event had a terrifying effect on Virginians. As they learned the details of the killing spree, they became agitated. Before long, the whole South began to view the incident as an attack by the North. They did not know that the details of the attack had been planned by just eight men– men who were agents of a wider British conspiracy.

One of the eight was a man named Gerrit Smith. When he heard of the failure of the plan he had helped implement, he went insane and was admitted to an asylum. Several of the others fled to Ohio and Iowa where the governors of both these states refused to extradite them for trial, claiming that the South had brought this retribution on itself because of all the violence that had occurred in Kansas.

Boston newspapers portrayed John Brown as a martyr and Louisa May Alcott even called him St John the Just. After Brown was quickly tried and sentenced to be hung, Ralph Waldo Emerson said that he would "make the gallows glorious like the cross." The extreme attitude of these radical abolitionist intellectuals did not typify the attitude among the common people in the North. Radical regional opinions had all been intentionally manipulated in order to produce a rift between North and South. Meanwhile, with the attack on Harper's ferry, the South became very fearful of the North.

Virginia's Governor Wise could have tried to mitigate the situation by commuting Brown's sentence to life imprisonment. But, instead, he played right into the hands of northern abolitionists who proceeded to turn Brown into a martyr and this further angered the South. With the frenzy created by the attack upon the arsenal at Harper's Ferry, in just a few days time, the enemy had quickly accomplished what thirty years of southern rhetoric never came close to accomplishing. An irreparable split in the Union had been forged.

1857-1859

26

MANAGED SOUTHERN SECESSION

"I have two great enemies, the southern army in front
of me and the bankers in the rear. Of the two, the
one at my rear is my greatest foe."

ABRAHAM LINCOLN

South Carolina had been the organizing nexus of southern secession for thirty years when Lincoln was elected to the presidency, in 1860. It was the first state to secede from the Union after he was elected. Its governor, William Gist, had been trained in insurrection ideology at South Carolina College when the British agent, Dr. Thomas Cooper, was president of that college. Disloyalty to the Union had been a tradition in Cooper's family for generations. After Cooper helped forge South Carolina's decision to secede, that state began calling for other southern states to hold conventions. At these conventions, ordinances of secession similar to the one drafted in South Carolina were forged.

Mississippi was the second southern state to organize a state convention. Young America revolutionist, John Anthony Quitman had been active in Mississippi disunion for many years. He had died, but his Young America followers ran the Mississippi convention. Mississippi's native son, Jefferson Davis, however, urged caution. Even though he had espoused Calhoun's southern rhetoric for decades, still, he did not look upon secession favorably. He wanted the South to work the slavery problem out legislatively. But Mississippi agent-organizers ignored him and pushed ahead to draft a Mississippi

Ordinance of Secession. It passed the vote. L.O.C. Lamar, a member of the Tory family that established the Bank of the Republic in New York City, had personally written it.

On the same day that Mississippi decided to secede, John Floyd, Buchanan's secretary of war and "favorite pupil" of revolutionist, Thomas Cooper, ordered the shipment of cannons to the unfinished, and yet undefended, U.S. forts in the harbors of both Ship Island, Mississippi, and Galveston, Texas. There they were quickly seized by insurrectionists.

In Florida, a small sampling of voters determined by a three to two majority that that state should secede. Young America operatives had both run the voting and tallied the results. However, the will to remain in the Union was very strong in that state. In fact, it was so strong that a portion of the population tried to break off from Florida to establish their own loyal state, but enemy agents squelched their initiative.

In Alabama, in a repeat performance of the same phenomenon, a narrow margin of a small sampling of people voted to secede. All over the southern Gulf Coast, similar things happened. In Georgia, the secessionists claimed a small, but questionable, margin of victory, but so many Georgians wanted to remain in the Union that it took fiery motivational speeches by both Howell Cobb and Bob Toombs to get Georgians to "move for their independence." In Louisiana, transplanted New York political boss, John Slidell, successfully engineered a move for secession by the same narrow kind of margin.

In Texas, the Lamar family, backed by the thuggish enforcement of the Knights of the Golden Circle, called for secession, but that state's patriotic governor, Sam Houston, said no to it. Undeterred, these secessionists then pulled a political coup, deposed Governor Houston, and called for a sham vote. This was all happening while Lincoln was waiting to be inaugurated. The narrow margin by which the South seceded, confirmed Lincoln's avowed belief that the work of secession did not represent the will of the southern population. Lincoln knew that it was a planned political operation managed by a minority core of British agents.

After determining to secede, the above states met at a convention in Montgomery, Alabama, under the direction of Northern Scottish Rite Freemason, Howell Cobb. There they announced the Southern Confederation and appointed Jefferson Davis president of their revolutionary government. During the month before Lincoln's inauguration, they had tried to compel other southern states to join them, but failed. Only later, under the sway of emotional momentum, did others states join the Confederacy.

During all of this, Howell Cobb worked on John Floyd's nerve. Then when Buchanan made it clear that he would not interfere with all of their treason, Floyd dispatched more guns and supplies to the enemy. This enabled the Confederates to build batteries all around Charleston Harbor. Meanwhile, the Knights of the Golden Circle began to plan for the assassination of Lincoln and the seizure of Washington. But, anticipating trouble years in advance, General Winfield Scot had moved army headquarters to an out-lying area surrounding Washington. Because of this foresight, at his inauguration, Lincoln was surrounded by sharpshooters and inaugurated without incident.

Lincoln's cabinet was full of men who believed in compromise and this habit of character had turned them into virtual traitors. Lincoln personally appointed them, so that he could "keep his eye on them." He would solicit their opinions, watch their responses and then make his own decisions. William Seward was secretary of state. From that position, he counseled Lincoln not to reinforce Fort Sumter. He told the President that if he "let South Carolina to go quietly" she would come quickly back to the Union. Then he advised Lincoln to start a war with France and Spain, telling Lincoln that that wider war would provide a "distraction" from all the nation's domestic problems. In reality, Seward wanted to be president himself. Believing that Lincoln was weak, he thought that Lincoln would just step aside and let him make all the decisions. But Lincoln, always ahead of these traitors, kept his own counsel and proved that he was more of a man than anyone had thought. Knowing how to bring the best out of people, Lincoln eventually won Seward's loyalty. Later, Seward even wrote to his wife and confessed that he had never met anyone quite like Lincoln.

Four months before Lincoln's inauguration, South Carolina had begun an intense military buildup. Then, two weeks prior to Lincoln's successful 1860 election, with knowledge that enemy agents were planning an insurrection in Charleston Harbor, Seward stood by as thousands of rifles were sent to South Carolina's Governor Gist. Later, after President Lincoln had become determined to defend Fort Sumter by sending reinforcements there, Seward held a series of meetings with enemy agents in South Carolina. At that meeting, he falsely assured them that Lincoln would not send reinforcements. Then, while Lincoln was focused on sending relief to Fort Sumter, Seward suggested that Lincoln secretly reinforce Fort Pickens in Florida, hoping that, with that plan in place, Lincoln might change his mind about relieving Fort Sumter. While Lincoln proceeded with plans to relieve Fort Sumter in Charleston, the secret plan for relieving Fort Pickens was also in place. And because it had been launched as a secret mission, orders became confused, so the squadron proceeded to Florida and aid to Fort Sumter was greatly delayed. General Anderson sustained the fort for thirty-six hours, but, low on food, he eventually had to surrender. The whole mission proved disastrous. Had Seward not interfered, Lincoln might have successfully confined the insurrection to the lower South.

The majority of Lincoln's cabinet incessantly advised him to compromise with the insurgents, but Lincoln stuck to what others considered his narrow view of the conspiracy and acted with unexpected strength in meeting the existing emergency. Not only did he launch a mighty war machine, but, at the same time, he also built a thriving northern economy. He did all of this by restoring the original principles of the American system— the system of government-sponsored credit designed by Alexander Hamilton. As a result, by the end of the Civil War, the United States was well on its way to becoming the world's leading superpower. With his protectionist program, Lincoln wrought mighty advances in technology. New inventions of all kinds flourished. By building a transcontinental railroad, he launched a spin-off steel industry. Through the efforts of the scientific community established in Philadelphia, after the war, all of this continued. We shall tell the story of the Philadelphia Interests in later chapters.

1860-1861

27

A PRESIDENT WHO KNEW HIS ENEMY

Leaving Springfield, Illinois, on February 11, 1861, Lincoln spoke these words to a crowd that had gathered to bid him good-bye: "I now leave, not knowing when, or whether ever, I may return, with a task before me greater than that which rested upon Washington. Without the assistance of that Divine Being, who ever attended him, I cannot succeed. With that assistance, I cannot fail. Trusting Him, who can go with me, and remain with you and be everywhere for good, let us confidently hope that everything will yet be well. To His care commending you, as I hope your prayers will commend me, I bid you an affectionate farewell."

The election of Abraham Lincoln to the U.S. Presidency marked the beginning of southern secession. Before he could even be inaugurated, South Carolina, Georgia, Alabama, Mississippi, and Florida had all seceded and Governor Sam Houston, of Texas, had been overthrown for his refusal to consider it. Buchanan's administration had bankrupted the government through its free-trade policy and his secretary of war, John Floyd, had secretly shifted Union armaments to the South to arm the Confederacy.

As Lincoln made his way from his home in Illinois to Washington in February, 1861, insurrectionists were capturing military forts all over the South. Southern arsenals, dock-yards and customs-houses were also falling into enemy hands. As the U.S. Mint in New Orleans was being plundered, a plan was hatched to seize the capital in Washington, D.C., in order to block the transfer of the presidency to Lincoln.

Very reliable sources, among them General Winfield Scott, were reporting assassina-tion threats on the life of Lincoln. In order to foil one such Maryland plot, a trusted circle of Lincoln supporters, including Philadelphia economist and adviser to the president-elect, Henry C. Carey, devised a plan for Lincoln to assume a disguise and take an undis-closed train route through the night from Harrisburg, Pennsylvania, to Washington, D.C. On his way to Washington, Lincoln had stopped to attend a dinner given by Pennsylvania governor, Andrew Curtain. There, the alternate route to Washington had been suggested. Lincoln initially protested, but then chose Colonel Ward Lamon, his close friend from Illinois, to accompany him on that journey. Lamon was armed with an array of pistols and knives, and so, with the president-elect's safety established, the two men set off on their nighttime journey to Washington. Years later, Lamon would recall the harsh realities of what Lincoln confronted when he took office. Never was there a day, from the moment he was elected, that Lincoln was not under threat of assassination. Chief among his body-guards, Lamon had directed Lincoln's presidential protection right up until that fateful night at Ford's Theatre when there was a break in security and Lincoln was killed.

Under the heavy guard of General Winfield Scott and his artillery of sharpshooters, following his inauguration, Lincoln bravely stood before the people to address the many unruly disunionists dispersed among the crowd that had gathered to hear him speak. Tenderly, he beckoned them back to the Union by saying: "In your hands, my dissatisfied fellow-countrymen, and not in mine, is the momentous issue of civil war. The govern-ment will not assail you. You can have no conflict without yourselves being the aggres-sors. You can have no oath registered in heaven to destroy the government, while I shall have the most solemn one to preserve it. I am loath to close. We are not enemies, but friends. Though passion may have strained, it must not break, our bonds of affection."

Up until the time of the inauguration, the North's resolve to maintain the Union had been weak. The military was limited to no more than 12,000 regular army troops and a widely scattered navy. But, with bold leadership, the day after the surrender of Fort Sumter, Lincoln began to fulfill his campaign pledge to preserve the Union by calling for 75,000 army volunteers. Lincoln's actions were followed by an outpouring of patriotic support that transcended party allegiances.

As troops poured into Washington from the North, subversive agents in the disloyal city of Baltimore, Maryland, disabled bridges, blocked railroad tracks, and attacked sol-diers. The traitorous Maryland governor, Thomas Hicks, prohibited federal troops from passing through Maryland and even wrote to the president, putting him on notice of this prohibition. Then he made an appeal for mediation. He wanted Lord Lyons, British ambassador to the United States, to preside over this mediation, but, of course, Lincoln was too wise to agree to such an idea.

Congress had adjourned indefinitely and Washington was in a state of siege. Telegraph lines had been cut and mail service had been interrupted, so Lincoln took a series of war measures. He ordered General Scott to observe the Maryland State Legislature which was about to convene. If that body voted for the armed attack of Washington, General Scott was instructed to bomb Maryland's cities. Then Lincoln ordered naval blockades of southern ports and by April, 1861, he had suspended the writ of haebeus corpus all the way to Philadelphia. Suspected insurrectionists could then be held by law without trial at the discretion of army officers. Congress had disbanded indefinitely, so, Lincoln took advantage of the departure of enemy-controlled representatives and easily secured the passage of the Morrill Protective Tariff. This act doubled duties on imports into the country and helped strengthen the domestic economy.

Then Lincoln went before Congress to define his mission. He would save the country from its domestic enemy. Lincoln had seen through the pretense of the slave-holding states in their attempt to break up the Union and he maintained that it was the project of a small group of traitors who had "been drugging the public mind of their section for more than thirty years." He claimed that the whole secessionist movement posed the question of whether or not a minority of discontented individuals, unable to lawfully promote their agenda, could arbitrarily break up the Union and put an end to the practice of free government on the earth. In his address, he also defended the Constitution saying that it had created the states as part of a federal union. That union, he said, could not be broken up by a minority of men who were unhappy with their circumstances. Without a willingness to work their problems out legislatively, civil war, he said, would become the determinant of whether or not a free people could have a government for their own benefit, free of rule by the powerful elite. The Constitution of the United States, he added, was a tool to be maintained for the purpose of uplifting the living conditions of man on earth, so that all might have a "fair chance in the race for life." Then, he added that he was most happy to feel the patriotic impulse of plain people who understood that this noble government had been created for them. He then cited their willingness to fight for it. Many in high military office, he said, had deserted the hand that had pampered them, but not one common soldier among all of the recruits he had just summoned to action, had deserted the flag under which he marched. He said he was happy to share their sentiments!

Then Lincoln boldly issued a warning to the enemy telling them not to join with their Confederate partners in any crimes against the Union. Lincoln knew that financing the war would be the most crucial issue he faced, so, while Congress was out of session, he sent Salmon P. Chase, secretary of the treasury and a confirmed free-trader, to the Gallatin-run Associated Banks of New York to make a request for a loan of $150 million in specie (gold.) Over the years, the U.S. government banking system had been hijacked by European bankers and their Wall Street partners and they had been profiting handsomely by financing U.S. government operations through the sale of high interest-yielding bonds. Through this illegal operation, they had effectively mortgaged the United States economy to British Empire interests. Then they had purposely bankrupted the U.S. as part of their attempt to take it over. With their accrued power, they then demanded such high rates of interest on the loan that Chase tried to negotiate, that Lincoln knew it would never be possible to pay them back. So, he decided to independently finance the upcoming war.

In order to organize support for his alternative financial plan, Lincoln then charged his economic advisor, Henry C. Carey, with a letter-writing campaign designed to promote the re-establishment of the nationalist policies of Alexander Hamilton. Then he secured congressional passage of the Legal Tender Act which gave him the authority to create legal government money called greenbacks.

Lincoln then augmented his finance plan by drafting a National Banking Act. It authorized the government to issue credit for the buildup of industry and revived Hamilton's early policies. Lincoln also arranged for the sale of long-term low interest bonds (5:20s) to both the general public and to the nationally-chartered banks he intended to create. Through this Hamiltonian-style plan, Lincoln intended to finance both the war and a new vibrant economy. The people would be the beneficiaries of the debt they owed only to themselves. With time, the economy would flourish, the standard of living would be elevated, and the debt would be paid off naturally. The banking cartel would not profit in any way. **With these bold actions, Lincoln had called for a showdown with the enemy and he knew it.** Like a soldier in a war between two competing ideologies, he had chosen to uphold the one which he described as the "last great hope for man."

Lincoln also revived a plan that Henry C. Carey had proposed to Henry Clay years earlier. It called for the construction of railroads into the South, so that that region could be industrialized. The southern hill region, rich in minerals, was inhabited by independent southern laborers who were impoverished. Carey's old plan for bringing railroads to that region intended to create a strong force of free men engaged in the pursuit of mining and manufacturing. This plan would have not only alleviated their poverty, but it would also have targeted the British plantation system for eradication.

Lincoln's 1861 speech urged Congress to finance Carey's renewed plan by bringing a new railroad system into the heart of the enemy strongholds of North Carolina, Kentucky and Tennessee. In this speech, Lincoln also took the opportunity to defend the government policy of befriending labor. He said that "no men living are more worthy to be trusted than those who toil up from poverty—none less inclined to take, or touch, ought that they have not honestly earned." He then urged Congress to re-enact his revived American-style plan.

Just as expected, though, before Lincoln could get this National Banking Act passed, James Gallatin and his Allied Banks cronies reacted by suspending specie payment on pre-existent bonds. Then they approached Lincoln with an "alternative" plan of their own, but Lincoln could see that it was nothing more than a return to the same old system of financial usury that he planned to escape, so he turned them away.

To get his new National Banking Act through Congress, Lincoln relied upon Thaddeus Stevens, House Ways and Means Chairman, old colleague of John Quincy Adams, and follower of Henry C. Carey. The initial bill drafted by Stevens called for the sale of 5:20 bills to the citizenry with no provision for payment of interest in specie because the British controlled the gold market. These imperialists had also arranged for the value of gold to float in order to maximize their profits through speculation. **Because Lincoln's National**

Banking Act made no provision to tie the greenback to gold, it had severed ties with the usurious foreign bankers who wanted to take over the United States and destroy her freedom.

Alarmed by Lincoln's bold move, the enemy banking cartel immediately mobilized to defeat the Stevens bill by dispatching their agents, James Gallatin and August Belmont, to Congress, in 1862, to lobby on behalf of the cartel. By bribing members of the Senate, they then arranged a deal that allowed bonds to be purchased with greenbacks, but only under conditions that required the interest on the bonds to be paid in specie. With this modification in the bill, the greenback was then effectively tied to gold and this allowed the bankers to manipulate its value. Congress passed the bill by a slim margin of only two votes.

Thaddeus Stevens was so angered by the modified bill that he told the Congress that the bankers had so "disfigured and deformed" the bill that "its very father would not know it." Lincoln and Carey were well-aware of the compromise that had been forced upon them, but they were still determined to defeat the enemy. So, while the war waged on, they waited and Lincoln worked with the handicap that had been imposed upon him, using every means he could conceive of, to finance a war that had become very expensive.

It took time, but eventually Thaddeus Stevens again came to Lincoln's aid by authoring a bill that outlawed the sale of gold in the New York Gold Room and when it passed, this curtailed speculation in gold at home. The enemy was not happy. Under enemy direction, Hugh McCullogh, Comptroller of the Currency and an enemy agent who had been pushed on Lincoln as part of the compromise bill enacted in 1862, then issued an attack upon Lincoln by writing an open letter to Carey in the *Chicago Tribune*. It called for an immediate reduction in the protective tariff and a return to specie control through the elimination of the greenback all together. Enraged by this letter, Lincoln then brutally chastised McCullough. Three days later, he was murdered. With Carey, Lincoln had been making plans to completely eradicate some of the most criminal British-aligned banks on Wall Street. They had already restricted much of their speculative activity.

Just prior to his assassination, Lincoln had also requested that Carey write a series of Open Letters to Speaker of the House, Schuyler Colfax. In these open letters, entitled "How to Outdo England," Carey constantly referenced the fact that, in order to prosecute the war, Lincoln had been repeatedly forced to compromise with the enemy by signing bills that he considered to be against the best interests of the nation. Carey then used this fact to argue for a national body under executive control that would plan national policy. Lincoln then set up the Independent Revenue Commission and appointed David Wells as its first head because, at the time, Wells appeared to be a devoted follower of Henry C. Carey. After Lincoln's death, though, Wells would reveal his true allegiance by helping the enemy re-infiltrate the U.S. banking system.

In these letters, Carey also insisted that only through industrializing could the U.S. effectively outdo Britain. Protective tariffs, he said, were the tool that would rapidly promote this industrialization. Then, once the economy was in full-swing mode, U.S. technology could be exported and this would eventually destroy the British system worldwide. Completely severing U.S. currency from that of Britain was intrinsic to the process.

The enemy assassinated Lincoln because they could, by no other means, deter him from severing these ties.

The results of the American system policies that Lincoln put in place, during his brief tenure as president, did not die with him. Within ten years of the close of the Civil War, they emerged to dazzle the world! Under the policy of protectionism, the Transcontinental Railroad had been created and this brought an American steel industry into existence. During the span of years between 1860 and 1880, there was a thousand-fold increase in U.S. steel production. In the same twenty-year period, through the joint efforts of government, industry and education, railroad miles tripled, the number of patent applications tripled, and coal and wool production quadrupled. Both the petroleum and electrical industries were also created.

Lincoln also created the U.S. Department of Agriculture in order to elevate farming to a science. And, he sponsored free government-created state colleges to teach this science. He also actively sponsored the recruitment of immigrants with the intention of settling the American West all the way to the Pacific.

During Lincoln's presidency, Benjamin Franklin's great-grandson, Alexander Dallas Bache, became Lincoln's principal scientific military adviser. In the tradition of his great grandfather, Bache coordinated alliances with leading European scientists like Gauss and Humboldt. By 1880, in order to promote the rapid development of the U.S. economy, the Franklin Institute in Philadelphia had formed the Philadelphia Interests. They rescued Thomas Edison from the clutches of the big banks and gave him a laboratory in Menlo Park, New Jersey. From that laboratory, he invented electricity. With the help of Bache, a widening circle of both American and European scientists and inventors then spread electricity throughout much of the world. We shall earn more about their efforts in later chapters.

Like his nationalist predecessors, Abraham Lincoln advanced the progress of man on this planet. With the war victory, he abolished slavery and pulled American society out of the state of human degradation that the elite had been fostering for thirty year. Sadly, with his murder, the enemy regrouped. For his brave efforts, by consensus, though, Lincoln remains the pre-eminent American president. For his dedicated commitment to the American system and his bold courage, Lincoln is loved by all patriots. After his untimely death, Andrew Johnson succeeded Lincoln as president. Johnson, as we shall see, though, was not the man that Lincoln was. So, after he became president, he changed sides in order to support unrepentant Confederate rebels as they re-infiltrated southern state legislatures in an attempt to return to a position of power.

1861-1865

ABRAHAM LINCOLN
SIXTEENTH PRESIDENT OF THE UNITED STATES

*"Government {by} possessing the power to create and issue currency and credit as money...
should not borrow capital at interest as a means of financing Government work and
public enterprise. The Government should create, issue and circulate all the currency and
credit needed to satisfy the spending power of the Government and the buying power of the
consumers. The privilege of creating and issuing money is not only the supreme prerogative
of Government, but is the Government's greatest creative opportunity."*

*A partial statement from Lincoln's monetary policy issued in 1865 and recorded in Senate
document 23, page 91. Following this, and other bold unswerving statements of opposition
to the enemy banking oligarchy's attempt to perpetuate its involvement in the finances of the
United States, Lincoln lost his life.*

28

PHILADELPHIA, THE HUB
OF THE NATION

"Corporations have been enthroned and an era of
corruption in high places will follow, and the money
power of the country will endeavor to prolong its
reign by working on the prejudices of the people
until all wealth is aggregated in the hands of a few
and the Republic is destroyed. I feel at this moment
more anxiety for the safety of my country than ever
before, even in the midst of war. God grant that my
suspicions may prove groundless."

ABRAHAM LINCOLN
IN A LETTER TO COL. WILLIAM F. ELKINS, NOVEMBER 21, 1864

Philadelphia had been chosen as the strategic center of American counterintelligence activity from the early days of Franklin's youth. He was dispatched there in 1723 by Cotton Mather to help plan and coordinate the coming colonial insurrection against Britain. Later, Philadelphia would grow from a center of strategic wartime endeavor to a nexus of planned technology advance.

By the time of the Civil War, the political and intellectual associates of Henry C. Carey, son of Matthew Carey, and Alexander Bache Dallas, great grandson of Ben Franklin, had created an extensive network of government and private-sector business contacts in that city. The goal of the patriots had remained unchanged from the days of Franklin.

Through implementation of economic progress, they would advance the long-established American plan for world freedom. In the spirit of a true nationalist, Lincoln had courageously begun a huge technology start. After his death the "Philadelphia Interests" would continue Lincoln's work.

The nationalist power that was forged after the Civil War revolved around the Pennsylvania Railroad and the banking house of Jay Cooke. Built during the 1840s, one quarter of the coast of financing the Pennsylvania Railroad had been incurred by the city of Philadelphia when it bought stock in that railroad. Before the Civil War, its president, Edgar Thompson, had hired a young engineer named William Palmer and he had converted the engines of the railroad from a wood-burning to a coal-burning system. In 1857, the Pennsylvania Railway was America's largest corporation. It had six thousand miles of line.

During the Civil War, under the direction of Lincoln, Philadelphia nationalist, Jay Cooke, helped finance the Lincoln war effort by selling one billion dollars in war bonds directly to U.S. citizens. In this way, Lincoln by-passed the London-allied Wall Street fiends who were trying to blackmail and bribe him into surrendering to them. Desiring to sever financial connections with the enemy, the determined Lincoln would play no part in their plan to control U.S. finances. So, he created his own government financing to fund both the war and the economy. After the war, Cooke continued to market the sale of U.S government bonds.

By the years 1871-72, a unified group of industrial companies had formed a partnership known informally as the "Philadelphia Interests." Among the members were Edgar Thompson, Thomas A. Scott, Andrew Carnegie, William J. Palmer, Matthew Baird, Samuel Felton and others. They ran such companies as the Pennsylvania Railroad, the Baldwin Locomotive Company, the Denver and Rio Grande Railroad, the Philadelphia Steel Company, the Kansas Pacific Railway, the Mexican National Railway, the Automatic Telephone Company, and other railroads, iron forges, coal mines, and machine-building companies. Partner Andrew Carnegie forged the J. Edgar Thompson Steel Works in Pittsburg, Pennsylvania. At that time, it was the largest modern steel mill ever built. The Pennsylvania Railroad had just installed Westinghouse air brakes on their trains.

Henry Carey's student, Joseph Wharton, founder of Bethlehem Steel Company, led the lobbying in Washington that protected these industries through high tariffs. This succeeded in blocking British interference in American development. Then, just as things appeared bright, in 1871, some City of London bankers established a Philadelphia-New York-London banking alliance in order to orchestrate the destruction of the profound American industrial leadership that had emerged in Philadelphia. It happened when London banker, Junius S. Morgan, placed his son, J.P. Morgan, into a position of influence in the Drexel banking house of Philadelphia. This created the beginnings of a new Drexel-Morgan banking alliance which would later become J.P. Morgan Company, the U.S. branch of the foreign House of Morgan.

Here is the story of the beginning of the takedown of the American system that Lincoln had established: Anthony Drexel owned the *Philadelphia Ledger* and its editorial department shared a correspondence with the editorial department of the *London Times*.

Together, these papers began to promote slander about Jay Cooke, the main banker of the U.S. government and the Philadelphia Interests. By alleging that Cooke was going bankrupt, they succeeded in destroying Cooke's reputation. Then, depositors panicked and withdrew their money in such large amounts that rumors alone caused the collapse of Jay Cooke and Company. It closed its doors in 1873. Within days, railroad construction came to a near halt and new steel mills shut down. Other banks soon closed and the stock market crashed. In true imperialist fashion, London had engineered a panic with ensuing depression.

When the economy slowed, the Philadelphia Interests withdrew from the railroad business. Then other less nationalist men took over the management of the industry. As a result, for a while, the Philadelphia Interests had to abandon their planned dream of spurring new industry all along the western routes of the Transcontinental Railroad System. They had envisioned the development of whole cities engaged in productive enterprise all along those routes and even down into Mexico.

Then in 1879, the year Henry Carey died, after years of deliberation, Congress passed the Specie Resumption Act and, in doing so, actually ceded U.S. sovereignty over finance to the international banking cartel. Then the allied banking syndicate houses of Morton Bliss and Co., Seligman Bros., the Rothschilds, and Drexel-Morgan all obtained contracts for refinancing U.S. debt. With the Species Resumption Act, the law then stipulated that payment of debt had to be made in gold. The cartel, you will remember, liked to permit the value of gold to float, in order to create a market for speculation. In the process, they not only enriched themselves, but they also manipulated sovereign economies. Lincoln, you will also recall, had attempted to prevent the cartel from interfering in U.S. financial affairs by almost completely severing the greenback's tie to gold. It took many tears to orchestrate the Specie Resumption Act, but when it was passed, the cartel, again became empowered to create banking collapses at will. Empire-created depression stymied the efforts of the Philadelphia Interests for a while, but they would mount another progressive push when a nationalist entered the White House in 1881. In the next chapter, we shall tell the story of how the banking oligarchs re-engineered the takeover of the U.S. financial system through a return to a controlled gold-backed currency.

1723-1879

29

SPECIE RESUMPTION

"Let me issue and create a nation's money and I care not who writes the laws."

MEYER AMSCHEL ROTHSCHILD

Union victory in the Civil War had made Lincoln very popular. As a second term peacetime president, had he been allowed to live, the prospects for future prosperity would have been staggering. Lincoln had demonstrated to the enemy that he was committed to strengthening the Hamiltonian-style American system of credit expansion he had put into place in order to win the war and advance progress, so they murdered him. Andrew Johnson then succeeded Lincoln as president. At the Republican National Convention in 1864, as part of the presidential nominating process, Lincoln had acceded to the suggestion that Johnson become his vice-presidential running mate because Johnson, a life-long southern Democrat, had professed a dedication to the Union. Having determined that Johnson's example could be used after the war, to further a spirit of reconciliation between North and South, Lincoln then moved forward with plans to heal the nation's wounds.

Unfortunately, though, Johnson's "allegiance" to the Union proved to be a mere pretense because, after he became president, he suddenly changed sides in order to support unrepentant southern rebels who had re-assumed control over newly-forming southern state legislatures. Many southern rebel insurgents—the same men who had precipitated the Confederate insurrection—were also then given complete presidential pardons for their war crimes. Emboldened by this beneficent treatment, they then proceeded to victimize poor loyal southern Unionists, while they also subjected newly-freed vagrant blacks to the worst kind of criminal indentured servitude. Before his murder, Lincoln had established the Freedman's Bureau in anticipation of the need to alleviate the poverty that war had created, but Johnson allowed Confederate rebels to pervert its purposes and personally profit from it.

With his masterful statesmanship, Lincoln had built a strong coalition of Republicans who were ready to follow his leadership during the difficult process of reconstruction that he knew was coming. Johnson's unexpected defection to the rebel cause destroyed this coalition, so the country started to again become factionalized under the old North/South political constraints that Lincoln had intended to heal. Hugh McCulloch, Comptroller of the Currency then began pushing for a contraction of the greenback supply, while the followers of Henry C. Carey wanted to use the expanded supply of greenbacks to further advance the technology start that Lincoln had begun when he built his Transcontinental Railroad.

Treasury Secretary McCulloch was one of many traitors who had surrounded Lincoln during his presidency. After Lincoln's death, he boldly stepped forward to display his allegiance with the interests of empire by falsely claiming that government wartime spending had been out of control and had caused inflation. So, rather than urge the stay of financial independence that Lincoln had chartered, he came to the aid of European banking oligarchs and insisted that the U.S. quickly pay down its war debt in order to maintain a good standing among European financial circles. He then introduced this platform among sympathetic congressional circles.

In 1868, as a result of the victory he had won for the Union during the Civil War, Grant was elected president. Grant had been wonderfully successful as a general and, as a president, he may have been well-intentioned, but he was not schooled in the American System of Political Economy and, without this training, he lacked true leadership ability. In forming opinions on many matters, he consulted with many advisers, but he lacked the ability to ascertain wise guidance from flawed rhetoric, so he proceeded to listen to enemy agents who were calling for a contraction of credit. Then, as president, he pushed the nationalist banker, Jay Cooke, into a "refunding measure" that allowed Britain to buy existing U.S. war bonds. While he lived, Lincoln had adamantly fought this enemy strategy.

Enemy-agents, such as David Welles and August Belmont, then led a consolidated push for a return to a gold-backed currency. Through the organized efforts of their Cobden Club, the enemy also called for the abandonment of protective tariffs in order to completely hijack the U.S. economy. In an atmosphere of moral corruption, without the influence of Lincoln's guiding presence, for personal gain, many elected officials were then easily bribed into abandoning the fair moral American system Lincoln had espoused. In the process, they forfeited the well-being of the country. Some Americans knew exactly what was going on, but they felt powerless to do anything about it.

From before the Civil War, the American clergy had penetrated the ranks of higher education, especially among the prestigious institutions like Harvard, Yale, Princeton and Amherst in order to train the minds of the youth in empire banking practices. Their British-inspired texts also reached the general public. In the midst of the confusion that started to prevail after Lincoln's death, the clergy then helped to orchestrate a great controversy over specie resumption. Despite their propaganda push, however, the Civil War technology start that Lincoln had created was very strong. So, by 1869, the country began to experience a new burst of economic growth sparked by a railroad boom and this effectively put the push for specie resumption on hold. The followers of Henry C. Carey then voiced the opinion that this renewed prosperity would not have come along had the U.S., early on, returned to specie. The paper that was in circulation, they claimed, had actually fueled this boom. So, with the acceptance of things just as they were, the Grant administration brushed the specie resumption issue aside.

Then, as we have already documented, after Grant was re-elected, the British began circulating rumors about the insolvency of Jay Cooke & Co. and, by rumor alone, they collapsed that bank in 1873. Since Jay Cooke had been the chief banker of the U.S. government, the railroad boom then came to an abrupt collapse and five years of depression ensued. The banking oligarchy had personally orchestrated the whole mess in order to place "the currency problem" back in the forefront of public opinion.

Following the panic of 1873, as faith in the greenback began to falter, the enemy began a renewed financial assault. Clergymen then again began "warning" about the dangers of a debased currency even though the increase in the number of greenbacks had been moderate. They even called greenback supporters agents of the devil.

As British supporters advocated for a return to specie, attacks upon the National Banking Act also began to circulate. John Murray Forbes, one of the most active of these radical agents of "reform," then established a weekly publication called the *Financial Record* in order to widely disseminate British propaganda. Enemy-organized protest rallies against the greenback were also held in both Boston and New York.

Once again in ascendency, the syndicate of international bankers then threatened Grant with a credit boycott and a mass dumping of U.S. stocks if he refused to support their attempt to repeal national banking through the Specie Resumption Bill. So, even though Grant had previously been a supporter of national banking, he then capitulated to the enemy and vetoed an existing attempt to save Lincoln's National Banking Act. He also attached a clause to his veto that supported a repeal of the Legal Tender Act. Then the Specie Resumption Bill was passed and it stipulated that after July 1, 1875, all debt contracts had to be redeemed in specie. When that date arrived, the bankers then began redeeming their bonds, so gold flowed out of the U.S. Treasury. In 1876, after the greenback was eliminated altogether, federal bank notes linked to gold were created. Then, the oligarchy, back in control of the circulating medium, effectively controlled U.S. credit once again.

Through all of this, Representative William Kelley of Pennsylvania tried to preserve U.S. sovereignty over banking through a bill that would have kept bonds tied to the greenback. In a long speech before Congress, he defended the greenback calling it the tool for maintaining U.S. independence. Congressman Kelley was a devoted follower of Henry C. Carey, so with the support of other nationalists, he made an attempt to pass high tariff legislation and push for an expansion of the economy through the issue of sovereign government credit, but, being part of only a small congressional minority, he failed.

The greenback could have continued to circulate as legal tender for debt after the Civil War and, contrary to popular opinion, it did not need to be linked to gold. The greenback had functioned effectively during the war and it could have continued to function after it, just by linking it to public contracts. The Constitution gives the U.S. government the right to issue its own currency. High interest-bearing bonds do not need to be sold to the enemy in order to finance U.S government operations. That plan is an enemy self-enrichment scheme that unnecessarily saddles the American people with huge debt. Lincoln lost his life because he intervened to end this scheme.

The enemy knew that the American System of Credit expanded the currency in a good way—a way beneficial to everyone, but they were not interested in promoting the common good. They wanted to promote the interests of empire, so they spread lies and so much confusion that the distinctions between their monetary system and the American System of Credit became muddied.

Let's clear up the issue. The enemy's system is a strictly money-oriented system. Through it, the self-appointed elite amass huge amounts of money through usurious lending practices and through speculation. Once they have all the money, they enslave everyone else, forcing them to work at supplying all their needs.

The American System uses money to create credit and this credit is invested in production. In the process, jobs are created and man learns to use his mind creatively.   This advances the general welfare. As business expands, a stable society results and domestic happiness prevails. This credit-created currency expansion is the fruit of the American system—the system of the founders—an equalizing system that was designed to create freedom from want. It drives progress.

After the Civil War, had the followers of Henry C. Carey been influential enough to stay the public on the course Lincoln had set, vast amounts of debt would not have been sold to foreigners for speculation and the American people would not have become burdened by needless interest payments. The government could have continued to print greenbacks and use that money supply as credit to expand the economy. The war debt would then have been paid down as a matter of course as the economy expanded. All the while, people would have been employed and depressions would have been averted. By extending credit to the South and with the help of tariff protection, that section, too, would have prospered and the country might then have quickly come together as a united prospering nation. With a buildup of the southern regional economy, racial equality would also have quickly ensued.

With the universal application of the American System of Credit nationally, Lincoln's vision of One Nation would have been quickly realized. But, instead, during ensuing years, there were only sporadic periods of prosperity because, through financial manipulation, the enemy created many recessions. Had Lincoln lived, he would have undoubtedly strengthened the national banking system by extending national banks throughout the South and the West. Under the enemy's plan, banks were purposely concentrated in the North in order to promote an enemy monopoly over commerce. Other regions were always complaining about the unfair restriction of credit that this policy had imposed upon them. Lincoln would also probably have established a national public education system in order to school the people in the American system of sovereign financial independence. Not until 1896, when William McKinley became president, was the leadership void created by the murder of Lincoln, filled. Later chapters will tell the story of William McKinley.

1864-1876

30

THE HUB EXPANDS GLOBALLY

"Let us hope..., that by the best cultivation of the physical world beneath and around us, and the best intellectual and moral world within us, we shall secure an individual, social, and political prosperity and happiness whose course shall be onward and upward, and which, while the earth endures, shall not pass away."

ABRAHAM LINCOLN, FROM AN ADDRESS TO THE WISCONSIN STATE AGRICULTURE SOCIETY, 1859

In the pre-1879 heyday of their might, through their influence in government, U.S. nationalists, operating as the Philadelphia Interests, helped promote the U.S. policy which "opened up" Japan to the outside world and brought her from a backward feudal society to the brink of modern nation status. Commodore Matthew Perry delivered a railroad train and a telegraph system to Japan. Then, in 1872, Japanese Prince Iwakawa and his delegation came to the U.S. for a stay at the Philadelphia home of Jay Cooke. There his delegation negotiated a trade treaty with the U.S. and a $1.5 million loan from Jay Cooke and Co. to finance Japan's development. Immediately afterward, Cooke began to negotiate for an Asian connection to the U.S. Transcontinental Rail System. The vision of a global alliance of nationalists was slowly beginning to take shape.

At the same time, Henry Carey's scientific community was mobilized. Geologist and industrial planner, Benjamin Smith Lyon, and economist, E. Pershine Smith, were dispatched to Japan to identify mineral resources, plan railroads, and draft tariff schedules. Then beginning in 1873, the U.S was blessed with a fiercely anti-British ambassador to Japan, John Bingham, and, until 1885, he battled the British for influence in Japan. A covert war of diplomacy was being waged between two conflicting ideologies, the American pacifist system of economic nation-state advancement vs. the backward British system of colonial exploitation. Then, when the British cunningly orchestrated a U.S. financial collapse that began with the Panic of 1873, Japan's hopes for technological advance were dashed.

The Philadelphia Interests had also targeted Russia for technological advance. From as early as the days of that country's involvement with Britain in the Crimean War, Henry Carey had tirelessly written in the American press about the long-standing friendship between the U.S. and Russia and he succeeded in reviving it. Then Carey personally went to Russia in 1859 to secure an alliance with that country just as the U.S secessionist crisis was deepening. This alliance with Russia actually helped prevent the British from intervening on behalf of the Confederacy during the Civil War. In a show of Union support during that war, Czar Alexander II sent Russian fleets to both New York and San Francisco as a warning to the British to stay out of the war.

In 1869, former Pennsylvania governor, Andrew Curtain, then the U.S. ambassador to Russia, went to that country to propose that the Czar build a trans-Siberian railway that would link Russia with the U.S. Then George H. Barker, ambassador to Russia from 1875-1878, further implemented the plan by drawing up an official joint venture agreement with Russia.

The Russians then chose nationalist banker Wharton Barker as their financial agent and, in 1878, he had four battle cruisers built for the Russian navy. Then he personally went to Russia to plan iron and coal mines as well as forges and factories. With the transformation of Southern Russia underway, he then proposed that the Russians ally themselves with the U.S. for an economic war to defeat their common enemy, the British Empire!

Wharton Barker also accomplished a wonderful thing at home. He secured the nomination of the nationalist, James A. Garfield for President of the United States. Duly elected in 1880, Garfield was sadly assassinated after only two hundred days in office. Czar Alexander II was also assassinated that same year. Then, his successor, Alexander III, struggled to continue his policies, but the British agent-in-place, American President Chester A. Arthur, curtailed American involvement in Russian development and things fell apart for a while.

Then, in the 1890s, Count Sergi Witte, student of Frederich List and advocate of European nationalism, eventually built the Trans-Siberian Railway and brought the beginning of modernization to Russia. Eventually, the British-sponsored Communist Revolution overthrew Witte, so Russian ties to the United States were then again severed and the battle with empire continued.

The U.S. had its hand in Irish politics, too. Years after Matthew Carey had become an Irish revolutionary, his son Henry C. Carey revived the one hundred year-old Irish struggle for independence from British oppression. In 1875, Henry C. Carey formed an association with William Carroll, Irish immigrant physician to the United States. Dr. Carroll became the chairman of the Clan na Gael, commonly referred to as the Fenians, an Irish revolutionary group. Carroll and his colleagues, Knights of Labor Chief, Terrance V. Powderly, and University of Pennsylvania economist, Professor Robert Ellis Thompson, sent cash and guns to Ireland. Then, in 1878, Carroll toured the British Isles and reunited the bickering Irish underground. Twenty years later, the formation of the Sinn Fein freed most of Ireland from British rule. Another of Carroll's Irish partners, John Devoy, became foreign editor of the nationalistic *New York Herald* and he used that newspaper to promote the genius of Thomas Edison. We shall learn about Thomas Edison in another chapter.

1879-1890

31

THE RAILROAD LEADING TO MEXICO

"With malice toward none, with charity for all; with
firmness in the right as God gives us to see the right,
let us strive on to finish the work we are in...."

ABRAHAM LINCOLN, FROM HIS SECOND INAUGURAL ADDRESS

Grant was elected president in 1868 just as the Philadelphia Interests were organizing for continued technology advance. Through their efforts, the economy then started to boom. In 1869, the Transcontinental Railroad was completed and new railroad lines were then laid all over the West. Geological surveys had detected rich mineral wealth in Colorado and, armed with this knowledge, the Philadelphia Interests planned for the buildup of a thriving industrial center in that area. They also forged a plan to lay a railroad line from the Rocky Mountains down into Mexico to create a huge dense agro-industrial zone which would help free Mexico from the ravages of empire and make her an ally in the U.S. fight to free the world. Mexico had overthrown Maximillian, the puppet emperor installed by the British during the Civil War, and Benito Juarez, long time friend of Lincoln, was again president of Mexico.

As we have mentioned, Samuel Felton was one of the key nationalists associated with the Philadelphia Interests. He was the owner of the Philadelphia, Wilmington and Baltimore Railroad and had been a friend to Lincoln during the Civil War. Before his inauguration, when Lincoln's life had been threatened, Felton had helped secure Lincoln's safe arrival in Washington by creating a diverted railroad trip to that city. While serving in the army during the Civil War, he had again offered Lincoln the services of his railroad.

In 1869, with his young engineer friend, William Palmer, Felton began to lay railroad tracks all across the western prairie. Then they moved into Colorado to begin construction of the Denver and Rio Grande Railroad in order to extend the growing U.S. rail grid down from the Rocky Mountains to Mexico City. There it was to link up with the Mexican National Railroad. Connected by rail to the U.S economy, the Mexican economy would then prosper.

In Colorado, Felton set himself up making steel rails with the new Bessemer steel making process that his friend, Andrew Carnegie, had learned about in Britain. With access to copper-rich ores, he also began to produce copper telegraph line. A grand strategy had been planned for Colorado. It involved reclaiming unused land, making it suitable for farming, and tripling the size of the habitable United States. The West would bustle and boom. The U.S. had forged alliances with republican governments in Russia, Germany and Japan and they, too, looked forward to an international hookup with the U.S railroad grid. A world-wide boom was contemplated!

A precarious economic situation, however, soon developed as America's already jealous enemy, got its financial arm, the London/New York banking cartel, prepared for economic warfare. As we have already mentioned, by 1879, the cartel had worked its way back into American banking by buying up U.S. debt. This effectively gave them renewed control over U.S. finances.

There were other unsettling developments, too. In 1876, the House of Representatives had to decide the winner of a too-close-to-call presidential election and they chose Rutherford B. Hayes. But, to keep Southern Democrats happy (and the enemy, too,) they agreed to remove federal troops from the South. Those troops had been protecting black voting rights, so, when they were removed, the black man's voting rights were jeopardized, southern society was destabilized and old North/South regional enmity was revived. Texans then even began to once again call for the annexation of Mexico.

With an eye to reviving the plan for a huge South American plantation system, the British then moved back into Mexico. There they formed an alliance with the Church and played upon the superstitions of the ignorant Mexican people, proclaiming that railroad development would open Mexico up to foreign conquest and ruin her standing with God. The poor superstitious Mexicans were then deceived. They hadn't realized that these propagandists were themselves aiming to conquer and exploit Mexico. Mexico's leaders then annulled their business agreements with American companies, so Americans were forced to retreat from Mexico. Then they had to try to find a new way to weaken the enemy.

In 1778, Henry Carey was an old man, but he mustered up enough strength to call for a council meeting of the Philadelphia Interests. At that meeting, members organized for the election of Terrence Powderly, Irish patriot and labor rights organizer, as the next mayor of Scranton, Pennsylvania. From that position, Powderly became the head of the Knights of Labor and taught laborers about nationalism. This was during the beginning of the heyday of John D. Rockefeller. Powderly had watched Rockefeller's consolidation and takeover of American business with horror, calling him a notorious "foreign agent and procurer of terrorism" because Rockefeller would systematically take over rival businesses by covertly enticing their employees into acts of violence. The Philadelphia Interests tried every means at their disposal to curtail U.S. enemies like Rockefeller, but, with Congress divided, nothing could stay his plans to hijack and consolidate American business. Government intervention was badly needed, but leadership was no where to be found.

Then, to stifle the progress of the Philadelphia Interests, the Baring Bank in London undertook the funding of a Boston "firm" for the purpose of entirely derailing the Mexican project. This Boston "firm" was nothing but a fancy front for a bunch of blue-blood criminals who were partners with the Barings in the China opium trade. They then revived the old Atchison, Wilmington and Topeka Railroad and two of their agents, Thomas J. Coolidge and John M. Forbes, bought up blocks of Denver and Rio Grande stock from panic-stricken Philadelphia nationalists who saw what was going on and feared the loss of their investments. After initially making large amounts of money, Coolidge and Forbes then "squeezed" the Denver and Rio Grande Railroad into bankruptcy.

Before implementing their credit squeeze, this Boston "firm" had used armed men to seize control of the Raton Pass, the Denver and Rio Grande's only pass south across the Rockies to Mexico. At one point, in order to block rail-laying, the enemy put heavily armed men into the Royal Gorge, but the courageous General Palmer put his own men in place to face them down. Then, for several years, there were skirmishes in both the field and in the courts. In 1879, because the Boston group was ignoring a court order, General Palmer led an informal alliance of Denver and Rio Grande railroad workers, some local coal miners, and a few friendly sheriffs to take back control of their lines and train stations. But the enemy was persistent and, in 1880, the criminal, Thomas Coolidge, obtained a court decree that prevented the Denver and Rio Grande from building any lines south of Denver for ten years. So, the nationalists again retreated, but they still continued to plan for the buildup of the Denver area into the planed new Rocky Mountain industrial center. The plans with Mexico though had to await the election of the next patriotic president— James A. Garfield.

1868-1879

32

THE WIZARD OF
MENLO PARK

"We don't know a millionth of one percent
about anything."

THOMAS EDISON

William Palmer had been a Union officer in the Civil War and his cavalry had
successfully routed and captured a whole rebel regiment in Alabama. After
the war, when he became a full-time partner with the Philadelphia Interests,
he converted the Pennsylvania Railroad to a coal-burning system. Then, in 1866, the
partners dispatched him and his telegraph expert, Edward H. Johnson, on a mission to
build the Kansas Pacific Railroad. On grants of land obtained from the U.S. government,
they then proceeded to survey untracked wilderness areas and eventually built a line from
Kansas City, Missouri, to Denver, Colorado. Then, they began laying line from Denver
toward Mexico City. They also surveyed wilderness areas in New Mexico and Arizona and
brought lines in that area to the Pacific Coast.

Johnson not only built telegraph lines, but also served as Palmer's secretary. Together
they had become determined to implement the development of modern U.S. manufacturing, bring it to Mexico and eventually extend it to the emerging republics of South
America. But, Wall Street was watching and organizing to covertly subvert all progressive U.S. enterprise. We have already documented how their support of Boston Brahmin
criminal thugs literally resulted in fighting which destroyed Palmer's Denver and Rio
Grande Railroad project to Mexico City.

In 1870, the Philadelphia Interests established the Automatic Telegraph Company in New York City in order to organize some competition for Western Union. Controlled by Wall Street banking tycoons, that company had been buying up inventions and burying them in order to stifle progress and thwart the burgeoning U.S. economy.

Palmer sent Johnson to New York City to supervise the Automatic Telegraph Company. There he snatched the inventor, Thomas Edison, from the clutches of Wall Street and hired him to **actually invent technology for the new company**. The twenty-four year old Edison had been working as a contractor developing telegraph devices for Western Union. The Automatic Telegraph Company gave Edison $40,000 to set up an independent shop. They also put him on a salary. For the next twenty years, Johnson served as Edison's business manager and he engaged both Josiah Reiff and Colonel Gouraud to work for Palmer as international representatives of Edison. Colonel Gouraud went to work in England contending with British elements that wanted to steal U.S. inventions.

Thomas Edison came from a background of resistance to British oppression. His father, Samuel Edison, a Canadian emigrant to the U.S., fled Canada, in 1837, with British troops in pursuit of him. When he reached the U.S. border, he crossed over into Michigan. From there he moved to Ohio to settle. Thomas Edison was born in Ohio in 1847.

At the Automatic Telegraph Company, Edison's first project involved finding a way to send multiple high speed messages simultaneously over the same telegraph line. In a race with time, Edison poured over books on the subject and worked on the project day and night. Finally after a long arduous process of trial and error, he obtained the speed he was seeking.

In 1876, he moved into his newly constructed "invention factory" at Menlo Park in New Jersey. There, he immediately went to work perfecting Alexander Graham Bell's telephone, an inferior device good only for short distance messages. By 1877, he had invented the carbon transmitter and microphone and these inventions led to the first practical telephone. Bell had been backed by Boston Brahmin, John Murray Forbes, Baring Bank ally and member of the Brahmin Boston-China opium syndicate. Edison, Johnson and Col. Gouraud created a company to rival Bell Telephone and fought bravely for its survival, but failed miserably when Bell Telephone succeeded in buying up stock in their company.

Palmer, Edison, Johnson and Gouraud were all moral men. Palmer was a practical dreamer who had envisioned a railroad under the control of trusted owners who would keep wages fair and expenses low, but the immoral foreign-inspired thieves in American business never allowed his dream to become reality. Edison had even criticized national banker, Jay Cooke, saying that money was of paramount interest to him, so he put it above all other concerns. Edison said that his conscience seemed to be atrophied and he speculated that this might have been because he had spent so much time associating with the Wall Street thieves who had no conscience at all.

After he perfected the telephone, Edison met George F. Barker, a physics professor at the University of Pennsylvania and chief resident at the Franklin Institute. Barker became Edison's mentor and encouraged him to invent the phonograph, a voice-recording device. Once the phonograph was perfected, the Philadelphia Interests arranged a demonstration of it at a meeting of the National Academy of Sciences in Washington, D.C. At the gathering, a packed audience listened as the phonograph recording device introduced itself with the words: "The Speaking Phonograph has the honor of presenting itself to the Academy of Sciences." That same evening a second demonstration was held at the Washington Bureau of *the Philadelphia Inquirer*. And the following day, national republican leader, James Blaine, held another demonstration for congressmen at the home of his niece. Suddenly Edison had become world famous.

Edison's next planned invention would be a device designed to produce light from electricity. There were multiple issues to contend with. First he had to create a light bulb. This involved enclosing a filament in glass, heating it, and then causing it to glow, yet not be consumed. Afterward, he had to devise a way to make a series of these bulbs run off the same power source. He also had to make the new invention work as inexpensively as the gas light system then in use.

Edison started this project in June of 1878. By October of that same year, he announced to the newspapers that he had invented the electric light. He then proclaimed that he would create both power sources and electric lights in every city in America and go on to light the rest of the world. With his invention, he proudly proclaimed that he had moved civilization upward.

Unfortunately, the Philadelphia Interests had been squeezed tight financially, so they were unable to finance Edison's project. Of course, the banking cartel was eager to be involved, but not for humane reasons. Alarmed by this new spirit of progressive American invention, they were anxious to buy up the rights to the inventions and suppress them.

J.P. Morgan and his partner Anthony Drexel, along with Rothschild representative, August Belmont, all went to Menlo Park to view Edison's latest invention and negotiate for the rights to it. Morgan actually went to that meeting with papers of incorporation for the Edison Electric Lighting Company and tried to conduct a deal in secret. This aroused Edison's suspicions. He rightly feared that they aimed to suppress his work.

Since he was then already famous, Edison had influence with the press, so, he began to expose the deal and educate the public about the invention at the same time. The *New York Herald* proved particularly helpful. They published a detailed article about the history of the project and described in vivid terms the quality of the bright beautiful light that the new method produced.

The British scientific establishment then immediately went to work degrading the project—claiming that electric light was impossible and that electric power was dangerous. The pro-British *New York Times* even ran an article on the merits and importance of gas lighting. They also repeated the false contention of British scientists that lights connected in a series could not each burn with steady luminescence, but that the lights had to diminish in brightness in proportion to their number. Then the banking interests bought the patent rights to the electric light bulb and just held it, refusing to manufacture any light bulbs. So, Edison sold his stock in the Edison Electric Light Company and set up a new company called The Edison Lamp Company. Then he went to work manufacturing his own light bulbs.

In 1880, on the eve of the election that promised to make James Garfield president of the United States, Edison hung a string of lights outside his home and made the announcement that he would light them if Garfield was elected. Then, with Garfield's successful election, and with public support strongly behind him, other sources of financing became available to Edison. He was then able to loosen the stranglehold of the cartel by getting municipalities to issue their own bonds for the purpose of constructing municipal power generating stations. Then, not only did the number of installations grow in America, but soon power-generating stations spread to South America and Japan. Then Professor Barker went to work in Germany with the industrialist, Emil Rathenau, and together they took on the British-controlled Siemens Company which was using electric dynamos of only 40% efficiency and they replaced them with Edison's dynamos which were 90% efficient. Rahtenau's German Edison company then electrified German industry.

Edison's scientific investigations were conducted in the spirit of the great European scientists, Gauss and Humboldt. Today, a bust of Alexander von Humboldt sits in the historic Edison laboratory in West Orange, N.J. There Humbolt's notebooks are on display. They contain thousands of experimental notes in a wide spectrum of scientific studies. Humboldt had studied the nature of gravity and electromagnetism. And, in the tradition of Johannes Kepler, he studied the nature of the origin of the earth's rotation in relation to the sun.

Edison's notoriety made it possible for him to attract dedicated researchers to his modern research and development laboratory. Along with Edison, these researchers embraced the tradition of the U.S. founders and called for scientific advance to lift the world upward. And, in the tradition of Leibniz, they called for linking manufacturing to R&D labs, so that prices could be held low and monopolies could be averted.

Unfortunately, though, as we shall see, monopolies gained a stranglehold over the U.S economy. Without any competition, they were then able to inflate prices and keep them high. Edison always maintained that prices had to be kept down in order for invention to flourish and he constantly complained of the handicap that inflation had placed upon him. He likened it to a "lead collar."

Edison ardently continued to hope for a decline in prices. Had the usurious British imperial monetary system been held at bay, this indeed would have happened. In the absence of financial exploitation, science and invention would have flourished. Unimpeded, creativity would have then continuously impelled America upward!

Thomas Edison personally trained Henry Ford, the creator of the automobile industry. He also trained Frank J. Sprague who worked with him on electric trains, and, with Edward Johnson, they developed electric subways, the elevator, and many electrically-powered industrial tools. Unfortunately, all of Edison's companies were eventually usurped by British-style oligarchs who had the backing of City of London/Wall Street financiers.

All of the industrial development that blossomed after the Civil War can be attributed to the planned scientific and industrial efforts of the Philadelphia Interests. Wall Street never helped to invent anything. Its interests have always been selfish and predatory. Americans are today largely oblivious to the wonderful legacy of invention that Lincoln personally spawned when he used constitutionally sanctioned U.S. credit to fund invention. But now you understand the profound changes Lincoln initiated when he used the power of the U.S. Constitution, to fund technology advance, don't you? That constitutional power can still be called upon today—and it must be called upon if man is to progress and create a better world!

1866-1879

33

THE NATIONALISTS FIND
A PRESIDENT

"Whoever controls the volume of money in any
country, is absolute master of all industry
and commerce."

JAMES A. GARFIELD

It was 1880 and time for the next presidential election, so the Philadelphia Interests
conferred with the powerful nationalist, James Blaine, and he urged the presidential
nomination of his colleague and friend, James Garfield. Wharton Barker, Henry
Carey's publishing successor, then went to work promoting Garfield's nomination at the
Republican Party convention. The prospects looked good, so the partners conferred with
Matias Romero, former Mexican Secretary of State, who was then living in the United
States. Looking forward to a promising American presidency, Romero then traveled home
to Mexico to inquire about the possibility of resurrecting the railroad from Mexico City.
Then, in 1881, just two months after Garfield's inauguration, the Diaz government signed
a contract with the Philadelphia Interests and new plans were forged for the revival of the
Mexican National Railroad.

The railroad from Mexico City was only the second railroad line to have ever been
built in Mexico. In order to exploit the resources of Mexico and intent upon keeping the
Mexican people in a backward state, the British had built a line from the Atlantic port
of Veracruz to Mexico City, but it carried only a handful of passengers and charged high
rates for the transport of freight. As a result, in negotiating with the Americans for a new

railroad, the Diaz government placed strict regulations in the new U.S. railroad contract. That agreement stipulated that the Mexican National Railway could not raise its rates and that it had to carry the Mexican military as well as Mexican foodstuffs at discounted rates. Mail had to be carried for free and Mexican telegraph lines had to be maintained by the railroad.

James Garfield was inaugurated as president amidst severe political tensions. Nationalism was on the rise in the world and an eruption in technology was expected. As a result, the British Empire began to fear for the life of its old evil system of exploitation. Lincoln ally, Tsar Alexander II, had copied the U.S by building a rail line in Russia and he anticipated linking it up to the U.S. rail grid. He had just freed the Russian serfs when, in March, 1881, he was murdered by a bomb.

Garfield made James Blaine his secretary of state and from that post, Blaine was taking sides with all the emerging nationalists in South America. The British had set their sights on stealing the mineral wealth of South America, so they organized a proxy army in Chile and it had invaded Peru and Bolivia, so that Britain could grab their nitrate deposits. They were also attempting to crush Peruvian nationalism. So Secretary of State Blaine sent Lincoln's old counterintelligence agent, Stephen Hurlbut, to face down the British diplomats who were demanding that Peru cede its richest provinces to them. The Peruvian army had collapsed because it was entirely dependent on the British Lima-based W. R. Grace merchants who controlled all the shipping along South America's west coast.

Blaine had an American nationalist upbringing. As a teenager, he had lived with his close relative, Thomas Ewing, while he was U.S. Secretary of the Treasury. In that post, Ewing had enjoyed a close relationship with the staunch anti-British statesman, Henry Clay. Later, under the influence of Blaine, who was his close friend, President Garfield re-instated the high tariff policies of the deceased nationalists Lincoln and Clay.

Meanwhile, during this same period, Garfield's future assassin, Charles J. Guiteau, wrote to the President. Characterizing Secretary of State Blaine as a "wicked man," he demanded that he be dismissed. He also insisted that Garfield and the entire Republican Party would "come to grief" if Blaine was not fired. Guiteau shot Garfield just weeks later.

As Garfield clung to life, Hurlbut, recently arrived in Peru, recognized the Peruvian regime of Garcia Calderon who had been made president by the Peruvian nationalist underground. Then the *U.S.S Alaska* reached Peru with Calderon's brother who had money and instructions for Peruvian national resistance forces. The British, however, quickly captured him and took him away to Santiago, Chile.

While imprisoned for shooting Garfield, Guiteau revealed that he had been taken by his father, while just a teenager, to the occult commune established by British-allied operatives in New York State. There, he claimed, he was isolated and subjected to pro-gramming that severely debilitated him in both mind and spirit. Later, after he left the commune, he began spending time at Republican National Committee headquarters in Washington, even though he had never before shown any interest in politics. Then, after Garfield became president, he began hanging around the White House and the State Department, relentlessly seeking a political appointment.

After Garfield's death, the new president, Chester A. Arthur, replaced Secretary of State Blaine with Theodore Frelinghuysen, a man with deep ties to Wall Street and he immediately canceled Blaine's scheduled Western Hemisphere peace conference. The congressman, Perry Belmont, then chaired a congressional hearing into the supposed corruption of Blaine and Hurlbut. At that hearing, Blaine exposed the involvement of British bondholders in the recent war against Peru. He also cited the fact that Britain had furnished the ironclads that destroyed the Peruvian navy in an operation that had used the Chilean government as an agent of war in South America.

Construction proceeded on the Mexican National Railroad. By 1885, two hundred and fifty-five miles of rail had been laid northward from Mexico City and thirty miles of rail had been laid to that city from the Pacific Ocean. Then, the old Boston "firm"—really a gang hostile to U.S nationalist interests–proceeded to make a deal with British-aligned elements in the Mexican government, and they secured an agreement to take over the new North/ South rail route that had been built from El Paso, Texas, to Mexico City.

Then the London/Wall Street banking cartel began to further intrude upon U.S nationalist plans for economic advance by gaining control of the Denver & Rio Grande Railroad's board of directors, forcing General Palmer to resign from the company. They then planned to crush nationalist plans for an industrial center in Denver.

During the Civil War, both Britain and France had invaded Mexico. Then, when Napoleon III installed Maximillian as emperor, Britain recognized his rule and withdrew her troops. When Maximillian was overthrown in 1867, Mexico then again became a republic and quickly acknowledged Britain as her enemy. She also refused to have any diplomatic relations with Britain. This was a severe economic blow to the British because from before the Civil War they had dominated foreign trade with Mexico.

By the 1880s, the U.S. had more than recovered from the Civil War. Not only was she prospering and out-distancing Britain in industrial development, but she was also trying to help uplift the rest of the world. Britain feared that Mexico might copy the U.S., break free from British domination, and set an example for the rest of Latin America to emulate. Garfield had sanctioned just such a plan when he appointed James Blaine as his secretary of state. This is why they killed him.

Intolerant of progress, Britain's Queen Victoria tried to renegotiate a return to favorable trading status with Mexico by sending Sir Spencer St. John there in 1883. Matias Romero had become Mexico's ambassador to Washington, and in 1884 James Blaine was running for president. From his platform as a presidential candidate, Blaine openly challenged the British Empire. If elected president, he promised to renew the crusade he had begun in South America when he was secretary of state under Garfield. A lover of things American, he wanted to unite the republics of the Western Hemisphere in an association for mutual benefit and progress. The British were fearful that Blaine might be elected and, even though the enemy-aligned Democratic Party waged a particularly vicious and slanderous campaign that year, he came close. Except that the New York political machine prevailed against him, Blaine would have been elected.

By this time, Spencer St. John had restored diplomatic relations with Mexico and was actively seeking the restoration of commercial relations, too. And, of course, the banking cartel was actively seeking to further financially paralyze the U.S. Throughout the 1870s and 1880s, St. John had been running British operations in both Chile and Peru and he had promoted the British-financed invasion of Peru by Chile. As secretary of state, Blaine had defended Peru.

With the defeat of Blaine's presidential bid in 1884, the British were jubilant. They held a huge celebration in Mexico on New Year's Eve, 1884, to celebrate the restoration of their favored trade status in that country.

Then in 1885, the Mexican National Railroad fell into the hands of British bond-holders and its control passed into the hands of a syndicate of British bankers with Wall Street partners. Among them was John D. Rockefeller's brother, William, and his Texas relative, James Stillman. Stillman had amassed a fortune supplying British contraband to the Confederate army during the Civil War and then he invested this money in Mexican mines and plantations. To amass further wealth, he then used financial leverage to control the Mexican rail lines and this helped eliminate competition, so Mexican progress was curtailed.

In 1900, during the presidency of another Blaine protégé, William McKinley, Edward Doheny pioneered the beginnings of the petroleum industry in Mexico, just as he had done in California. He planned to use petroleum to power electrical-generating stations and they, in turn, were going to fuel Mexican trains and factories. Then McKinley was assassinated and Doheny was over-whelmed by Wall Street just as Edison and Carnegie had been. Later, Wall Street also took over Henry Ford's operation.

The strength of the nationalists was waning. By 1910, General Palmer's Colorado Coal & Iron Co. had fallen into the hands of J.D. Rockefeller and he renamed it the Fuel & Iron Company. In a later chapter, we shall document the fact that Rockefeller used his control over the Colorado State Guard to send guardsmen into Ludlow, Colorado, a town just north of the Raton Pass. There, in an attempt to put down a miner's strike, they slaughtered mining families.

In 1899, old Thomas Coolidge formed the United Fruit Company and, with New Orleans-based Mafia muscle and Boston syndicate money, they set up tropical planta-tions all over Central and South America. In 1929, they merged their Old Colony Trust Company, an extension of United Fruit Company, with the First National Bank of Boston. With their boards interlocked, a powerful enemy alliance was forged. The First National Bank of Boston's predecessor, the Bank of Boston, had been founded by John Lowell in 1784. It had a long history of using Tory money to fund American involvement in early enemy syndicates. The nationalists had begun an early start toward world freedom, but, as we shall see, they proved to be no match for the well-organized enemy forces of empire that later succeeded in prevailing against them.

1880-1881

JAMES A. GARFIELD
TWENTIETH PRESIDENT OF THE UNITED STATES

Intellectual, teacher, college president, and self-ordained minister, James A. Garfield was a self-made man and brilliant orator who would have made a monumental president. Sadly, only months after he was elected, an assassin's bullet deliberately stopped him from forging an ever-widening circle of American influence with his newly-appointed secretary of state, the nationalist, James G. Blaine. Garfield once said of himself: "I love agitation and investigation and glory in defending unpopular opinion against popular error."

34

THE ROBBER BARONS

"As we view the achievements of aggravated capital,
we discover the existence of trusts, combinations,
and monopolies, while the citizen is struggling far in
the rear, or is trampled beneath an iron heel.
Corporations, which should be the carefully
restrained creatures of the law and the servants of the
people, are fast becoming the people's masters."

GROVER CLEVELAND, 1888

In 1865, John D. Rockefeller was a young ambitious Cleveland, Ohio, merchant who wanted to go into the petroleum business, so he opened an oil refinery in Cleveland and incorporated it as Standard Oil Company. Then he began to ruthlessly buy up other oil companies and oil-carrying railroads in the area. He had shrewdly reasoned that by owning all the refineries, he could set both the regional price of crude oil and the cost of refining it.

Corporations had first emerged during the Civil War, but afterwards they began to be commonplace. The Philadelphia Interests had organized partnerships that were focused on promoting science and invention in order to raise the standard of living, but, British-inspired corporations like Standard Oil were focused exclusively on profit. Greedy men then became politically influential, so British-style corporations began to dominate the business landscape in America. As the public began to protest, some states began to try to regulate them.

In an attempt to limit the size of these corporations, the state of Ohio passed legislation that prohibited Ohio companies from owning plants in other states. They also prohibited them from holding stock in out-of-state corporations. But, J.D. Rockefeller was bent on creating an empire, so he charged one of his attorneys, C.T. Dodd, with the task of finding a way around this legality. In order to circumvent the law, Dodd then created the trust as a new legal designation for the corporation.

John D. Rockefeller first organized his corporation, the Standard Oil Company, into Standard Oil Trust in 1882. Then by consolidating it with thirty-eight other corporate refineries located in different states, he created a monopoly of the oil industry. In an agreed upon arrangement of the thirty-nine merged corporations, a board of nine trustees emerged to operate the trust, but the controlling interest rested with Rockefeller who sat at the head of the board. Standard Oil Trust then controlled over ninety percent of the oil industry in the United States. Rockefeller's success caused other businessmen to follow his example. Soon there were meat trusts, barbed wire trusts, whiskey trusts, sugar trusts, etc. Even the necessities of life were not beyond the reach of the trusts.

The managers of trusts fixed high prices for consumers while they established low wages for laborers. Then during the 1890s, as people became frightened by these huge monopolies, they complained again. Fear was not just confined to the common people. Even men in high places complained. For example, Justice Harlan of the U.S. Supreme Court said that the U.S. had abolished one kind of slavery, but was faced with the real danger of the emergence of another kind. He called it "the slavery that would result from aggregations of capital in the hands of a few individuals running large trusts and controlling, for their own profit and advantage exclusively, the entire business of the country, including the production and sale of the necessities of life." Sounds a bit like the return of the British Empire, doesn't it?

Soon states began to prohibit trusts, but, in order to retain control, unscrupulous men like Rockefeller got lawyers to work out yet another designation to replace the trust! It was called the holding company. Then, in 1899, the Rockefeller Board of Trustees dissolved the Standard Oil Trust and reorganized under a holding company called Standard Oil Company of New Jersey. This new holding company was still the same monopoly, but now, under new technicalities, anti-trust laws could not prevail against it. Skillful lawyers had secured a coup for J.D. Rockefeller and others.

The British financial arm of the empire then conspired to further disarm the people of the United States by diverting their attention away from legislating against these monopolies to focus on the "good" that agents like Rockefeller were doing with their money. In this way, these sham reformers rescued Rockefeller from the wrath of the people.

One enemy-agent, Frederick Gates, came up with an ingenious scheme to save Rockefeller's power and advance the strength of the empire at the same time. So, he counseled Rockefeller to use some of his vast wealth to finance the University of Chicago. It opened in 1892. Now you might ask the question, "What was wrong with using this wealth to finance a university?" Well, there would be nothing wrong with it if the university was going to promote American values and help the people progress, but that is not what happened! The educational model of this university and others, like Columbia

Teachers' College, which followed, did not embrace the American humanist tradition, but instead promoted treasonous British political ideology. Rather than teach about the pacifist founding principles of the nation and advance real science in service to the people, they taught students about free trade in order to skillfully promote it throughout the world.

Through our careful inspection of U.S. history, we have seen that free trade is a foreign-inspired doctrine that **always** causes Americans to suffer. Americans only prosper when they first promote their own manufacturing, grow strong and independent, and then set out to form trade agreements with other nations. Through these cooperative agreements, it is then possible for an already prosperous U.S. to help other nations prosper, too. This is the American way! In past chapters, we have documented that, when the American system is implemented, the results are both immediate and dramatic. In succeeding chapters we shall tell of the unbridled success President William McKinley achieved when he applied protective tariff legislation to the U.S. economy. During his presidency, the U.S, economy boomed and this made him one of the most successful and popular U.S. presidents of all time.

1896

35

THE PEOPLE'S PRESIDENT

"Let us ever remember that our interest is in concord,
not in conflict; and that our real eminence rests in
the victories of peace not those of war...
Our earnest prayer is that God will graciously
vouchsafe prosperity, happiness and peace to all our
neighbors, and like blessings to all the peoples and
powers of earth."

WILLIAM MCKINLEY, SEPTEMBER 5, 1901

Beginning with Grant in 1868 and ending with Harding in 1922, seven Ohio-born citizens held the high office of President of the United States. Pre-eminent among them was William McKinley. History has falsely portrayed McKinley as a lack-luster president who catered to big business and Wall Street. Actually, though, he was a president in the tradition of the greatest American nationalists—men like Washington, John Quincy Adams, Lincoln, FDR and JFK. The facts of his life substantiate his greatness. The last of a group of Civil War veterans-turned-statesmen who loved Lincoln, from early in his political career, McKinley purposefully set out to emulate Lincoln. He once described his hero with these words: "Lincoln had that happy peculiar habit, which few public men have attained, of looking away from the deceptive and misleading influences about him—and none are more deceptive than those of public life in our capitals—straight into the hearts of the people. He could not be deceived by the self-interested host of eager counselors who sought to enforce their own peculiar views upon him as the views of the country. He chose to determine for himself what the people were thinking about and wanting to do, and no man ever lived was a more accurate judge of their opinions and wishes."

Born in Ohio in 1843, William McKinley had a thoroughly middle class upbringing. During the early days of the establishment of the public schools in Ohio, at his mother's insistence, when he was nine years old, the McKinley family moved to Poland, Ohio, so that the children could attend its academy. It was at home though where McKinley's values were forged. Subscribing to the best periodicals of the day,—the *Atlantic Monthly,* (young Will's favorite), *Harper's Monthly,* and Horace Greely's *New York Weekly Tribune,* each evening the family gathered together in the sitting room and took turns reading out loud. Considered western Whigs, the family's sentiments were deeply nationalistic and this perspective helped congeal McKinley's life-long uncompromising commitment to a pro-active government committed to promoting the general welfare. The McKinley family belonged to the locally popular Methodist Church, but they were very tolerant of all religious faiths. They also regularly read abolitionist literature.

Just eighteen years old at the outbreak of the Civil War, McKinley heard Lincoln's first national appeal for volunteer army recruits and responded by quickly enlisting in the Poland, Ohio, guards. His Twenty-third Regiment fought in the bloody Battle of Antietam. There, during the fighting, when several units were cut off, having been placed in charge of the commissary, the nineteen year-old McKinley, wanted to get food and rations to the stranded men. So, under his own initiative, he put together a wagon-full of supplies and personally drove the wagon through open enemy fire. The rear of the wagon was taken off by a small cannonball, but the aid arrived. For this act of bravery, McKinley received the first of a continuing series of promotions which made him a major by the end of his three-year enlistment. McKinley forged many friendships during his years in the Twenty-third Regiment. Future president, Rutherford Hayes, numbered among those life-long friends. After the war, Hayes urged McKinley to pursue a business career, but McKinley always knew that he was destined for a life in politics.

As the protectionist policies of Lincoln and Carey were gradually abandoned after the Civil War, business interests began to be consolidated in the form of trusts. Labor suffered horribly under these conditions, so strikes often broke out. Federal troops were called in to break them up. Always pro-labor, in 1876, after he had launched a successful career as a Stanton County attorney, McKinley volunteered his services in the defense of striking coal miners despite the fact that friends said it would hurt him politically. Thirty-three coal miners had been imprisoned for rioting during that strike. McKinley's defense freed them all. Later, when they had raised the funds to pay for their defense, McKinley refused the money.

During his congressional years, McKinley personally presided over many labor disputes. Then he became governor of Ohio in 1891, and in that office, he was responsive to the growing needs of labor. When strikes occurred, he would often mobilize the state militia and send them to the scenes of protest where, just by their presence alone, violence would be averted. Critics would cite the cost of mobilizing such large numbers of troops, but McKinley always followed his own instincts. When, in 1894, he had to repeatedly send the Ohio state militia to scenes of miner violence, he often stayed in his office until

3 a.m., watching from a distance the movement of troops for periods of as long as sixteen days. Every life mattered to him.

With the intention of establishing the means for peaceful mediation, while he was a congressman, McKinley had proposed a national system for the arbitration of labor disputes. And, although this national legislation failed to pass, it did contribute to pioneering just such a system in Massachusetts. Later, when he became governor of Ohio, McKinley made Ohio the second state to establish arbitration.

In January, 1895, when miners in Hocking Valley sent word to Governor McKinley that they were living in a destitute situation, he immediately began to assemble relief for them. By 5 a.m. the next morning, a railroad car full of provisions had been dispatched along with a message from the Governor insisting that no one was to go hungry. McKinley had personally paid for the emergency supplies. When further investigation revealed persistent devastation, he immediately made a statewide appeal for charity that resulted in relief for ten-thousand people. Legislatively, he also went to work bettering working conditions by establishing one-thousand dollar fines for employers refusing to let employees join labor unions. This kind of legislation was rare in the 1890s.

In 1896, McKinley successfully secured the republican nomination for President of the United States on the first ballot and he did so without personally submitting to the forces of the eastern political machine. Today, McKinley is relegated to the dustbin of forgotten lost American personages, but in the 1890s, he was the dominant political personality of his time. His rise to the top of American politics was patiently forged by masterfully building a solid reputation and an immense popularity. With this popularity, when he became president, he not only faced down the political party establishment of his day when necessary, but he also faced down the trusts. In 1900, for example, in the face of outrageous steel prices, he threatened to have the Navy Department build its own armor plate facility. Prices soon came down.

Like Lincoln before him, after his inauguration. McKinley called a special session of Congress in order to enact a protective tariff. When the Dingley Tariff became law, it quickly began to usher in a period of profound prosperity. With his vision of Lincoln-style global advance in mind, McKinley tried to fix international currency exchange rates by establishing an international agreement to include silver, along with gold, as an acceptable backing for the major European currencies. When these negotiations failed, McKinley passed the Gold Standard Act of 1900 and fixed the dollar to gold at $20.67 an ounce. European nations did not fix their currencies to gold until 1917.

Then McKinley appointed an ambassador to Russia and charged him with gaining contracts for U.S. firms in the new Russian Manchurian rail project, an extension of the Siberian project first initiated when Lincoln was president. By the fall of 1898, Russia had ordered locomotives from the Baldwin Locomotive Company. Threatened that this Russian Manchurian project would ruin their international trade by extending Russian trade to China, Britain then mobilized to defeat the project. In a later chapter, we shall learn about the Russian nationalist, Sergei Witte, and his grand attempt to "Americanize" Russia.

McKinley also worked for racial harmony. Lincoln had formally emancipated the slave, but he was murdered before he could forge the policies that would practically emancipate them. McKinley took up where Lincoln left off by vowing to make emancipation, as he said, more than "the cold formality of constitutional enactment." He wanted it to be a "living birthright." Because emancipation had been compromised from as far back as 1876 when Tilden and Hayes had vied for the presidency, McKinley knew there was much work to be done. You will recall that that election had been close, so Congress had to intervene and they chose Hayes. In the process, they made a compromise with Southern Democrats, the political remnant of the old Confederate enemy. As a consequence, federal troops, which had been protecting the voting rights of southern blacks, were withdrawn from the South. After this Tilden/Hayes compromise, freed from the watchful eye of the government, enemy-aligned elements in the South maintained segregation there until the 1960s.

In 1896, the year McKinley was elected president, civil rights suffered another setback when the Supreme Court officially legalized segregation by a "separate but equal" decision and this further challenged black voting rights. It also restricted Republican Party vote-gathering in the South. But, McKinley overcame this disparity in true Lincoln style, by championing the general welfare. This brought people together and re-awakened a commitment to American ideals. The people greatly loved McKinley for championing these ideals.

McKinley always claimed that he knew from his youth that he would one day become president, so he spent his whole political career preparing to emulate the policies of Lincoln should his vision become reality. Lincoln's historic policies were a revival of the sovereign national policies of Alexander Hamilton who, as we have mentioned, spent his early career researching the problems involved with freeing the nation from financial domination by empire. As a student of Hamilton, John Quincy Adams and Henry Clay, Lincoln had revived these protectionist policies to not only defeat the British-organized Confederacy during the Civil War, but to also create a great U.S. technology start. Within ten years of the end of the Civil War, this start bore fruit causing the U.S. to emerge as the world's foremost industrial power. When he became president, McKinley successfully resumed the start that Lincoln had begun.

After the death of Lincoln, many in the United States largely understood that Britain was their nation's long-standing enemy. As a congressman, from as far back as 1888, McKinley had branded the opponents of protective tariffs as domestic agents of Britain. Then, during the presidency of Benjamin Harrison, when McKinley achieved the passage of his McKinley Tariff Law, that domestic enemy—the same enemy that had consolidated the trusts—responded by artificially raising domestic prices, so the tariff failed to attain its goal. This was enough to fool many people, and so they voted the Republicans out of office. During this period, McKinley suffered the only defeat of his whole political career. In a predictable response to it all, he claimed that many great acts had met with this kind of conspiracy. They were, he said, designed to fool a "duped and deceived pubic."

Well-aware that protectionism fostered independence from the historic enemy, during his first term in office, President McKinley used the prosperity he had created to inaugurate the start of the second phase of the U.S. founding plan for world freedom—the export of American prosperity to the emerging republics of South America. The U.S was manufacturing a surplus of goods, so, McKinley intended to export them to South America where they would be exchanged for raw materials.

Like Lincoln before him, McKinley was a moral man whose determination to advance the founding U.S. goal of peaceful world cooperation could not be stopped. In order to stay one step ahead of the enemy, he generally kept his long-range plans a secret. But, despite this policy, the enemy could perceive his dedication to American founding principles, so they murdered him. Had McKinley managed to stay alive, peace might have begun to prevail in South America and **a gradual, but consistent, elevation of the standard of living may have arisen there.**

When Garfield was elected president in 1880, he had committed himself to the very same peace-oriented policy by appointing Senator James G. Blaine of Maine as secretary of state. Blaine understood the strategic situation in Latin America very well. As a congressman, he had actually been the first member of his generation to propose the idea of trade reciprocity agreements with South America. Under Garfield's direction, Blaine began to plan for the spread of the American system to South America by organizing a Pan-American Conference. But, these progressive nationalist plans were too much for the organized enemy, so, within two hundred days of Garfield's election, they assassinated him. British stooge, Chester A. Arthur then succeeded Garfield as president and immediately reversed his policies. Blaine was then removed from the office of secretary of state and the Pan-American Conference was delayed until he once again became secretary of state under Benjamin Harrison in 1888.

James Blaine was a popular leader in his own right. Nominated for president in 1884, he was defeated by Grover Cleveland through an array of dirty political tricks. Very aware of the forces conspiring against him, Blaine later described his defeat as "a coup by the Confederacy." Blaine had first suggested trade reciprocity agreements to McKinley when he was head of the Congressional Ways and Means Committee during the Harrison administration. Pennsylvania congressman, William D. Kelley, one of Henry C. Carey's closest collaborators, had passed the American system political torch to McKinley before retiring. McKinley then took over Kelley's responsibilities as the American system spokesperson and collaborated with Blaine to establish reciprocity as part of his 1891 McKinley Tariff. Later, when McKinley became president, he successfully re-applied tariff law to the American economy and ushered in a grand prosperity. Later, after McKinley was elected to a second term as president, he prepared to extend trade reciprocity agreements to South America in an attempt to economically defeat the enemy. Like patriots before them, McKinley and Blaine saw the implementation of this U.S. trade policy as the way to fulfill the intentions outlined in the Monroe Doctrine.

In 1900, just before his murder at the Pan American Exhibition, in what he confided to friends as the most important speech of his career, McKinley cited reciprocity as the "natural growth of our wonderful industrial development." And, true to his natural habit of always giving credit to others for their ideas, he mentioned the then deceased Blaine and said that the exhibition would have "touched the heart of that great American statesman whose mind was ever alert and thought ever constant for a larger commerce and a truer fraternity of the republics of the new world." For planning to implement the wholesome plan of Lincoln, refined for their day by Blaine, McKinley was murdered through an enemy-orchestrated plan to stop him.

McKinley had obviously given much thought to the manner by which the economic development of South America could be executed. Ever since 1850, there had been international discussion about building a canal in Central America in order to enhance world commerce. McKinley wanted to make sure that Britain did not obtain dominant interest in that canal because, opposed to the spread of American prosperity, she would have used her control to block regional progress. McKinley actually wanted to build the planned canal through Nicaragua, rather than Panama, because, from as far back as the 1840's, a successful railroad had been operating through the Darien Gap in Panama. With the canal located in Nicaragua, McKinley would have been free to sponsor an expanded U.S. railway system from the Darien Gap all the way to the tip of South America in order to facilitate American-style commerce throughout the continent.

Aware of the domestic enemy's imperialist plans, McKinley was committed to fostering the American founding plan for world peace through promoting the advance of science and technology. The enemy, however, was busy forging plans for an Anglo-American imperial collaboration in order to strengthen the empire. McKinley, as we shall see, opposed imperialism and tried to implement peaceful political solutions to every problem he faced. He did not want the U.S. to fall into this British-set trap. We shall speak more of this in following chapters.

1896-1901

JAMES G. BLAINE

Eminent U.S. Statesman and
Two Time Secretary of State

In a eulogy before the House of Representatives, February, 1882, James G. Blaine aptly memorialized the final days of his colleague and friend, the martyred President James A. Garfield, with these beautiful words: "Gently, silently, the love of a great people bore the pale sufferer to the longed for healing of the sea, to live or die as God should will, within sight of its healing billows, within sound of its manifold voices. With wan, fevered face tenderly lifted to the cooling breeze, he looked out upon the ocean's changing wonders; on its fair sails whitening in the morning light; on its waves rolling shoreward to break and die beneath the noonday sun; on the red clouds of evening arching low to the horizon; on the serene shining pathway of the stars. Let us think that his dying eyes red a mystic meaning which only the rapt and departing soul may know. Let us believe that in the silence of the receding world, he heard the great waves breaking on a farther shore, and felt already upon his wasted brow the breath of the eternal morning."

36

ROUGH RIDER

"Speak softly and carry a big stick, you will go far."

TEDDY ROOSEVELT

During McKinley's first term as president, British-sympathizer, Senator Henry Cabot Lodge paid the President a visit and asked him to appoint Teddy Roosevelt to the post of Undersecretary of the Navy. For a long time, TR had been banging around the state of New York in various political capacities annoying many people, but his British handlers had plans for him, so they wanted him to get some national exposure. When McKinley appointed TR as undersecretary of the navy, he did not know it, but, on behalf of his British handlers, TR was aching to go to war.

From that post, in true imperialist fashion, while secretary of the navy, John D. Loring, was out of town for a few hours, Teddy put the U.S. Pacific fleet on alert and told Admiral George Dewey to be ready for an attack in the Philippines. Before long, Dewey engaged in a brief fight with the Spanish that locked the U.S. into a presence in the Philippines that lasted until 1902. Over the years, many Americans were killed in fighting there.

Teddy Roosevelt was pushed on McKinley a second time when, in 1900, he had been "suggested" as McKinley's vice-presidential running mate. Years later, Mark Hanna, McKinley's campaign manager, recollected the time when he and McKinley had learned of the possible nomination. Aware of TR's reputation as a hothead and distrustful of him, McKinley had laughed and Hanna had cursed and banged his fist on the table.

TR was a British-style imperialist who came from a family steeped in a long history of treason. In 1883, his favorite uncle, James D. Bulloch, had brazenly published an historical work about British secret intelligence called, <u>The Secret Service of the Confederate States in Europe</u>. Bulloch had been one of two coordinators of the British secret service plot to kill Lincoln and, from his youth, TR had regularly conferred with his beloved uncle who was exiled in Britain for his Confederate war crimes.

Prior to McKinley's 1900 re-election to the presidency, there had been reported rumors of assassination threats upon his life. After his re-election, Hanna had told him: "Your duty to the country is to live four more years from next March." The New York City police commissioner had been warning that the Henry Street Settlement House, in New York City, was full of anarchists. Intent upon destroying all U.S. foreign alliances geared towards promoting prosperity in the world, especially the successful U.S. alliance with Russia, the enemy had engaged in promoting radical insurgency. But, like his nationalist predecessors, Lincoln and Garfield, McKinley underestimated the enemy and refused to worry. When, at the Pan American Exhibition, a body-guard was suggested, McKinley rhetorically asked, "Who would want to kill me?" Optimistically focused on creating prosperity and unflinchingly committed to American ideals, McKinley dismissed the suggestion and instead focused in on giving his important Pan American Exhibition address.

Then, the day after this address, McKinley proceeded to hold his customary public reception. This is when the brainwashed anarchist, Leon Czolgosz, entered the reception line and twice shot McKinley. One bullet was removed immediately, but because the surgical techniques of the day were limited, the second bullet could not realistically be removed. The doctors waited! After several days, President McKinley rallied, sat up and had some tea, so they began to hope that the President might recover and be able to live with the bullet in him. But soon, gangrene set in and he declined again. After seven days, the beloved McKinley died.

The extent of intellectual development that had arisen under McKinley's presidential leadership could be viewed at the Pan American Exhibition he had just attended. A huge display of incandescent lighting was slowly turned on at sunset during the evening before the close of the exhibition. It brought tears of joy to the large crowds that had assembled to witness it. They had never before seen such a large display of lights! Buffalo had been chosen as the site for the exhibition because of its proximity to Niagara Falls. There, a newly-built hydroelectric facility had been built. At the exhibition, there were a variety of exhibitions on display—even newly-invented infant incubators. They held real new-born babies!

After the successful murder of McKinley, TR, the unregenerate racist and fanatical Confederate sympathizer, entered the office of president and destroyed all of McKinley's plans for world progress. The imperialists then took charge of America's destiny by opposing all real American advances in technology—advances that aimed at freeing the world. Instead, they focused in on creating novel toy-like inventions to amuse and placate the public. Always interested in creating subjugate slaves, they, the self-styled privileged few, were hell-bent on reaping all financial rewards. Solely consumed with accumulating money, they could not, or would not, espouse the truth that money is not meant to be hoarded or spent merely on pleasure. Under the American System of Credit, money is principally used to forge progress through scientific advance. A real physical economy then develops and that economy drives a universal prosperity and a universal happiness. When a nationalist American president arises to challenge the empire's regressive monetarist policies, they murder him in order to continue to perpetuate the empire's ages-old notion that money alone should be the determinant of value.

After McKinley was assassinated, Roosevelt drastically slowed immigration and reversed the American system policy of developing the West. History has falsely bestowed upon TR a reputation for being a trust-buster, but the only trust-busting he ever engaged in was a phony charade designed to give the Morgan financial interests power over true industrialists. Determined to make British foreign policy America's very own policy, on behalf of the empire, TR proceeded to break with the wise counsel of Washington. That counsel had advised Americans to stay clear of entangling foreign alliances. A lover of things British, as president, TR secretly aided all his covert aristocratic friends. Soon Wall Street would control both parties.

After he had served as president for nine years and decided that that was long enough, under orders given by his handlers, in 1910, TR again emerged as a candidate for president under his own Bull Moose Party banner. He had been given orders to run as a third party candidate in order to take votes from the republican candidate, the conservative Taft, who was running for re-election. The success of this scheme led to their mutual defeat and cleared the way for Woodrow Wilson, another British puppet-president.

A great U.S. moral decline followed the death of McKinley because later "leaders" lacked his moral integrity. Despite the growing medical bills of a wife who was a semi-invalid, McKinley always refused the many perks that he was offered. He insisted that accepting such extras created an inherent conflict of interest. During his years as a congressman, the opportunity to give a ten thousand dollar paid lecture series on protectionism arose. Despite the fact that this money would have augmented his then modest congressional pay, he turned it down. As governor of Ohio, he also turned down an invitation to join the board of directors of a major New York life insurance firm which paid eight thousand dollars a year for attending only one annual meeting. Always humble, as president, McKinley refused to let the army go forward in rewarding him with the Congressional Medal of Honor for Civil War bravery three decades earlier. His intense devotion went hand-in-hand with his morality. He was a consummate politician in the noblest sense of the word—always striving to bring people together.

By contrast, as president, TR blatantly alienated South America and fostered divisiveness. He also contributed to breaking up peaceful alliances with Japan, Russia, and Germany and dismantled the free pro-development system of Lincoln and McKinley. He also destroyed the independent platform of high wages that the McKinley Tariff Law of 1890 had fostered. Soon the legacy of Lincoln disappeared from American life. And, sadly, too, so did the hope of progress for South America—a hope that McKinley had tenderly nurtured. Not until the days of FDR and JFK would these sentiments and these hopes be revived.

1897-1910

37

THE MAKING OF AN IMPERIALIST

"We want no wars of conquest. We must avoid the temptation of territorial aggression. War should never be entered upon until every agency of peace has failed; peace is preferable to war in almost every contingency."

An excerpt from the first Inaugural Address of
William McKinley

After winning a second term as president, William McKinley was poised to spread the ever-widening U.S. prosperity to the republics of South America. Trade reciprocity agreements between many countries had already been negotiated. McKinley had been popular with Americans of both political parties. After his re-election, he had proudly proclaimed to his secretary: "I can no longer be called the President of a party. I am now the President of the whole people." Even the then Democratic mayor of Boston, "Honey-Fitz" Fitzgerald, had taken his daughter, Rose, mother of the future president, JFK, to McKinley's inauguration in Washington because he understood that the prosperity that McKinley had forged was a triumph over the stifling "blue-blood" agenda of the old Boston money. Too quickly though, McKinley was dead and Teddy Roosevelt was president. With a lover of things British in the White House, a clear path was then set for the British-controlled trust empire of J.P. Morgan to take over American business and otherwise promote the agenda of the empire.

The first proudly aristocratic president to ever assume office, T.R. had been groomed for that office by the British enemy and their circle of American counterparts. Raised in an aristocratic family and schooled at Harvard, TR loved the elite British lifestyle, especially the animal hunt, a traditional pastime among British aristocrats. On expensive holiday trips, as a child, he had been allowed to wield a shotgun and hunt defenseless animals. On one trip to Egypt, the near-sighted child shot animals until absolutely content and then proudly displayed them to his doting parents. Among the dead animals were small birds, mice, squirrels and large insects. After sifting through them, he saved the ones that were not completely destroyed to add them to his taxidermy collection. Perhaps he took after his father, an amateur naturalist who, with J.P. Morgan, had founded the American Museum of Natural History in order to promote the enemy's subversive anti-development agenda.

During his Harvard years, Teddy became acquainted with Professor Henry Adams, the aristocratic grandson of John Quincy Adams, who hated everything his patriotic grandfather had espoused. Aware of TR's love for hunting, the professor engaged Teddy in discussions of his favorite pastime in order to entice him into joining his Cosmos Club. Committed to advancing the interests of the British Empire through the promotion of false science, this club created a way for false scientists to infiltrate the political system and spread disinformation. This was part of the enemy plan to stifle American technological advance. At meetings of the Cosmos Club, TR met and befriended the Boston blue-blood, Henry Cabot Lodge, a fellow Harvard alumnus.

By the mid 1890s, Teddy had entered politics. Serving in the New York State Legislature for a while, he made a reputation for himself as a British-style "reformer," but his aristocratic conceit made him quite unpopular. Then he secured an appointment as New York City police commissioner and served in that office for a while. A stint as U.S. Civil Service Commissioner followed, but he never really accomplished anything significant in any of these offices. Then, in 1897, Henry Cabot Lodge, U.S. Senator from Massachusetts, approached President McKinley and asked him to appoint TR undersecretary of the navy. With McKinley's reluctant compliance, TR was then catapulted to the national political scene. This appointment proved fortuitous for TR's British handlers because it created a platform from which TR could begin to promote the advance of the enemy's imperialist agenda for the United States.

In Washington, Lodge and his friends had organized the Cuban Revolutionary Junta as a propaganda machine for promoting the first phase of the British-designed imperialist agenda for the United States—the "liberation" of the Spanish colony of Cuba. This junta was an association of British-Boston-New York merchants and bankers who met regularly in Washington at the home of Henry Adams. Having set their minds on initiating a war with Spain, they used their newspaper connections to intentionally agitate Americans over "atrocities" in Cuba.

You may recall that, in 1823, John Quincy Adams had formulated the Monroe Doctrine and, through it, he issued a clarion call for peaceful cooperation throughout the Western Hemisphere. McKinley was committed to the same principle. He also had other truly American ideas percolating in his mind. He was going to defeat the British

Empire in an economic war of advancement without firing any guns. During his years in office, McKinley had associated with the brilliant James Blaine who had been a long-time congressman and senator from Maine and twice the secretary of state. Together, in the tradition of Abraham Lincoln, they had originated a plan to modify U.S. protective tariffs by forging reciprocity treaties with select Latin American republics. Under these arrangements, tariffs were going to be lowered, so that nations wanting to engage in mutually beneficial commercial relations with the U.S. could develop economically. Economic advance was going to eradicate war!

This was all happening during the era of Counte Sergei Witte in Russia. As a student of Friedrich List, Witte had learned about the American System of Political Economy and he had intended to Americanize Russia through industrialization. America's example had also been copied in Germany and Japan, so its influence was spreading. Canada and Australia were also attentively watching these developments. All of this progress made the British imperialists extremely anxious. They had been watching the McKinley-Blaine collaboration ever since 1891 when it had produced the McKinley Tariff Law. The British knew that protective tariff legislation had the potential to drive their imperialism from the Western Hemisphere, so they repeatedly used their agents to infiltrate the U.S. government in an attempt to legislatively defeat protectionism. They had also tried, through repeated wars, first in 1775, then in 1812, and finally in 1861, to dismantle the progressive agenda of technology advance upon which America was founded. But, they had militarily failed each time and they were devoid of prospects for again defeating the U.S. through waging another war against her. If outright war could not be orchestrated, they had to go back to a plan for internal subversion and trick the American people into giving up the American system. A leadership void would first have to be created and then filled by a British sympathizer. And the ever-so-popular McKinley was only in his first term. How could they quickly get a British agent installed in the presidency? They had to kill McKinley! If, in the election of 1900, they installed TR as McKinley's vice-presidential running mate, TR would be in the default office when the murder occurred.

In the enemy's imperialist view, Teddy Roosevelt was the perfect choice for president because he viewed himself as a mighty soldier in the British aristocratic tradition. His favorite uncle, James D. Bulloch, had been exiled in Britain after the Civil War for the part he played in arming and supporting the Confederacy. He had also helped plan Lincoln's murder. His war crimes had been considered so egregious that he had been ineligible for exclusion under Lincoln's generous post-war amnesty program. Bulloch had not only organized and manned the Confederate navy during the Civil War, but he had also served as a Confederate spy. With his treasonous help, during that war, Confederate vessels destroyed Union ships and killed American sailors, while they crippled American trans-Atlantic commerce. Uncle Jimmy had been TR's favorite uncle!

Teddy's revered uncle was, in his mind, an authority on naval power and geopolitics. In exile in Britain, he had written a two-volume set of books called <u>The History of the Confederate Secret Service</u>. Teddy had so admired it that he had copies of the volumes printed up for personal distribution. Like his uncle, the fanatical TR believed in the

British system of "managing" inferior races. He did not espouse the American ideal of equality and universal freedom from want.

After graduation from Harvard, Teddy married Alice Lee, the daughter of Boston Brahmin, Henry Cabot Lee. (The "elite" always try to inter-marry.) You will remember that the aristocrats were not confined to just Boston and New York. They has infiltrated the South in advance of the Civil War to promote their planned program of civil insurrection, so, in this regard, both Teddy and Alice were blue-bloods. Teddy was from the southern tradition and Alice from the northern one.

Teddy loved the company of Alice's father, a partner in the Boston Brahmin banking firm of Lee & Hutchinson. In the years before the Civil War, his bank had helped finance both terrorists in the South and radical business abolitionists in the North. The Lees were proud descendants of the Essex Junto, the arch-Tory league that had tried to sever the nation as early as 1796.

Teddy's family itself had banking connections in nefarious imperialist enterprises. Uncle James' father, Archibald Gracie II, was president of the Baring Bank office in New York. And Uncle James' brother, Archibald Gracie III, was a Baring Bank representative in Alabama and a noted Confederate author. The Baring Bank had financed and managed the Anglo-American trade in East Asia, the most profitable part of which was the illegal opium trade in China. These banking and trade connections made the Roosevelts well-connected agents of empire. A considerable number of Roosevelts and Bullochs had been Tories since the time of the American Revolution.

When President McKinley appointed TR as undersecretary of the navy, he could not have imagined how ready Teddy would be for naval action. Then, in 1898, a ship just "happened" to run into trouble in Havana harbor just as James Bulloch's ship had done, in 1854, when he was serving there as a Young America revolutionist. This second ship, *The Maine*, exploded. No one has ever determined who was responsible for this explosion, but it killed over two hundred Americans. While President McKinley was vested in trying to find a peaceful diplomatic settlement with Spain, Teddy, anxious to exploit the opportunity the explosion had presented, was aching to go to war. Finally, President McKinley, under relentless pressure from Congress, reluctantly declared war on Spain.

Teddy then had himself installed as a lieutenant colonel in the army, joined with Colonel Leonard Wood to raise a volunteer cavalry of golf players and cowhands, and took off with them to San Juan Hill to fight the black slaves the Spanish had just liberated. Even though Roosevelt's Rough Riders were badly beaten by these black troops, the press glorified TR's "heroics." After the war, with this new press-created reputation as a victorious soldier, Teddy was then catapulted into the office of governor of New York. There he was out of McKinley's way for two years. Then, after serving two unpopular years as governor of New York, in 1900, TR became McKinley's vice-presidential running mate. After McKinley's murder, TR became the enemy's puppet-president.

With Teddy as president, the J.P. Morgan trust empire drastically extended its control over American business. Never afraid to oppose the trusts, had McKinley lived, he would surely have opposed their expansion. Before his death, he had not only bemoaned a

Supreme Court decision that legalized a trust purchase of two sugar refineries, but he had also voiced the wish that the Sherman Anti-Trust Laws had been sustained by Congress.

After McKinley's murder, with TR as their installed puppet-president, J.P. Morgan and his allied bankers consolidated much more of the free American economy. On the day of TR's inauguration, one hundred independent steel companies were consolidated into the mega-giant, United States Steel Company. Morgan and his friend, George W. Perkins, also eventually formed the International Harvester Trust by buying out all major farm machinery companies. With his select friends, J.P. Morgan also took over the largest railroad companies. When General Electric made an agreement with Westinghouse, Morgan then became the dominant partner in the electrical industry, too. By sanctioning all of this activity, TR helped the foreign bank of J.P. Morgan and Company become owner of the American economy. He also destroyed the conditions for world prosperity that his patriotic predecessor, William McKinley had created.

Trust buster is a bogus label that has been bestowed on TR. It is part of the falsified view of history that has been fed to Americans. During his presidency, T.R. gave his commissioner of corporations, Henry Knox Smith, the task of investigating International Harvester, but this sham investigation proved inconclusive. When challenged to reveal the records his administration had garnered through this investigation, Teddy staunchly refused. Instead he locked them up and then challenged the House to impeach him. There the matter rested.

TR is also known for the inauguration of the practice of Conservation. He actually originated the term and created the whole movement in order to tie up U.S. western lands and prevent their development. Toward this end, he created the United States Forest Service and appointed Gifford Pinchot as its first chief. In another chapter, we shall tell the story of the rise of Conservation.

1897-1901

38

WHO WON THE WAR
WITH SPAIN?

"God bestows supreme opportunity upon no nation that
is not ready to respond to the call of supreme duty."

WILLIAM MCKINLEY

It is said that no one present at the Ohio Society banquet in 1900 ever forgot the
challenge to imperialism that McKinley posed that evening. Rapt in silence, his
audience listened as he said: "There can be no imperialism. Those who fear it are
against it. Those who have faith in the Republic are against it. So that there is universal
abhorrence for it, and unanimous opposition to it.......those who do not agree with us have
no confidence in the virtue or capacity or high purpose or good faith of this free people
as a civilizing agency, ... the century of free government which the American people
have enjoyed has not rendered them irresolute and faithless but has fitted them for the
great task of lifting up and assisting to better conditions and larger liberty those distant
peoples who through the issue of battle have become our wards. A self- governed people
will never permit despotism in any government they foster and defend. The burden is our
opportunity; the opportunity is greater than the burden."

With these sentiments, McKinley embraced the pacifist ideals of his forefathers. In
1898, when public sentiment for war with Spain had been manipulated to a high pitch,
McKinley tried to delay. It had been his hope that with delay Spain would free Cuba.
McKinley wished that he could have defused Congress, but they were relentless. In secret,
he had admitted that, if there had been a way to get the legislatures of both countries out of

the way, he could have himself negotiated a peaceful resolution with Spain's prime minister. Yet despite his wishes, he knew that war would come. In clamoring for war, both the Hearst and Pulitzer newspapers had been telling atrocious tales of slavery and repression in Cuba. They had manipulated public opinion to such a high pitch that the American people became convinced that war with Cuba was necessary. Far-sighted and wise, McKinley knew that problems would come as the U.S began to annex foreign territories. He did not relish having them. He knew they would be difficult problems, but powerful anti-American forces had taken hold of the day, so he resolved to make the best of the situation.

After the war got underway, during the actual fighting, the newspapers made a hero out of Teddy Roosevelt by dubbing him the "hero of San Juan Hill." But, on the war front, McKinley actually directed every military move on both land and sea. Like Lincoln before him, night and day, he followed every battle and was on top of every plan. In one particular incident, in July, 1898, after the U.S. had engaged in a long exhausting battle driving the Spanish over San Juan Hill, the American commander, fearful of a Spanish counter-attack, questioned if his men could withstand another fight, so he cabled McKinley in Washington about the situation. McKinley urged, but did not order, him to hold the hill. Rather than decide the action himself, after giving this counsel, he told the ground commander that he was there on the scene and because of that he knew best. Then, he placed his confidence in the decision his commander would make. The commander, however, recognizing McKinley's wisdom, stayed his recommended course and led the American soldiers to a swift victory.

From their high position on the hill, the Americans then fired upon Spanish ships and they fled the harbor. The real hero of San Juan Hill was not TR, but McKinley. History has been falsified. The Rough Riders did not win the war with Cuba, the U.S. Army and its commander-in-chief won that war.

When it was time to sign an armistice with Spain, McKinley was humble. He did not feign the attitude of a conqueror. Instead, he viewed the position he was in as an uneasy and tenuous one and sought the counsel of almost everyone he knew. And he formed a peace commission to study the problems involved in promoting peace. During his time as president, McKinley developed the art of appointing government fact-finding commissions to a high level and he placed his confidence them. In this instance, the only advice he gave to them was to be "magnanimous." He wanted all their deliberations to be in harmony with the great benevolent mission of the U.S. Even though he had been cornered by the imperialists into fighting a war he had not wanted, he could let a just peace with Spain reflect well on the U.S.

Then McKinley proceeded to make speeches and write letters promoting peaceful world cooperation. Afterward, he laid back to watch and wait for the reaction of the people he represented. McKinley had supreme confidence in the common sense of the average American and he listened to them. On many occasions, he said, "The people will choose." He was interested in how the Filipinos and the Cubans felt, too. Ever the peacemaker, McKinley always had a gut instinct for the right course of action. Respectful of the people, he was always the patient guide of the country he loved.

After the war, when McKinley found himself saddled with the new U.S possessions that the British Empire had thrust upon him, he found that he was unsure of what to do. He was particularly troubled about the Philippines. In his biography of McKinley, Charles S. Olcott tells of a visit some Methodist ministers paid McKinley, in November of 1898. At that time, McKinley took them into his confidence. He told the ministers that, after having sought counsel from Democrats as well as Republicans, he had still been unclear about what to do, so one evening, while anxiously walking the floor, he said, he dropped to his knees and prayed in earnest to the Almighty, seeking His counsel. Then, in a flash, he said, it had come to him. Everything became clear. He saw that he could not give the Philippines back to Spain after winning them away from that country. Neither could he turn the Philippines over to any other country. And, because they were incapable of self-government, he could not leave them to themselves. He had to stay there, educate and uplift them, and teach them how to rule themselves. With his mind at rest, he then slept peacefully that night.

Historians have always claimed that McKinley was no intellectual giant. He certainly did not have an eastern education. But McKinley made no claim to greatness or specialness of any kind. He had no airs about him. He just knew who he was—a servant of the government of the United States. Like nationalists before him, he knew that his country had been founded as part of a great experiment. McKinley strived to advance the experiment with the tool he had perfected. That tool was tariff law. The study and perfection of tariff law had been the work of his life.

Cartoonists of the day used to have a great time portraying McKinley as the "Napoleon of Protection," but McKinley was no Napoleon. In character, he bore no resemblance to that historical person. There may have been a physical resemblance—he may have had the same build or a resemblance in facial features—-but that is where the resemblance ended. McKinley had no imperialist ambitions. He never courted disaster like Napoleon. He was sure and steady and thoroughly American. He was kind, but never weak.

During his five years in the White House, his secretary, George B. Cortelyou was very close to him. When once asked what McKinley's chief characteristic was, without hesitation, Cortelyou said, "Courage."

McKinley always stood firm on principle. After his inauguration, his friend, Mark Hanna, approached him with a request to appoint Henry C. Platte, Republican organizer from Wisconsin, to the position of postmaster general. McKinley declined Hanna's request because Payne had been a lobbyist for the Northern Pacific Railroad and he was opposed in principle to appointing lobbyists to government office. But McKinley's reply to Hanna was couched in kindness. He said that he would love to do it for him because he could see that it was important to him, but a lobbyist in his cabinet was impossible. That was the end of it. Five years later, when elected president himself, Teddy Roosevelt appointed Payne without compunction.

The newspapers of the day always liked to declare that Hanna controlled McKinley. This was a falsehood. McKinley would frequently solicit opinion from others, but then he would make his own decisions. That was part of the greatness of the man.

1898-1900

WILLIAM MCKINLEY
TWENTY-FIFTH PRESIDENT OF THE UNITED STATES

*His often repeated phrase, "The people against the bosses" can
be likened to the war cry of a devoted foot soldier in the fight
to advance the republic of the United States.*

39

THE SOCIALISTS MOUNT
A CHALLENGE

"Out of modern civilization, economic royalists carved
new dynasties. It was natural and perhaps human that
the privileged princes of these economic dynasties,
thirsting for power, reached out for control over
government itself. They created a new despotism
and wrapped it in the robes of legal sanction...And, as
a result, the average man once more confronts the
problem that faced the minute-man..."

FRANKLIN DELANO ROOSEVELT

In 1901, railroad tycoon, Edward H. Harriman bought the Southern Pacific Railroad
and, through this purchase, gained control of land that had earlier been granted to the
Oregon and California Railroad by the United States government. This land had been
allocated for the construction of a line from Portland, Oregon, to California. Under this
agreement, Congress had specified that, after the railroad was built, the surrounding land
had to be sold to settlers in lots of not more than 160 acres and at a price not greater than
$2.50 an acre. But, in 1903, E.H. Harriman illegally withdrew from sale almost three
million acres of the land he had obtained by public sale and for public use, in order to sit
on it and speculate on its rising price. The theft of this land caused such a public outcry
that prospective settlers went to squat on the land expecting the federal government to
fairly redress the problem by getting the land back from Harriman. But Teddy Roosevelt

was then president and he took no action against him. As a result, the land stayed idle until 1916 when the federal government finally won a suit to get the land back. But then, instead of selling it to the people, the government placed the land under the Bureau of Land Management. Today, in Oregon, gangsters reap large profits cultivating marijuana on both government land and the land owned by the huge Weyderhauser Company!

Teddy Roosevelt left office in 1909. During his years as president, the press garnered for him a reputation as a progressive trust-buster, but his successor, the conservative, William Howard Taft, actually launched more anti-trust suits than did Roosevelt. TR actually had made prearranged understandings—"gentleman's agreements," with J.P. Morgan and his cartel—for sham "investigations" of their monopolies to placate the public and insure that these monopolies would remain in tact. TR was afraid that if he did not promote the outward appearances of investigation, the railroads and other utilities would end up being owned by the government. During his administration, the men who planned the monopolies always evaded prosecution by bribing elected officials. In this way, they gradually rendered elected officials subservient to big business.

Initially opposed to the organization of labor, big business eventually came to view labor unions as inevitable, so, they began to infiltrate them in order to conservatively organize them. In this way, they reasoned, their monopolies would survive. But socialists continued to call for progressive reform, so big business began to fear the advent of a socialist system. In 1910, a member of the Socialist Party was elected to Congress and by 1911 there were seventy-three socialist mayors.

With socialist doctrines growing in strength, the enemy then began the careful orchestration of a campaign of "education" aimed at eradicating this opposition. This campaign stressed the sanctity of both private property and legal contracts and depicted the capitalist system as the preserver of individual liberty, while socialism was characterized as an opposing oppressive system.

Despite all this propaganda, the Socialist Party continued to grow and, in 1913, one year after Woodrow Wilson was elected president, a bitter violent coal mine strike broke out in Colorado at the Rockefeller-owned Colorado Fuel & Iron Corporation. Following the murder of one of their labor organizers, workers had initiated a strike against low pay, dangerous working conditions and the nearly complete takeover of their town.

After the strike began, the miners were evicted from their shacks, and so they went to the nearby hills to set up a tent city. From there they carried on their strike. Then the Rockefeller interests hired the Baldwin-Felts Detective Agency and, armed with Gatling guns and rifles, they raided the tent city. They also hired strikebreakers to go in and put the strike down, but the strikers fought them off in a gun battle. With the miners refusing to give in, the Governor of Colorado called out the National Guard, but Rockefeller paid for the support of the guard, so they were effectively working for him. Unaware of this, the strikers greeted the arrival of the guard with cheering and flag waving. Then guardsmen proceeded to beat and arrest the miners and burn down their town. In the process, they killed innocent women and children. The strikers still refused to give in and armed workers then marched in from other areas to help prepare for a larger battle by destroying mines and killing mine guards. Then the local militia received orders to go to Ludlow to engage there in a fight, but they refused to go. Soon cries went out for the arrest of the guard members who had conducted the killing spree. All over the country there were protests and meetings. Picketers marched in front of the Rockefeller offices in New York City. Newspapers were reporting the events worldwide.

Meanwhile, President Wilson focused his attention on a diversionary bombing of Veracruz, Mexico. Mexico had arrested the American soldiers of a U.S. ship that had dropped anchor in Tampico, a city that was under martial law. Even though they were quickly released and the Mexican government extended an apology for the incident, U.S. Admiral Mayo demanded a twenty-one gun salute to the American flag and Wilson backed him up. When the Mexicans refused the salute, President Wilson then invaded Veracruz.

The Mexican diversion didn't work for long though and soon, under mounting criticism, Wilson had to send federal troops into Colorado to subdue the strike. Members of the guard were never prosecuted for their killing spree. A spirit of rebellion continued to grow—a mass strike rebellion against the old forces of oligarchy that had worked its way back into the internal affairs of the nation. These forces had created a business monopoly that was causing much suffering among Americans. Soon, a senseless British-inspired war in Europe would become the focus of American attention and eventually the United States would be drawn into that war. That war was part of a covert British plan to break the hold the American system had secured on the minds of nationalist leaders in Europe. In typical British fashion, that war's devastation succeeded in deterring the world's sovereign industrial advance. For a while, it also deflected America's attention away from its domestic problems and its domestic foe.

1914-1918

40

THE ROYAL FORESTER

"There can be no greater issue than that of
conservation in this country."

TEDDY ROOSEVELT

As we have seen, the succession of Teddy Roosevelt to the U.S. Presidency was the culmination of an organized British plan to place an enemy agent in the executive seat of U.S. government. Under Teddy's watchful guidance, the empire was then empowered as he proceeded to implement a British East India Company-style scheme to withdraw prime U.S. western land from use. Regressive in nature, this plan had already been used in India to set valuable lands aside and keep them undeveloped. The Indian people, as a result, had remained in a backward state of perpetual impoverishment. From the start of his presidency, to stall U.S. development, Roosevelt was determined to implement the establishment of the same kind of reserves in the United States. Towards this end, he enlisted the help of Gifford Pinchot and appointed him chief forester.

Gifford Pinchot was the son of a wealthy New York real estate speculator who, in later years, founded a forestry school at Yale University. In 1880, while he was an undergraduate at Yale, under his father's counsel, Pinchot had determined that he would become a "forester." Together, father and son then actually created the profession. Before this time, no one in the U.S. had ever heard of a forester. To train for this self-created profession, Pinchot interned with the British, first in India and later in Cambridge, England, where he was schooled in British conservation rhetoric.

After Pinchot completed his training with the British, he returned to the United States to manage a North Carolina forest estate that belonged to the Vanderbuilt family. Then, during Cleveland's second term as president, he began to lobby Congress for the removal of U.S. "forest" land. By the end of Cleveland's administration, 21 million acres of western land had been removed and placed into government reserves. Then, when TR became president, together with Pinchot, they made the movement an official U.S. program and called it Conservation.

Pinchot enjoyed easy access to President Roosevelt. No one else in the president's cabinet could so easily summon TR's attention. The two spent long hours working together on their program. Later in life, TR called Conservation the most important accomplishment of his presidency. In 1905, TR converted the Bureau of Forestry into the U.S. Forest Service and put this new department under Pinchot's management, so that Pinchot could control the nation's forests. By the end of TR's administration, the U.S. Forest Service had removed 172 million acres of land from development.

A romantic campaign of widespread publicity then used TR's professed "love of the wilderness," to brainwash the American public into believing the hoax of Conservation. That movement falsified facts by claiming that the wide-scale removal of land to forest reserves was necessary to prevent the erosion of soil. All the while, the land that was removed was neither mountainous nor forested. The whole movement was a clandestine organized plan to disrupt U.S. technological progress.

As we have seen, after the Union victory in the Civil War, a great government-directed effort was launched to promote development in the West. Bolstered by the findings of several geological surveys commissioned by the federal government, Colorado was determined to be a region of vast mineral wealth. The Philadelphia Interests then targeted it for development by creating a climate for invention. These inventions, in turn, raised the U.S. standard of living.

Millions of immigrants then came to the United States and moved west to settle on farms in agro-industrial complexes the Philadelphia Interests had established. There, scientific methods were applied to farming and the rate of invention was so rapid that new harvesting equipment became available almost as quickly as it was created. A successful government-protected steel industry arose, too, and it produced low-cost steel rails that were laid down all over the West. All patriots were optimistic and happy. The long-awaited true American republic was in sight.

All the while, the power-hungry imperialists were anxiously despairing over all this progress, so they forged business takeovers and withdrew capital from investment. Then they began to speculate and concentrate on growing their own personal fortunes. Unlike the nationalists, they cared little about elevating the living standard of man or fostering creative work. Then, when the Conservation hoax was implemented, under the pretense of protecting the environment, conserving raw materials, and keeping wilderness areas pristine, many Americans were unwittingly duped into going along with this plan to curtail American progressive advancement. A halt on U.S. technological advance ensued.

The establishment of Conservation was part of a planned enemy scheme first initiated in 1897, when British-agent, Cecil Spring-Rice, advised TR, then undersecretary of the navy, to begin the inauguration of an American imperialist partnership with the British Empire. Towards this end, TR initiated a war in the Philippines and began to plan for a war in Cuba. The success of these wars forged the beginning of this desired imperial alliance. Then, with the success of the enemy's covert coup of the presidency, TR went to work furthering British ideology in the United States by establishing the British-inspired doctrine of Conservation as official U.S. policy.

Analogous counterparts aimed at thwarting development were then also established in both Canada and South Africa. In South Africa, a newly established republic had emerged in 1880 when a brief Boer War was fought in its Transvaal region. This successfully re-established the independent republic that had been lost there in 1877 when that tender republic had given up its independence in exchange for British help fighting the Zulus. After this 1880 British defeat, Cecil Rhodes and his fellow criminals planned a second Boer War of more dramatic intensity. Initially they hesitated to launch it though because they feared that Germany might intervene on behalf of the Boers. So, Britain sought an alliance with the U.S. military. The American war in the Philippines and the subsequent inauguration of Teddy Roosevelt as U.S. president forged this alliance and with it empire confidence grew.

In 1899, the British proceeded with their plans for a second Boer War. This war proved to be a bloodbath of alarming horror. In response to a Boer guerrilla campaign of lengthy duration, the British interred the native civilian population in gruesome prison camps where civilian death and suffering was so awful that it broke the Boers of their determination to win the war. The British then prevailed in South Africa. This war had been planned for the purpose of gaining control of the lucrative gold and diamond mines at the tip of the continent of Africa.

From 1888 on, Cecil Rhodes had been chairman of the Rothschild-backed DeBeers Consolidated Mines, the largest corporation in the world. Then, in 1899, the British government granted Rhodes a charter for the establishment of the British South Africa Company. Modeled on the British East India Company, it staked out a territory extending up the Zambesi River into what would later become Rhodesia and, later still, Zimbabwe. The incorporation of this charter conferred great power on Rhodes and his cohorts and succeeded in giving his company, along with the British East India Company, unlimited power over huge colonial territories in both Asia and Africa. With British backing, and using all that had been done in India as a model, the British South Africa Company then raised an army to guard their looting rights in these "fiefdoms." As a result, just a few imperialist families came to own entire countries.

By winning the Second Boer War in 1902, the British conquered South Africa, but they found themselves faced with a voting majority that was not British. So, they began to promote the emigration of Chinese indentured servants to South Africa in order to have both laborers for their mines and a British voting majority. After creating a monopoly on industry, they eventually converted the native black population, too, into a source of cheap slave-labor. A thriving lucrative raw materials looting operation ensued.

These British imperialists **have always desired to extend their looting operation worldwide.** The United States, however, has traditionally been a holdout. Historically, up until that time, even with covert infiltration of the American government, under ordinary circumstances, the British could never succeed in just turning Americans into slaves, so they had to plot to demoralize the American people and make them entirely unfit to rule themselves. Towards this end, they infiltrated the pubic schools and universities of the U.S., established false science and false facts, and then set the people on a path of sensual gratification. With the successful establishment of Conservation, the people became focused on preserving the environment, so the fantastic upward economic growth that the nationalists had envisioned was largely abandoned. In the next chapter, we shall explore the workings of the empire in Canada.

1897-1902

41

REBELLION IN MANITOBA

"The government of the world was (Cecil) Rhodes'
simple desire."

SARAH GERTRUDE MILLIN

Canada had been established as the seat of subversive British action against the North American colonies from before the American Revolution. From there, the British had encouraged the Indians to mount raids upon settlers in New England and New York. During the Revolution, Tory-loyalists to the British Crown had fled New England to go to the loyalist bastion of Nova Scotia. Then, after the U.S. established itself as a nation, the British Empire planned, organized, and funded the Confederacy from Canada. When the South seceded from the United States, many loyal southern imperialists transplanted themselves to Ontario where they received land grants from the British Crown. British agents in Canada were sure that the U.S. would degenerate and eventually be re-conquered. Canada would then become the organizing nexus of empire in the Western Hemisphere.

Later, at the turn of the twentieth century, after Cecil Rhodes established his empire in Africa and added it to the empire's Asian holdings, Canada became the British center for the subversion of nationalism. Canada had a history of colonial exploitation dating back to the year 1670 when Charles II had given a charter to the Hudson Bay Company that enabled it to go to the New World to trade in furs, minerals and other commodities. King Charles had also given a charter to both his brother, the Duke of York, and to Prince Rupert of Germany to establish the Royal African Company, the first full-scale British venture into the African slave trade.

Except for the lower southeast corner, the Hudson Bay Company owned all of Canada. More than half the size of Europe in its total extent, until 1869, this holding was know as Rupert's Land. When the Hudson Bay Company went into this area, it corrupted the native Indians by addicting them to alcohol in much the same way that the East India Company had addicted the Chinese to opium. They also engaged with the Indians in trading furs for guns. Then the armed Indians were used to terrorize and murder American settlers who were trying to move beyond the western frontier. **For two centuries, in Canada and in what became the United States Pacific Northwest, the Hudson Bay Company did everything it could to prevent western settlement and curtail progress in North America.**

Disgusted with all of this, many Canadians joined the ranks of the Union army during the U.S. Civil War to fight for freedom from this system. The success of that military fight, along with the beginnings of the huge technological advance initiated by President Abraham Lincoln during that war, then raised the possibility that Canada might emulate the U.S. example or that the U.S. might even annex Canada. So, to prevent such a happening, in 1867, the Hudson Bay Company got the British government to create a Confederation of her Canadian colonies north of the U.S. border and they were given quasi rights of self-government. In the process, the Crown bought land form the Hudson Bay Company and generously compensated them for it. Soon they had a country to rule.

Still all was not well, though, because a rebellion broke out in the province of Manitoba where unhappy settlers of the Red River country north of Minnesota took up arms, captured a fort, and spoke of either joining the U.S.A. or proclaiming their independence from Britain. The British government faced a real threat, but could do nothing to put down this insurrection because they had kept the land in such a state of underdevelopment that there were no traversable roads. So, they called upon the Hudson Bay Company to help them secure the area and, in the process, acknowledged their need for their help. Without it, they had no way of maintaining control over their loosely connected provinces. Just like the East India Company had done to the British Crown in 1763, the Hudson Bay Company then coerced Britain into allowing them to establish financial rule in Canada. Then they proceeded to loot the country.

The Hudson Bay Company's CEO was a man named Donald A. Smith. Later knighted, he became known as Lord Strathcona, the political boss of all of Canada. In 1864, during the American Civil War, Strathcona had invested some of the company's money into financing the blockade-runners who supplied arms and equipment to the Confederacy. With these ventures he earned huge profits for his company.

Then, on his 1870 trip to Manitoba to put down the rebellion on behalf of the British government, Donald Smith, aka Lord Strathcona, met James J. Hill, a thirty-one year-old Canadian merchant living in Minnesota. Engaged in intelligence work for the Canadian government, on its behalf, Hill had shipped arms from Minnesota to the area of the Manitoba rebellion. Lord Strathcona, the majority stock holder in the Hudson Bay Company, then engaged Hill as a partner and he worked as a shipping agent for the company. Together, in 1878, Lord Strathcona and James J. Hill bought a bankrupted

Minnesota railroad that had been heavily subsidized by the U.S. government, and, with funding from the Bank of Montreal, they expanded the railroad northward to Winnipeg, then southward down into the Dakotas, and west to the Pacific Coast at Seattle. This railroad eventually became the Great Northern Railroad and, under empire management, it strengthened ties between the Minnesota-centered grain trade and the empire's oligarchical corporate power in Canada.

The company then used its influence to cheaply buy up land adjoining the railroad for the purpose of setting up grain-holding silos all over the countryside and eventually they secured a monopoly in the trade of grain. This monopoly evolved into the Cargill grain cartel. In 1880, before the advent of the Great Northern Railway, the only rail outlet from Minnesota to the East Coast led through Chicago, but, the Hudson Bay Company changed all of that by establishing a new rail connection eastward from Minnesota to Saulte-St. Marie. From Saulte-St. Marie goods were then shipped by rail straight to Boston.

Eventually, Lord Strathcona also took control of another railroad, one heavily subsidized by the Canadian government—the Canadian Pacific Railway. He also became president of the Bank of Montreal. By 1896, the Hudson Bay Company interests had become the controlling "establishment" in Canada. When Cecil Rhodes went to war in South Africa in 1899, Lord Strathcona sponsored and paid for a company of Canada's own "Rough Riders," known as Strathcona's Horse, to sail all the way to South Africa to fight there on behalf of British world imperialism.

By the time Cecil Rhodes died in 1902, he had amassed a great fortune. One of the executors of his trust was Albert Earl Grey and he was appointed Governor General of Canada in 1904. From that post, he worked with political boss, Lord Strathcona and his Round Table to advance the British One World imperialist agenda and they succeeded in defeating the government of Canadian Prime Minister Wilford Laurier in 1911. Laurier had made an attempt to forge trade ties with the United States, but the Canadian establishment had quickly put this down. Meanwhile, J.P. Morgan, of the British House of Morgan, helped Hill obtain control of another railroad—the Northern Pacific. Hill also obtained 50 million acres of U.S. land through U.S. government land grants.

Lord Strathcona then helped the British-installed Teddy Roosevelt administration launch the covert British Conservation program and, as we have seen, it succeeded in withdrawing millions of acres of habitable U.S. land from settlement by placing them into "forest" reserves. Then, in 1908, in order to get around mounting western opposition to Conservation, Hill spoke at a U.S. governor's conference sponsored by Teddy Roosevelt and Chief Forester, Gifford Pinchot. As principle speaker at that conference, Hill then inaugurated the British popular campaign on wasted resources and managed to dupe American governors into accepting the Roosevelt administration's Conservation program. At the same time, James J. Hill's neighbor and fellow imperialist, F.E. Weyderhauser, was allowed to sign a lucrative deal with the U.S. government that gave him the right to harvest timber at low prices on government land. This eventually established him as a "timber baron" in the states of Oregon and Washington. By the end of Roosevelt's presidency, rules for cutting timber on government land became so strict that small timber companies regularly went out of business. The Weyderhauser Company, however, thrived. In 1909, there were three giant landowners in the American Northwest: James J. Hill, the Weyderhauser Family and the railroad tycoon, E.H. Harriman. We will speak of Harriman in a later chapter.

1869-1909

42

PLANS FOR A
TRANSOCEANIC CANAL

"A free man cannot be long an ignorant man."

WILLIAM McKINLEY

I n 1902, Congress authorized President Theodore Roosevelt to negotiate with Columbia for the construction of a canal through the Isthmus of Panama. Panama was then part of Columbia. Congress stipulated that if an agreement could not be forged with that nation, then the President was to construct a canal through Nicaragua. This was the canal route that President McKinley had favored.

With congressional approval for the Panama Canal in place, J.P. Morgan and E.H. Harriman then proceeded with plans to reap all the profits from the construction of the canal. Their trust lawyer, William Nelson Cromwell, had helped J.P. Morgan forge the mega-trust, U.S. Steel Corporation, and he had also helped Harriman forge a monopoly of rail interests in Panama—the Panama Railway Company. Cromwell had also represented the mysterious unidentified "French" interests who had already failed in an attempt to dig a canal through Panama. He then used his influence to insure that the canal would be located in Panama, so that these interests could salvage their investment in the canal project.

TR then proceeded to sponsor a canal treaty favorable to these interests, but unfair to the Colombians. Then, when the Columbians refused to ratify the proposed treaty, William Nelson Cromwell organized a local "revolt" using employees of Harriman's railroad to lead a secession of the province of Panama from Columbia. In the wake of this successful coup, TR sent American gunboats to the Canal Zone to intimidate Columbia and to make sure that the zone remained in the hands of the criminals. This "gunboat diplomacy" established the new nation of Panama. A canal treaty was then quickly established and ten days later it was signed in Washington.

The Wall Street lawyer, Cromwell, and the U.S. President, Teddy Roosevelt, then orchestrated and sanctioned the payment of $40 million to the private covert "French" interests who wanted to sell worthless rusting assets lying around in the Canal Zone to the U.S. government, yet Columbia was paid nothing for the land that had been stolen from her. William Cromwell's fee was $600. Teddy Roosevelt refused to disclose the identity of the French interests. During all of this, one U.S. Senator, John Mitchell of Oregon, bravely stood up and objected to this swindle. He not only claimed that it robbed taxpayers, but he also said that it had injured relations between the U.S., Columbia and all of Latin-America.

Mitchell was a patriot and popular Lincoln-style republican from Oregon. He had immigrated to Oregon in 1860. Along with Senator Edward Baker, he had also fought the Knights of the Golden Circle when they agitated for a separate pacific coast republic to be aligned with the southern Confederacy. His efforts had kept Oregon in the Union during the Civil War. After the Civil War, he stood with the Philadelphia Interests in their push for government-sponsored western development. He served his state as senator off-and-on from 1873 until 1905.

In 1902, during congressional debates over the transoceanic canal, Mitchell demanded that Congress determine the choice of the canal route. At that same time, he also exposed the 1879 Wall Street banking fraud that had given private banks financial control over the provisions in the Constitution that had established U.S. fiscal independence. This coup, he said, had succeeded in promoting the interests of big business in violation of the constitutional pledge to uphold the general welfare. Congress then gave timid canal guidelines to TR, but he ignored them, so Mitchell lost his congressional fight to establish control over the canal project.

Then, in 1903, to stir up trouble for Mitchell, Roosevelt ordered Secretary of the Interior Ethan Allen Hitchcock, to conduct a sham investigation into Oregon land fraud, and Hitchcock, in turn, sent detectives to Oregon to gather information for the purpose of indicting politicians. In the process, the government arrested a petty criminal named Stephen Puter. Puter had been engaged in a scheme that had seduced individuals into falsely claiming to be homesteaders, so that they could procure government land grants. Then, for a fee, they turned these grants over to railroad tycoons and lumber companies. After he was jailed for this crime, Puter was asked to cooperate in indicting Senator Mitchell. So Senator Mitchell was charged with accepting $1700 in fees for helping clients secure claims to public land even though he had not intended to promote any fraud. During all of this, no one in Washington ever stepped forward to help Senator Mitchell. In 1905, while awaiting the appeal of his conviction, he died of a "tooth extraction." Right up to his end, he ceaselessly spoke of the swindle that had occurred over the Panama Canal, but the only notoriety the press ever gave him was for his indictment as a criminal in TR's fraud extravaganza. While in prison, Stephen Puter wrote a book about the merits of the Roosevelt/Pinchot Conservation drive and then he received an early release from jail on a pardon by the President.

When the press used the Oregon land fraud indictments to gain more notoriety for the Conservation hoax, additional western lands were withdrawn from development. The state of Oregon never made any challenge to the withdrawal of large tracts of land in her state.

1902-1905

43

BRITISH GEOPOLITICS

"Power...which is secured by oppression or usurpation
or by any form of injustice is soon dethroned."

WILLIAM MCKINLEY

In the years following Lincoln's murder, we have documented the rise of the nationalists and we have spoken of their vision and their efforts to elevate the standard of living in the United States and in the rest of the world. We also chronicled the gradual re-emergence of the control of banking and finance by the London/Wall Street banking cartel. Then, after the murder of President McKinley, we witnessed the advent of American imperialism under Teddy Roosevelt. This U.S. involvement in British Empire imperialism eventually put an end to the pacifist dream of world cooperation envisioned by McKinley and earlier American patriot presidents.

Under the policy of protectionism initiated by McKinley, American productivity had skyrocketed. Then, as other nations, like Germany, Japan and Russia, began to emulate the U.S., they surged ahead of Britain in industrial development. American commerce also began to penetrate British colonial areas, further threatening the empire's world financial domination. Intimidated by all of this new United States-sponsored progress, British oligarchs then ushered in a new phase of evil planning in order to secure their planned domination of the world.

The British navy had long held dominion over the seas, but being a small island nation, Britain had never attempted to militarily conquer large land masses. Oh yes, she held colonial territories for exploitation, but she always operated from their major ports and left inland areas largely undeveloped. She had never attempted to militarily conquer

Europe's heartland, but she had maintained hegemony there through covert espionage and incessant warfare. This had established a balance of trade in her favor.

At the turn of the twentieth century, as United States industrial development began to influence Germany, German nationalists began planning for a Berlin to Baghdad Railway that they eventually hoped would extend down into Africa. Russia had also forged a Trans-Siberian Railway that "threatened" to link the whole world in commerce. The pacifist protectionist policies of President Lincoln had inspired all of this progress. Alarmed by it, the entrenched British oligarchy resorted to an old ploy—warfare—-in order to create the circumstances that would pit Germany against Russia and ruin both nations.

France, too, had embraced a progressive ideology. In 1894, her foreign affairs minister, Gabriel Hanotaux, had forged a platform of aid to France's colonies by publicly stating that France had an obligation to her colonies that involved helping them advance economically. By assuming this new character, France challenged Britain's old feudal practices, so Britain planned to unseat Gabriel Hanotaux by launching a series of initiatives that began in Egypt.

France had controlled Egypt ever since the days of Napoleon, but her dominance there was strengthened by Ferdinand de Lessep's construction of the Suez Canal. By 1875, however, she had become involved in the empire-orchestrated Franco-Prussian War and when that war ended, she was in debt. The Rothschild banking house, because they had financed her involvement in that war, then levied a huge indemnity on France, and this indebtedness created an opportunity for Britain to gain shares in the Suez Canal.

Then, in 1882, during an empire-orchestrated nationalist uprising in Egypt, that country decided that it wanted to sell its share of stock in the canal, so a French diplomat—really an enemy operative in the employ of the Rothschilds—by-passed his own government and alerted Rothschild intelligence circles to this potential sale. The Rothschild's then advanced money to prime Minister Disraeli, so that Britain could buy up these Egyptian shares and wedge France out of the canal area. These wars and uprisings had all been covertly incited by British secret intelligence. This is the way the empire works. In this book, we have documented similar subversive British undertakings.

In 1894, British intelligence operations also conspired to ruin the growing entente between France and Germany by creating a French scandal called the Dreyfuss Affair. Dreyfuss was a French military officer arrested for allegedly selling French military documents to the Germans. One of the letters used to frame him was later identified as having been written by an agent of a Hungarian aristocrat with long-time financial backing by the Rothschilds. This agent had worked as a spy for the Germans and he was the one who gained the French intelligence information, but, when the German government went public with the fact that it had procured this intelligence, they referred to someone identified as "D" as the agent who had fed them the secret French information. Soon a case was built against Dreyfuss. The scandal not only created anti-German sentiment in France, but succeeded in weakening Hanotaux, the target of the whole scandal.

Hanotaux's cooperative alliance with Germany was influencing developments in Africa where the two nations had ruined a British/Swiss treaty made in the Congo. Hanotaux had also been busy forming an alliance between Russia and Turkey that gave control over Abyssinia back to France. Then, in 1896, Hanotaux won special recognition from Austria for France's rights in Tunisia, an area the British had covertly usurped. Other nations then started to come to the aid of France. Things were not going well for the British Empire.

Despite the ill-will created by the Dreyfus affair, Germany kept trying to maintain her progressive alliance with France. Towards this end, the German foreign secretary visited the French ambassador to propose an agreement aimed at "limiting the insatiable appetite of England." He stressed that it was high time that England be told that she could no longer rely on the promotion of German-French antagonism in order to seize what she wanted. But British covert intelligence kept up its pressure in both governments and eventually France rejected Germany's cooperative efforts. Hanotaux was then forced out of office in 1898. He was succeeded by a pretend nationalist who used the friendship Hanataux had cultivated with Russia to encourage Russian antipathy toward Germany. Sides were being set for a local war aimed at destroying progress in Europe, but, as we shall see, plans eventually spiraled out of control and led to World War I.

1875-1898

44

COUNTE SERGEI WITTE

"The railroad is like a leven which creates a cultural fermentation among the population. Even if it passes along the way, through an absolutely wild people, it will raise them within a short time to a level required for its operation."

COUNTE SERGEI WITTE.

Britain was not content with just destroying the alliance between France and Germany. She wanted to also bring Asia under her control because both Japan and Russia were industrializing and threatening her empire-hold over India and China. Japan, as you will recall, had copied the American economic system in 1868 when the Philadelphia Interests, under the guidance of Henry C. Carey, succeeded in opening up that nation to the West. Her progressive emperor, Meiji, then looked toward an alliance with Russia for the purpose of industrializing Asia and this threatened to break up British control in that region. You may also recall that, from as far back as the days of Caleb Cushing, the British had fought opium wars with China in order to debilitate and then control the Chinese. Through this Chinese debilitation, they maintained hegemony in Asia.

By the late nineteenth century, Japan's industrial leader, Prime Minister Okuma, was beginning to plan for the liberation of India. Boldly, he had announced that there were three hundred million natives in India waiting to be rescued from the British Empire. Towards this end, nationalist Japanese shipping interests were seeking to forge an alliance with the Indian merchant fleet in order to break the British monopoly of commerce in Asia. But, unfortunately, there was also an old feudal landholding faction in Japan and, allied with their aristocratic British counterparts, they were organized around export. So they came to the aid of the empire and blocked the planned Japanese alliance with India. To selfishly advance their own power, they also blocked plans for a Japanese alliance with Russia.

Meanwhile, in Russia, the pro-American government of Counte Sergei Witte had gained power and it was seeking to break up China's backward feudal dynasty in order to industrialize the mineral-rich region of Manchuria and connect it to Europe via the Trans- Siberian Railroad. So it, too, sought to forge an accord with the nationalist faction in Japan.

Hanotaux and Count Sergei Witte had together established the Russian-Chinese Bank in 1896 and with the collaboration of Okuma in Japan, this bank was going to independently accomplish the desired industrialization of Manchuria. But quickly the British organized for the defeat of this independent financing by placing the Dowager Empress back on the thrown in China. And, in Japan, they replaced Okuma with the pro-British Mitsui faction.

By 1902, Prince Edward Albert had become King Edward VII of England. He had a particular disdain for the "yellow races," but, in the interests of British geopolitics, he put his prejudices aside and made visits to Japan in order to forge an Anglo-Japanese accord. Japan had, by that time, already launched a war with China over the control of Manchuria and the Korean Peninsula. Recognizing her ambition, the King made an appeal to the emperor's vanity by comparing Japan to England saying that like England, Japan was an island nation destined for greatness. Then, in further attempts at brain-washing, he lied and said: "Where we rule over Europe, you shall rule over Asia." Subtly, he was aiming to pit Japan against Russia in order to set the stage for a war between these two nations. The accord he signed with Japan stipulated that, should either nation become embroiled in a fight with Russia, they would come to the aid of one another. Empowered by this pact, Japan then launched a sneak attack on the Russian city of Port Arthur in 1904. By war's end in 1905, the Russian navy was entirely crippled and Russia's economy was greatly weakened. Teddy Roosevelt presided over the peace treaty signed after the war. It gave Japan command of the eastern seas, and so she emerged in control of northern Asia. Later, in 1907, Britain forged an entente with a weakened Russia in order to add strength to the 1904 entente she had signed with France. Sides were quickly being formed for the upcoming European battle being planned by the British.

The British-orchestrated Russo-Japanese War entirely defeated the progress Russia had made, beginning in 1891, when Counte Sergei Witte rose to the position of Russian finance minister. Inspired by U.S. technological progress, he had inaugurated an impressive Russian development program. Russia had a legacy of admiration for the U.S. republic that dated back to Catherine the Great. To oppose Britain during the American Revolution, she had helped forge the European League of Armed Neutrality. Then, thirty years before the advent of Sergei Witte in Russia, Tsar Alexander II had shocked the British by allying his country with the U.S. wartime administration of Abraham Lincoln. The Tsar had announced that if Britain entered the U.S. Civil War on the side of the

Confederacy, he would intervene on behalf of the Union. Then he backed up his intentions by sending warships to both the eastern and western U.S. seacoasts.

Sergei Witte was an admirer of the American System of Political Economy. In emulation of Lincoln, during his sixteen years of power in Russia, he directed the construction of the Trans-Siberian Railroad. He also introduced monetary reform in Russia and created a climate for foreign capital investment. Many criticized this policy by saying that it would bring foreign domination to Russia, but Counte Witte said: "Only a disintegrating nation must fear foreign capital." At that time, Russia's Baku oil fields were as advanced as any in the world. Russia had also developed mining and steel industries. A program was also instituted to train peasants to engage in industrial work.

Years later, Lenin would continue Counte Sergei Witte's reform when, in 1922, he launched a Russian electrification and industrial development program. The British tried to discourage Lenin from pursuing his program by instead pushing a British-model program on his government, but Lenin rejected their model because it involved keeping the Russian peasants backward, ignorant and poor. When, in 1924, Lenin died under suspicious circumstances, his program fell apart and then the British-sponsored program was implemented. Many years later, under British direction, this same model would also be implemented in Mao's Red China.

The British Empire knew that Eurasia was a pivotal center rich in mineral wealth and they had always coveted it. But they were a maritime empire and it was inaccessible by ship, so they covertly conspired to prevent Eurasian inland development. Only the horse-riding hordes of Ghenghis Khan had ever historically accessed this area by land, but the proliferation of the U.S-inspired Trans-Siberian Railroad System was once more set to open it up to development. So, fearing the challenge that this rail system posed to her trade empire, Britain planned to curtail Russia's far-reaching technological promise. Without intervention, she feared that Russian influence might spread to Finland, Scandanavia, Poland, Turkey, Iran, India, and China. And if Japan again allied herself with Russia, Manchuria would be developed.

The Tsar backed Witte's policies right up until 1903. Then, when Witte's influence in Russia was compromised by the British-manipulated fall of both Hanotaux and Okuma, Tsarina Alexandra, great granddaughter of Queen Victoria, created an opening in Russia for British influence. Witte was then dismissed as finance minister. The London-bankrolled Russo-Japanese War then followed in 1904. After that war, a financially devastated Russia was then poised for British-planned revolution.

The 1905 revolution was bankrolled by the London banking cartel. It began when the British-controlled Jesuit priest, Father Gapon, incited Russian steel workers to strike. Then the Russian trade movement, the Bund, also provoked strikes, and after they were violently subdued, police repression followed. Most of the Bund leaders then fled to the U.S. Funded by the Rothschild/Warburg banking circle, the Bund later organized the Russian Socialist Democratic Party to promote more subversive activities.

After the Tsar was overthrown in the British-sponsored Russian Revolution of 1917, the Soviet emerged as the ruling body in Russia. Initially, it spear-headed reform, but it was soon internally weakened by the enemy. Once in control of the Soviet, the British then further weakened the country by promoting a finance plan designed to bankrupt the country by destroying Witte's old policy of welcoming foreign capital. Then the enemy-dominated Soviet withdrew gold from the treasury in order to pay the wages of government workers. From his minor position in government, Witte wondered how, under these policies, anyone was going to ever have confidence in the Soviet government.

After the Soviet government was financially paralyzed, the British deployed Muslim fundamentalist terrorists to Russia from their British strategic base in Iran to help further destroy the remaining productive base of the Russian economy. The British had strategically penetrated Iran from as far back as the 1880s in order to promote local unrest. Then they cultivated Iranian terrorist forces for deployment elsewhere.

From as far back as 1901, under Witte's policies, Russia had been producing one-half of the world's oil. By 1905, however, as a result of British-sponsored war and terrorism, three-fifths of Russia's sophisticated oil-producing region was in ruins because the over two thousand Armenian entrepreneurs, who were providing the skilled labor for the Baku oil fields, were eliminated. By 1906, Russia was bankrupt. The Russian government was then forced to accept British as well as French credits in order to function, so Russia became indebted to the empire for the first time since before the American Civil War. From his minor position in government, Witte spoke out and proclaimed that this "meant for the whole world a rapprochement of Russia with a political grouping which does not correspond to the interest of Russia or Germany."

The British then convened an Anglo-Russian Convention in 1907 to set the stage for World War I. Thoroughly confused, Germany then refused any loans to Russia and then compounded this mistake by erecting tariff barriers to Russian trade. Witte then left the Russian government entirely and never returned.

1891-1907

45

THE EMPIRE CRUSHES
PERSIAN NATIONALISM

"We shall be as a City on a hill. The eyes of the People are upon us........."

JOHN WINTHROP

When Edward VII acceded to the British throne in 1901, he actively began to implement a secret British plan aimed at destroying the influence of the quickly-spreading American-style nation state system. Toward that end, he forged alliances throughout Europe in order to subdue the growing spirit of cooperation between Germany and Russia. Industrialization in both of these countries had made the prospects of an alliance for U.S. world cooperation imminent.

To eradicate progress, the empire orchestrated the 1890 ouster of Otto von Bismark as chancellor of Germany. Under Bismark's counsel, the inept German kaiser had sanctioned a progressive relationship between Germany and Russia. But, rather than continue to listen to Bismark, Kaiser Wilhelm II, instead heeded the advice coming from his uncle, King Edward VII, and dismissed Bismark from his post. Bismark's departure then deprived Germany, and indeed, all of Europe of the only statesmanship capable of outsmarting the British. The Kaiser later regretted his actions.

By 1907, as we have seen, the British had orchestrated the bankruptcy of Russia in order to defeat the policies of Count Sergei Witte, an eminent supporter of the American system. Helpless, Tsar Nicholas II was then enticed, at the Anglo-Russian Conference, to sign a treaty that ended up strengthening the old spheres of influence that both the British and Russian empires had long sustained in Persia (modern day Iran.)

For a long time, Persia had been watching all the American-inspired cooperative progress that was being forged in Europe. For what seemed like eons, she had suffered the ravages of centuries of exploitation by both the British and Russian empires. But, during the heyday of United States-inspired progressive technology advance, she became hopeful that she, too, might forge an industrial economy. Towards this end, nationalist forces within Persia began to seek a way to establish a constitutional government. From as far back as 1856, the most able statesman in all of Persia's long history, Amir Kabir, had made an attempt to establish diplomatic relations with the United States, but not until 1883, did the first American minister, Samuel Benjamin, arrive in Persia. While in Persia, Benjamin wrote extensively about the forces deterring Persia's progress toward freedom. Not until 1902, however, did the Shah acquiesce to the creation of a constitution, a national legislature and an elective assembly.

Against the backdrop of world intrigue that had been forged by King Edward VII of Britain, emerged the American patriot, William Morgan Shuster. Trained first in Cuba, where he helped forge Cuban independence through the promotion of progressive American policies, Schuster was later dispatched to the Philippines where he worked, in a similar capacity, under its governor, William Howard Taft. Then, in 1911, a constitutional government was successfully launched in Persia. That country then made an appeal to the U.S. for a trained expert in finance, so Morgan Schuster was sent there to help forge a financially-independent Persian nation-state.

Upon his arrival in Persia, Shuster found that the chief Anglo-Russian enemy agent-in-place had conspired for the contraction of a loan from the London-controlled Bank of Persia. This had created an immediate Persian fiscal emergency. But, worse still, this agent had proposed a new law that would give him responsibility for managing and disbursing future Persian loans. Quickly, Schuster blocked this action. Then he drafted legislation that gave the deputies of the Persian constitutional legislature the authority to reorganize the country's finances. After this law was passed, they then officially appointed Shuster treasurer general. From this position, he drafted a national budget and placed government accounts under his authority. Tax collection was then taken out of the hands of corrupt tax farmers and put under the control of treasury officials. Shuster also created government treasury notes, so that the Persians no longer had to acquiesce to the Imperial Bank of Persia for currency.

Shuster also inaugurated the construction of a N/S national rail grid that ran from the Russian border to the Persian Gulf. It crossed the richest regions of Persia and was scheduled to eventually expand to a total of eight lines crossing the countryside. Designed to hasten the country's development, he hoped that it would eventually hookup with the Russian Trans-Siberian Railway. Eventually, this whole huge system might be extended to India. It would also be natural for it to eventually connect with the old German-built Berlin to Baghdad Railway. A vast regional elevation in the standard of living was contemplated.

In his relentless support of Persian nationalism, Shuster continued to implement projects that increasingly earned for him the hatred of the British imperialists and their new Russian allies. As he began to expose all the irregularities he found in the Persian government's financial records, Schuster drove enemy agents out of the government. Soon the problematic Russian-backed minister of war left the country and headed back to Russia. From there, he worked to help the British bring Shuster down.

British intrigue continued. See if you can follow it: Thousands of miles west of Persia, in the French-controlled Moroccan port of Agadir, a small German gunboat, *The Panther*, set anchor. The British then quickly claimed that Germany had violated the Triple Entente treaty that Britain had forged with France and Russia, so they threatened to make war on Germany. Then British Prime Minister, David Lloyd George, the man who would lead Britain into World War I, made a speech and, following that speech, Britain sent a naval deployment to that region.

In his speech, Lloyd George never even mentioned Germany, but constantly referenced the United States, complaining that Morgan Shuster, in the course of just two months in Persia, had disrupted the interests of Britain by ignoring the political realities of the conditions that both the British and Russian empires had imposed on Persia. Then he claimed that the Anglo-Russian Convention, which had divided Persia up into British/Russian spheres of influence, had been violated when Shuster's Persian military advisor had crossed Russian territory on a routine trip into Persia.

Lloyd George then got the Russians to declare formal charges against Persia and they released the imprisoned former Shah of Persia, Mohammed Ali, so that he could lead Russian armed forces into Persia. The Persians had no army, so they had to raise and pay for a mercenary army in order to defend their country. Then an assassination plot against the life of Shuster was discovered that was traced to the Russian legation. Shuster then dispatched a letter to President Taft alerting him of the return of the Shah and the near approach of Persian civil war. In his letter to President Taft, Shuster claimed that British foreign intrigue had caused these developments.

At a British diplomatic dinner, Shuster received a stern warning and was even offered a bribe if he pledged to stay passive while the Shah took over the Persian government. He was told that he could even remain in the Shah's government afterward, but Shuster said that he would never serve under the Shah. While dinner was proceeding, the Shah's forces moved into Tehran and, even though they were out-numbered, the Persian forces contained them. The empire then moved to crush the Persians completely by deploying more Russian troops to Persia. They also sent in troops from India, once again using foreign armies to fight their imperialist battles! Surrounded by Russian troops in the North and Indian troops in the South, Shuster then realized that the Persians would be slaughtered if they tried to resist, so he resigned.

Shuster's resignation generated an international outcry. Muslims throughout the world sent messages of support to Persia. For months, these Persian developments were front page headlines in the United States. The Taft administration then tried to get Senate approval for an arbitration treaty with Britain. Throughout the U.S., widespread support arose for the abrogation of a commercial treaty between Russia and the United States. Congress was deluged with letters of support for Shuster and the Persian government.

With British backing, the Russians then launched a reign of terror in northern Persia and a coup followed, so Schuster left Persia. In the United States, Shuster engaged in a speaking tour of major U.S. cities. **Before cheering audiences, he exposed the role of Britain's Triple Entente in crushing the Persian Constitutional Revolution.** The British-orchestrated defeat of Persian nationalism was a prelude to the war that was being planned in Europe. Although Persia took no official part in that war, its country was a battleground for three armies. In 1914, a Turkish-German army poured in from the East, the Russians entered from the North and Britain invaded that country from the South. Under these conditions, Persia lost one third of its population to famine and disease. Constitutional government would not be re-established there until 1951. Then, in 1953, the democratically elected prime minister of Iran, Mohammed Mossadegh, was assassinated because he nationalized Iranian petroleum assets. The United States CIA was involved in that assassination because, by then, the U.S. had become aligned with the forces of empire. In succeeding chapters, we will speak more about how this happened.

1911-1914

46

BALKANIZATION AND THE COMING WAR

"The more of the world we inhabit the better it is for the human race."

CECIL RHODES

Britain's long-range strategic plan for dominating Europe called for subverting industrial development through warfare. Germany and Russia were her particular targets because industrial development had already begun to transform these nations. The planned war was initially designed to be a local one, then, after those two nations had totally destroyed one another, Britain was going to step in, clean up the mess and rule Europe. But first balkanization had to occur.

A modern term for a very old British ploy, balkanization divides large territories in order to weaken them. This renders them subservient to the forces of empire. British intelligence had been at work trying to balkanize the United States from the time of the Essex Junto and the failed Hartford Convention. And then, later, British intelligence manipulated the two sections of the U.S. into fighting a devastating civil war for the purpose of dividing and weakening it. As a result, a separate plantation empire was supposed to emerge in the Western Hemisphere. Both these attempts at balkanization failed.

The twentieth century British balkanization plan involved Eastern Europe. Turkey had once ruled a vast empire in that region. Its territory had reached southward into North Africa, as far as Egypt and Iraq. It also reached northward up into Greece, Yugoslavia and Bulgaria. But, from 1830, it had been chopped up into French, German, British and

Italian protectorates. Then, in 1898, during the heyday of German industrial development, Germany reached an agreement with the Turkish Sultan that allowed her to construct a Berlin to Baghdad Railway right through the Turkish Empire. Completed in 1911, it was a boon to the economies of both Germany and Turkey. Not only did this railway open up prospects for a direct route to Middle Eastern oil, but it gave access to the metal resources in Anatolia and the supplies of wool, cotton and hemp from the Balkans and Mesopotamia. These raw materials fed European textile manufacturing. Because railroad supply lines were more direct and faster than British shipping lines, these rail lines also challenged British commerce.

The Germans were very progressive. They intended to fairly administer their railroad in order to promote international cooperation. Other nations were offered financial shares in the construction of the railroad and the Germans did not discriminate in carrier rates. From the start, Britain opposed the construction of this railroad and prevented Turkey from participating in it. Then they pressured Germany into signing an agreement that effectively curtailed its plans for progress and international cooperation. To protect the British monopoly over oil resources, the agreement stipulated that the Berlin to Baghdad Railroad had to terminate before it reached the Persian Gulf. With this agreement set, British intelligence then proceeded to prepare for war by arming anti-nationalist forces in Germany.

Despite British covert pressure to destroy Germany's planned international commerce, German nationalism was strong. It took the U.S. entry into World War I, in 1917, to entirely defeat it. As we have seen, with the successful assassination of President McKinley, the British Empire had succeeded in changing U.S. foreign policy, so that the U.S. could become a military arm of Britain. President Taft had remained somewhat independent, but Woodrow Wilson's presidential agenda was coordinated from London. Wilson then led the U.S. into World War I despite objections by the American people. Had Germany joined Britain's Triple Entente and focused on war with Russia as the empire originally intended, World War I would have been a local war for the defeat of Russia. Without German participation in the Triple Entente, however, Britain had to seduce anti-nationalist elements in the German government into waging a larger war in Europe.

When the U.S. entered the war, it did so in order to defend the agenda of the British Empire. **Had the U.S remained neutral during that war, the British Empire would have been defeated!** The U.S. did not even begin to prepare for war until Germany, under the direction of British secret intelligence, broke through the front established by French armed resistance and then violated Norwegian, Belgium, Dutch, Swiss and Italian neutrality. Then when the Germans sunk the Lusitania, American travelers on that ship were killed. Through published warnings in the U.S. press, Germany had cautioned Americans about traveling on that ship because it was carrying British munitions, but the warnings went unheeded. Wilson then had the excuse he needed to enter the war, so he stopped issuing written warnings to Germany and American isolationists began to accept the inevitability of war.

The change in the scope of the war meant that Britain had to quickly build up its military. Ironically, to do so, she abandoned her philosophy of free trade and adopted a Hamiltonian-style policy of protectionism. Her reversion to this policy proves that the empire knows that Hamiltonian principles strengthen and build up a nation and do so very quickly!

1911-1917

47

SECRET ALLIANCES PROMOTE IMPERIALISM

"The very word 'secrecy' is repugnant in a free and open society; and we are as a people inherently and historically opposed to secret societies, to secret oaths and to secret proceedings. We decided long ago that the dangers of excessive and unwarranted concealment of pertinent facts far outweighed the dangers which are cited to justify it."

JOHN F. KENNEDY, APRIL, 27, 1961

World War I did not end British plans to conquer Europe, nor did it prevent the empire from forging secret imperialist alliances. For nearly a whole century now, this Sykes-Picot system of British secret imperialist agreements has kept the Middle East in a continuous state of British-directed warfare for the purpose of controlling the natural resources of the entirety of Southwest Asia. Political control of that area, not only affects regional peace and development, but the extensive development of Europe and Africa, too.

Since the end of World War II, not a single decade has passed without a war in the Middle East between Arabs and Jews. Contrary to all that we have been led to believe, Arab-Israeli disagreement alone does not fuel the fighting. The fighting has been purposefully manipulated by secret agreements that promote the interests of empire.

Only the sovereign power of the United States government is great enough to prevail against this covert imperialist system. Once, this fact was widely recognized among many of the world's eminent statesmen. Now, however, because the United States government has bought into the empire's financial usury scheme to become an arm of that empire, constitutionally-sanctioned U.S. independence has been compromised.

At the end of World War I, there were forces in the United States that well understood the danger that the British Empire posed for the world. These forces, largely military, knew that the injustices spawned by the imperialist system would cause future wars unless its imposed system of financial usury was replaced by a return of the U.S. to the principles outlined in her Constitution.

After World War I, two American commissions were established to investigate the geopolitical reality that the secret Sykes-Picot imperialist system had imposed upon the Middle East. These reports and their findings have largely been forgotten, but, had their recommendations been acted upon, the world might be in much better shape today.

World War I was a war of empire consolidation orchestrated by the British, French and Russian empires, so that the British Empire could place the empires of Germany and Austro-Hungary under her rule. It also intended to carve up the vast Ottoman Empire—an empire that had once reached down into the Middle East all the way to Syria and Iraq—into small warring principalities. The Sykes-Picot agreement basically gave Constantinople to the Russians, Syria and Lebanon to the French, and Palestine and Iraq to the British. When Italy was later drawn into the war, she, too, was included in the Sykes-Picot system. And, in return for rebelling against his Ottoman overlords, King Emir Faisal Hussein of Saudi Arabia (and later King of Iraq) was also promised an Arabian mandate in the area.

When the United States entered World War I on the side of the Triple Entente, it declared war only against the German and Austro-Hungarian empires. It did not go to war against the Ottoman Empire. And, the United States never recognized any secret treaties, nor did it sign any of the post-war treaties between the British, the French, the Italians or the Ottomans.

World War I ended in 1918, but it never brought about its stated goal of ending war all together. That goal was a British hoax for, upon the war's conclusion, the British proceeded to covertly sponsor more wars and revolutions throughout Eurasia and Southwest Asia. Almost one hundred years have passed since the inauguration of the secret Sykes-Picot agreements and today the world is still engaged in British-style imperialist wars.

In 1919, Navy Lieutenant Commander Halloway H. Frost, from the staff of Planning Development in the office of the chief of Naval Operations, delivered a series of lectures on U.S. strategy in the Atlantic. In them, he referred to the desperate state of Britain's finances as a result of her engagement in World War I. He also mentioned the state of unrest that existed in many of her dominions. Her financial desperation, he said, might drive her into another war because her condition showed no prospects of improving without one. No nation that subsisted exclusively on trade like Great Britain, he said, could continue to exist with a growing annual trade imbalance of four billion dollars. The growing United States commerce, he said, was the direct cause of Britain's demise. It had turned the U.S. into Britain's major competitor and this had doomed her to commercial defeat. Before accepting defeat, he said, Britain would probably reach for another military solution to her problem.

In his lecture, Frost also documented repeated international requests to the U.S. government for action against Britain. In a 1919 criminal violation, a British military officer in Palestine had forced Standard Oil of New York's Arab partners to allow his group to enter the offices of Standard Oil in Jerusalem. There they went through company files and took maps and other data related to oil concessions that the company had purchased from the Ottoman Empire in 1914. This caused widespread concern that the British might prevent American petroleum companies from operating in any territory claimed by Britain after the war.

Despite a testy diplomatic exchange between the U.S. and British state departments after this incident, American companies were unable to obtain oil in any British territories until after World War II. In the interim, U.S. military planning was shaped by this development. At that time, the U.S. rightly considered Britain to be the greatest threat to her security. As we shall later see, FDR, too, understood this reality and, for as long as he lived, he was committed to liberating the world from the scourge of the British Empire. This book will later document the fact that after his death, the U.S. embarked upon a path of departure from the nationalist policies he had forged and, under Truman, engaged in a covert association with the empire. This has brought the world to its current existential crisis.

1917-1945

48

REPORTS OF THE TWO COMMISSIONS

"The real truth of the matter is, as you and I know, that a financial element in the larger centers has owned the Government since the days of Andrew Jackson."

FDR TO COL. EDWARD HOUSE, 1933

In examining the files of the Tsar's Foreign Ministry after the Bolshevik's took power in Russia in 1917, Leon Trotsky uncovered copies of secret empire-orchestrated treaties that Russia had signed and he released them to the world press. The Soviets then repudiated the treaties and declared their new government's anti-imperialist policy.

Colonel Edward House, adviser to President Woodrow Wilson, knew of the secret treaties. In 1917, after the United States had entered World War I, House held a meeting in Washington with British Foreign Secretary, Lord Balfour, and engaged with him in a conversation about these treaties and their acknowledged intent to allow English-speaking people to restructure the world after the war. Even House, avowed Anglophile that he was, spoke up and opposed them saying that they would lead to wide-scale destabilization and future wars.

World War I ended in November, 1918. By the beginning of 1919, the Paris Peace Conference had convened and the plan for restructuring the world got under way. At that time, there were Americans who were aware of the British Empire's plans for covert world conquest and they wanted to oppose it through the establishment of a cooperative worldwide sovereign nation-state system. But Britain prevailed over the peace conference and succeeded in laying the groundwork for her future imperialist plans.

At the peace conference, Wilson either willfully endorsed or was manipulated into endorsing a powerless League of Nations. The organization of that league had been a British scheme to place all of Europe under her control. Its harsh sanctions against Germany established the conditions that would lead to the next British-designed war between Germany and Russia. The United States Senate rejected the League's treaty because neither Britain nor France would allow for free commercial access to world markets. Secret agreements had assured that there would be no healthy world trade. When the U.S later objected to this secret system, the British Foreign Office said that, because she was not a member of the League of Nations, the U.S. had no right to complain.

The existence of secret treaties and their unofficial sanction by the League of Nations made a complete mockery of U.S. involvement in the British geopolitical war that had just been fought. **Had President Woodrow Wilson been a patriot, he would have kept the United States out of that imperialist war and the British Empire would have gone down to defeat.**

The U.S. was the only non-empire at the peace conference. At one of the many meetings, British Prime Minister Lloyd George tried to seduce the United States into accepting an offer of a slice of the Ottoman Empire, but she refused it. Then, when large oil deposits were discovered in the Middle East in the region of Iraq, the British restructured the Sykes-Picot map in order to gain control over the entirety of the extent of the oil. The French objected, but Lloyd George proclaimed that Britain had sacrificed the most in that region during the war and, so, she had the greatest claim to control of the oil fields. Britain then took the rights to the oil.

Wilson refused to recognize any of the provisions of the empire's secret agreements and proclaimed that they would lead to future wars. Then, he further upset the meeting by insisting that the Turkish people be allowed a say in what happened to the Ottoman Empire. France and Britain both outwardly agreed to this provision, but then met again in secret to reaffirm their refusal to go along with such an idea.

Then, in 1919, President Wilson commissioned two studies in the region. In the first of the two studies, Henry Churchill King and Charles Crane were appointed to compile information for the King-Crane Commission. They arrived in the Near East in 1919 and proceeded to tour the region of Syria which was, back then, a very large area composed of Syria, Lebanon, Palestine, Israel, Jordan and the Gaza Strip. The King-Crane Commission held meetings with local leaders and representatives to ascertain the local will of the people and discovered that they overwhelmingly desired independence. They also wanted the U.S. to oversee the process by which they would secure their independence. The people further expressed an honest fear of placing their welfare in the hands of the British because of their long-standing reputation for sanctioning colonial exploitation. The Americans, on the other hand, they said, had no territorial ambitions and, therefore, they could be relied upon to justly oversee the process. The example that the U.S had set in both Cuba and the Philippines had inspired Middle Eastern leaders to have confidence in her. They knew that the U.S. would remove herself from Syria, too, at the appropriate time just as she had done in these other areas she had protected.

Meanwhile, even though the Arabs overwhelmingly opposed it, the British-designed Balfour Declaration of 1917 had planned for a Zionist homeland in Palestine. It was part of an empire plan to chop up the whole region in order to promote regional strife. Unfortunately, or perhaps intentionally, the King-Crane report was not made available to the public until 1922. So, without the benefit of its findings, the U.S. Congress passed a joint resolution sanctioning the Balfour Declaration's proposal for the establishment of this Jewish homeland in Palestine.

By contrast, the King-Crane report had recommended a different approach. It wanted the U.S. to move in to occupy the entire region of Syria. It also recommended that European Jews go to Syria and simply live there as Syrian citizens. The establishment of a Jewish State, it insisted, could not be accomplished without gravely trespassing upon the civil and religious rights of existing non-Jewish communities in Palestine.

The King-Crane report also cited complaints that British forces occupying the region were restricting both speech and movement and it warned that British expansion in the area would open the region up to exploitation in both oil and agricultural commodities. A confidential footnote to the report disclosed that King Faisal Hussein was being bribed by the British to oppose a U.S. presence in the area. The British also refused to allow the U.S. commission to visit Mesopotamia (present-day Palestine and Iraq.) The Mesopotamians were then left powerless in the face of British regional aggression.

1917-1919

49

THE U.S. MILITARY BACKS TURKEY IN DEFIANCE OF SYKES-PICOT

"Without visiting the Near East, it is not possible
for an American to realize even faintly, the respect
and affection with which our country is regarded
throughout the region."

GENERAL JAMES G.HARBORD

After the King-Crane mission was complete, President Wilson dispatched a second U.S. commission to the Near East—The American Military Mission to Armenia. It was instructed to tour the non-Arab region of the Ottoman Empire—-today's modern Turkey—-to investigate and report on geographical, administrative, economic and other considerations of interest to American foreign policy. The commission was led by General James G. Harbord, Chief of Staff to General John Pershing. During World War I, Pershing and his staff had fought against empire schemes to deploy U.S. forces to theaters where they could be used to fight for imperialist interests, so Harbord well understood the problems the British had created for Americans.

When this U.S. commission arrived in Constantinople, it found that the new nationalist leader of Turkish resistance, Mustafa Kemal (Ataturk,) a former general officer in the Turkish army during World War I, had repudiated the British-backed puppet government of the Sultan, and had formed a nationalist government in Ankara. In his report, Harford quickly recognized the nationalist government of Mustafa Kemal and identified Turkey as an ally of the United States. Both the British and the French hated Mustafa Kemal.

Harbord had seen into the trap that the British had tried to set for Americans when, at the Paris Peace Conference, Lloyd George had suggested that the U.S. assume a mandate over Armenia. Britain wanted to take over the best lands in the region and leave the U.S. to oversee the problem areas they left behind. But, as a result of Harbord's foresight, the U.S. refused a mandate over Armenia and suggested instead that it be given either a mandate over the whole Ottoman Empire or a mandate over its non-Arab parts (modern-day Turkey.).

Kemal expressed full support for a U.S. mandate over Turkey. The Turkish Nationalist Party, he said, needed the aid of an impartial foreign country with no expansionist plans. Kemal was schooled in the concept of the sovereign nation-state and its commitment to advance the general welfare, so he knew that Turkey would prosper with the impartial help of the United States. His country had been weakened by foreign interference and intrigue, but he insisted that all that would change under U.S. supervision. The British considered Mustafa Kemal to be a rebel because he opposed their interests.

As part of a general attempt to balkanize the Ottoman Empire, the British wanted to create an independent Armenian state, but Harbord reasoned that Russia was about to emerge from revolution. When she stabilized her government, Armenians in Turkey, he said, might then be reunited with Russian Armenia. He knew that uniting Armenia as a whole ethnic people was in her best interests. The British had planned to keep the Armenian people separated and mixed with other ethnicities, so that they might effectively "manage" them. This has always been their policy. In a separated condition, it is difficult for ethnic peoples to rule themselves.

The British responded to the reports of the two American commissions with a renewed determination to crush all opposition to their plans for carving up the Ottoman Empire according to the Sykes-Picot Accord. After Harbord's report appeared in the Congressional Record in 1920 and exposed the empire's subversive plans, Britain, France and Japan immediately convened another secret conference, the Conference of San Remo, and proceeded to divide up the Ottoman Empire. The U.S. was not invited to participate in that conference.

Within two months, the French had erected a mandate in Syria and within five months the British established a mandate over Mesopotamia. All of this had been accomplished in contradiction to the expressed local wishes of the inhabitants of the region and the findings of the still suppressed King-Crane Commission. Public opinion in the U.S. was divided over this matter because an Arab majority in Syria had expressed a desire for an American mandate in the region.

Then, by secret agreement, the remainder of the extensive Ottoman Empire was divided into six different regions. Neither the League of Nations nor the United States endorsed these secret agreements. Then the scoundrels who forged these agreements unleashed war upon Mustafa Kemal and abolished the Ottoman Parliament. They also established the Ottoman Bank in order to control Turkey's debt and burden her with usurious rates of interest. Unable to repay this debt, Turkey would then effectively be under empire control.

Kemal, however, organized an army of Turkish liberation and successfully maintained Turkish resistance, so the empire was temporarily curtailed. Then he signed the Treaty of Moscow with the Soviets, in 1921, and this not only secured Turkey's northern border, but gave her access to arms and munitions. Soon, he also defeated the Greeks and the French and succeeded in driving a wedge between France and Britain. In 1923 a treaty was signed with Greece that secured Turkey's border with that country.

Harding was president during these years of friendship with Turkey. Then, in 1922, after Coolidge became president, former President Wilson authorized the public release of the King-Crane report and, by this time, its warnings had materialized. Shocked by the fulfilled predictions of the report, the *Editor & Publisher* trade journal printed the report in its entirety and its editor harshly criticized the U.S. for its failure to implement the report's recommendations. His editorial also stated that secret treaties had both caused and prolonged World War I and had destroyed the peace that was supposed to have followed that war. Out of secret treaties international distrust had grown. Under U.S. oversight of the Middle East, he said, secret treaties might have been reproved and a different reality might have emerged after the war.

In the wake of the published findings of the King-Crane report, the Turkish government approved an American concession for the construction of a railroad net in Turkey. Led by retired U.S. Admiral Colby M. Chester, this concession was designed to build an interlocking rail network from Ankara to Mosul, (now in Iraq, but then claimed by Turkey.) From this main east-west line, the railroad was to branch out north and south at various locations across the countryside in order to explore for oil and other resources. In doing so, it was to traverse and explore undeveloped land claimed by both Britain and France.

Like nationalists from the past, Admiral Chester knew that his railroad concession, the Ottoman Development Company, helped serve Turkish independence by promoting the development of Turkey's economy. Through the Ottoman Development Company, thousands of U.S.-made tractors were imported into Turkey in order to expand agriculture. At that time, the U.S. State Department was committed to protecting the interests of American companies engaged in promoting commercial freedom and this support gave the Turkish government badly needed leverage in fighting the unreasonable demands of the empire. This project eventually collapsed, however, because the empire got involved in its funding. Turkey then gave up the oil-rich region of Mosul to the British in 1926.

1919-1926

50

TOWARDS THE VERGE OF ANARCHY AND BACK

"We must reassert the doctrine that in this Republic the first obligation and first allegiance of every citizen, high or low, is to his government, and to hold that government to be the just and unchallenged sponsor for public welfare and the liberty, security, and rights of all its citizens. No matter what clouds may gather, no matter what storms may ensue, no matter what hardships may attend, or what sacrifices may be necessary, government by law must and will be sustained."

WARREN G. HARDING,
FROM A MESSAGE TO CONGRESS DELIVERED ON AUGUST 8, 1922

In 1920, Warren G. Harding became the seventh Ohio-born man to become United States President. From the day he determined to run for president, powerful forces tried to prevent the success of his election. But, like McKinley before him, his congenial kind personality had won him many friends and they had all determined that he was destined to be president. Chief among the men who promoted his election to office was Harry M. Daugherty, his shrewd campaign manager. Harding served only two years, but during those years, he discharged the obligations of the office of president patriotically and unselfishly and left a record of great accomplishment.

The nation had just emerged from World War I, and burdened by a huge war debt, the U.S. domestic economy was in chaos. All kinds of businesses were in distress and unemployment was extensive. Agriculture, too, was floundering. To deal with these problems, President Harding summoned Congress to an emergency session and kept it in session for nearly two years. Congress immediately enacted a new tariff law in order to spur both domestic production and the international sale of American-made goods. To protect labor, immigration was also restricted. Then a new internal revenue law was enacted and wartime taxes were reduced.

Foreign relations were unsettled because the U.S. had rejected the World War I Versailles Peace Treaty. And, in the Western Hemisphere, a long-standing dispute with Columbia over the Roosevelt-orchestrated theft of the Panama Canal Zone had made relations with that nation precarious. Under Harding, the U.S. paid Columbia for Canal Zone land and settled that dispute. Diplomatic relations with Mexico were also resumed. Ever the peacemaker, Harding also began to stabilize the post-war world by negotiating peace treaties with all the nations that the U.S. had just fought.

In spite of a universal desire for peace, the world was engaged in a competitive and expensive arms race, so, Harding convened an historic conference for armaments limitations in Washington, D.C. This historic conference drafted a treaty designed to settle future differences among the nations of the Pacific Ocean and canceled a war alliance between Britain and Japan. Then the world's five great maritime powers entered into a solemn covenant limiting warship tonnage and the armaments their ships could carry. When this treaty was signed, it promised to usher in the start of a new epoch of peace. Under this treaty, international trade revived and a better international understanding prevailed. The ancient nation state enemy was worried.

World War I had ended in 1918, but, in the last year and one-half of his presidency, Woodrow Wilson had been an invalid. So, at home, not a single legal action had been taken on war fraud profiteering despite a very loud clamoring for it. Under the cover of war, there had also been gross violations of the Sherman Anti-Trust Laws and these violations had largely gone unchallenged. To change this, President Harding re-organized the Department of Justice and created a separate branch just to prosecute these violations. Under the able leadership of Attorney General Harry M. Daugherty, law suits were filed that recovered $300 million from war contract profiteering. Up until Harding's presidency, no "American" had ever gone to jail for violating the Sherman Anti-Trust Laws. Harding's attorney general prosecuted these criminals. High-powered enemy-aligned organizations then began to spend large sums of money in an effort to try to discredit everyone in the Justice Department who had been connected with the prosecutions. But Harding continued to enforce these laws.

Harding also reorganized the prison system. When he took office, the prisons were crowded and inmates had nothing to do. So, to improve the lot of young first-time offenders, they were separated from hardened criminals and the government established work programs for them. There was a duck mill in Atlanta that made postal carrier bags, and, with that factory, the government organized a program for shipping piece work to prisons. At Leavenworth, a shoe factory was also established and a dairy and a slaughterhouse, too. As an incentive to industry, inmates were paid a small wage to work in these prison programs, and, upon discharge the government helped secure jobs for many model inmates. As a result, many inmates were effectively rehabilitated while incarcerated. At this same time, women prisoners scattered in state penitentiaries all over the country, were also rescued and placed in a West Virginia federal prison exclusively for women. There they were also given employment, good food, recreation and schooling.

When Harding became president, Eugene V. Debs, was in the Atlanta prison serving a ten year sentence for "obstructing the conduct of the war" because he had refused to register for Wilson's draft. While in prison, his record had been impeccable. An extremely peaceful person, he had had a good effect on prisoners. Imprisonment had not made him bitter, nor did he ever criticize the government. Daugherty interviewed him at the request of the President and reported that he had found Debs to be one of the most remarkable men he had ever met. A sincere believer in socialism, in the presence of the Attorney General, he had apparently defended the doctrine with eloquence. Harding released him from jail.

The great strikes of 1922 have faded into history with little notoriety, but they brought the country right to the verge of anarchy and put the Harding administration to a great test. This is the background to what happened: To foment the Bolshevik Revolution, enemy agents of empire had placed radical "Red" agents into Russian labor organizations for the purpose of creating anarchy. Many of those agents later came to the United States to infiltrate U.S. labor organizations. There they engaged in radical revolutionary speeches and circulated pamphlets. In April of 1922, they finally incited a strike of six hundred thousand mine workers who then proceeded to explode and flood mine shafts and take up arms. Behind this strike of coal miners, there also loomed the threat of a strike of four hundred thousand railroads workers. These strikes threatened the U.S. with a complete shutdown in commerce.

The coal miners' strike raged for five months and caused the loss of at least a hundred million dollars in revenue. As thousands of coal-laden cars were side-tracked, they piled up at switching points where they were vandalized. They then became immovable and this caused a stall in the distribution of the little bit of coal that was being mined. Suffering prevailed among the people. Every effort to reach a compromise between miners and management failed. The secretary of commerce tried to mediate and then the secretary of labor tried, too. Even President Harding tried, but all negotiations failed. To prevent the outbreak of total anarchy, the railroads needed to move again.

When Attorney General Daugherty suggested to Harding that they ask the governor of Kentucky to call out the Kentucky State Guard, so that the seventeen thousand cars that were blocking coal transportation in that state could be moved, the strike appeared to have been broken. But, the relentless enemy did not stop when the coal strike ended. They moved to start a railroad strike. The situation was grave.

Labor unions soon began demanding that the railroads be surrendered to them. Amidst union pressure to create a government partnership with the railroads, Secretary of Commerce Herbert Hoover brought a settlement proposal to the railroads, but they rejected it. Trains were being derailed all the time as bridges were blown up, tunnels were destroyed and rail switches were wrecked. The damage incurred from the railroad strikes reached one-half a billion dollars.

The enemy used its agents of lawlessness very well. Crime prevailed. Women were often attacked and dragged into the woods. There they were tarred and feathered. Many murders occurred. Finally, striking picketers surrounded both the White House and the office of the Attorney General in an effort to intimidate the Harding administration. Then, at a meeting with the President, the Attorney General presented the facts of the situation. Anarchy, he said, had not been the work of the average union man, but was rather the work of outside enemy forces that had covertly infiltrated the workplace with a new plan to destroy the United States. The Red army, organized by the British, was trying to convert labor unions into a fighting army for the purposes of taking over the country. Top-level directors of the conspiracy had infiltrated both liberal and radical labor groups and both groups had consolidated themselves into a news agency known as the Federated Press. With access to a total of two hundred newspaper publications in America and one hundred twenty in Europe, the Federated Press was writing articles designed to organize American labor unions into an insurrectionary fighting force aimed at promoting civil war.

Instinctively, Harding understood that there was no time to waste, so he charged Daugherty with filing an injunction in the court. Inspired to save the republic, they then stepped forward to see if the court system would come to the rescue of the country. Harding went before Congress to make an address. With his usual eloquence, he spoke of the need for the government to forcibly intervene in the strike in order to put men back to work. He said that radicals had temporarily gained the upper hand and were planning more strikes, but he was now taking forcible action to stop them. With every turn of his eloquent phrasing, Harding was cheered and applauded by both the representatives on the floor and the people who had packed the galleries. With a great fervor of patriotism, he asserted that he was determined to use all the power of the government to restore transportation, put men back to work, and reinstate the order of law. Without the order of law, he said, there could be no freedom in America. The situation had become so precarious that the legislative process would not suffice to solve it quickly enough. The courts had to intervene, use existing statutes forbidding conspiracy to hinder interstate commerce, and restore a free America. With his bold action, Harding made his enemies furious, but patriotic Americans lauded him for championing their well-being.

In response to Harding's address before Congress, the enemy stepped up its violence and lawlessness became so rampant that thoughtful Americans began to question if they still had a government. The Attorney General worked unceasingly to compile his case for the court. Harding was optimistic, but also anxious for action. Together, he and the Attorney General maintained the strictest secrecy about the government's actions. They did not want enemy agents to find out what the government was planning. The injunction was the government's last peaceful resort. Harding did not want to have to resort to calling out the army. That would surely have meant bloodshed. To avert needless delay, Daugherty was planning to argue the case himself. Harding was concerned about Daugherty's safety. He even feared that he might not make it alive to Chicago to begin his arguments. But, even though Daugherty was in great danger, he did not back down. With a commendation for the great service he was rendering his country, Harding sent him off on his mission.

After hearing the case, without a minute's delay, presiding Judge Wilkerson granted a temporary injunction to stop the strike. After the Attorney General returned to Washington, Harding convened a meeting of his cabinet and a lively "discussion" ensued. Daugherty was criticized by some, but Harding defended him by saying that he had acted with his full endorsement. Within forty-eight hours after the court ruling, the strike was broken and the railways began to function again without obstruction.

The enemy-controlled labor organizations then began to call for the immediate government takeover of the railroads. Wilson had done this during the World War, but that takeover had resulted in an appalling loss of money as a result of government mismanagement and corruption. Under the loss of one-half a billion dollars, the railroads had been brought to the brink of ruin. Upon taking office, President Harding had secured the return of the railroads to their owners, reasoning that since the owners had invested in constructing and equipping the railroads, they should manage them. Harding's attitude had not changed.

Sensing that Daugherty was advising the President, in desperation, labor leaders then began to call for Daugherty's resignation. Harding, however, defended him, saying that rats had gnawed their way into labor unions and had temporarily deceived Americans, but the deception had been exposed and the rule of law re-established by a court injunction. When the common laborer learned of Daugherty's bravery, they respected him, but the enemy persistently continued to call for his removal. When their efforts failed, they orchestrated the Teapot Dome scandal to try to completely discredit the Harding administration. Some years after the scandal, in order to vindicate both the deceased President and himself, Daugherty penned a book entitled, The Inside Story of the Harding Tragedy. In this chapter, I have summarized the details of what Daugherty had to say about the 1922 crisis and what the maligned and forgotten President, Warren G. Harding, did for the country. President Harding died in office without having the chance to vindicate his administration. Sadly, today he is remembered only for the Teapot Dome scandal. The circumstances surrounding his death are eerily similar to those surrounding the death of Zachary Taylor. In fact, the similarity is so striking that it causes enlightened people today to suspect that Harding, too, may have been poisoned. Like Harrison and Taylor, Harding was a nationalist. Could that have been the underlying reason for the suspected poisoning?

1920-1922

51

BETWEEN THE TWO WARS

"I know my limitations. I know how far removed I
am from greatness. Be that as it may, I intend to
approach every problem with goodwill in my heart
instead of hatred. Most questions which are settled
by armed force are never permanently settled...Peo-
ple may think of me as they please, but I shall continue to be just what I am, Warren G. Harding as he is
and as God fashioned him, a man who is trying the
best he knows how to throw into the discard age-old
discordant ways of doing things, ways which never
have succeeded in bringing happiness
into the world."

WARREN G. HARDING, JULY 2, 1920, MARION, OHIO

The Versailles Treaty was never meant to work. British agents from the secret Round
Table had infiltrated the conference for the purpose of orchestrating harsh German
reparation payments. At that peace conference, Wilson's secretary of state, Robert
Lansing, also lied by declaring that Germany had planned World War I when, all along,
the British monarchy, with the compliance of France and the complicity of Nicholas II
of Russia, had actually orchestrated that war. Under the pretense of false guilt, German
reparation payments were then sanctioned in order to recreate the conditions for another
war been Germany and Russia because the British Empire still wanted to destroy Russia.

After World War I, nationalism was re-emerging everywhere. In Russia, Lenin had taken over and he was reviving Witte's reform program, France was contesting Britain's influence in the Middle East, and free of the Kaiser's rule, Germany was once more contemplating industrialization. The U.S. had emerged from the war stronger than she was before it and the American industrialist, Henry Ford, was building cars and tractors that had the potential to change the world culture of British economic domination. The British Round Table was particularly worried about a resurgence of the U.S.-Russia-Germany alliance.

By 1922, Germany and Russia had signed the Rapallo Treaty and, through this treaty, Russia abrogated German war debt. With this treaty, the two countries also hoped to cooperate in a joint venture for the industrialization of Africa. Two years earlier, Lenin had announced plans to electrify Russia and, like Ford, Krupp had established a plant in Russia. Russian prosperity was looming on the horizon. Obviously the British-orchestrated Bolshevik Revolution hadn't worked. Without British covert opposition, nationalism might again emerge in Russia. The elite were worried.

On the western coast of the U.S., an industrialist named Washington Baker Vanderlip had organized a group of American nationalists and they were going to do business in Russia. In return for equipment like grain storage elevators, boxcars, typesetting machines, cars, trucks and motors, the Russians had offered these U.S. industrialists both coal and oil concessions in northeast Siberia. Vanderlip was very pleased with his negotiations. With his concession secure, he then began to bravely speak out against the British, accusing them of spreading unfair propaganda about Lenin. He said that British propagandizing was aimed at preventing the spread of American business interests to Russia. He also characterized former President Wilson as an autocrat in the British tradition. Then, he cited the long history of friendship between the U.S. and Russia. At this same time, the *New York Times* also printed an article that accused President Wilson of having opposed trade with Russia.

With Vanderlip's successful penetration of Russia, in an attempt to garner a share of it, both Britain and France then lifted their trade restrictions with that country. Then the British tried to intrude upon Vanderlip's negotiated coal and oil concessions. While Vanderlip was in Russia, H.G. Wells, organizing member of the British Round Table, went to that country to spy on him. While in Russia, Wells also met with Lenin and warned him not to industrialize Russia without British approval. To this, Lenin replied that the Bolsheviks were in charge of Russian development.

To make matters worse for the British, in 1923, Harry Sinclair, another American industrialist, secured a concession to develop the oil in the Baku oil fields. With the help of the Rothschild's, the British had attempted to secure the same rights, but they had been unsuccessful.

Meanwhile, President Harding became determined to recognize the new government of the Soviet Union. Then, while on a speaking tour of Alaska, he suddenly collapsed and became very ill. He displayed all the symptoms of strychnine poisoning, but officials blamed his severe "indigestion" on eating too many crabs, even though he never ate any crabs. Gravely ill, he revived once only to decline again just as Zachary Taylor had done years earlier. No autopsy was ever performed.

President Harding had changed the political climate in the United States. Wilson had been unpopular. Having encountered much resistance to the U.S. entry into Word War I, in order to get soldiers to fight in that war, he had instituted the draft. Many, though, had refused to comply with it, so they were imprisoned. The socialist, Eugene Debs, was one of these men. He was first locked up in the West Virginia State Penitentiary. Then later he was transferred to the Atlanta Federal Penitentiary where he was incarcerated for thirty-two months. Then, upon taking office in 1921, President Harding released him.

President Harding had also worked on civil rights issues and he had personally organized world peace conferences. He did not support the League of Nations, but did organize a World Court. With his death, the climate in the U.S. declined. The Coolidge administration which followed then withdrew the support Harding had given to American nationalist businessmen and, for ten years, a speculative climate favorable to British interests ensued. Then, in 1932, in the midst of a U.S crisis caused by the collapse of the Wall Street stock market, FDR was elected president and he began a renewed fight to reinstate the American System of Political Economy.

Concurrent with the death of President Harding, a scandal was about to erupt in the U.S. involving Harry Sinclair. Sinclair was accused of bribing Interior Secretary Fall for a concession to pump oil from reserves stored for the U.S. Navy on land in the Teapot Dome area of Wyoming, but it now appears that Fall was the true criminal. Sinclair was innocent, but the scandal, of course, proved timely for the British because when Sinclair was jailed, the deal he had secured for a Russian oil concession fell apart. Then the vulnerable Soviets, who were just emerging from the devastation war had created, were left on their own without any help. Their oil fields then remained undeveloped and their technological recovery was thwarted. The British were very pleased.

Then the situation in Russia was further aggravated by the suspicious death of Lenin in 1924. His death, too, was accompanied by symptoms of poisoning. In 1918, he had been the subject of an attempted assassination by the anarchist Dora Kaplan, but he survived it. The British were certainly behind that attempt on his life.

Finally, when the German industrialist and foreign minister, Walter Rathenau, was gunned down in 1922, the Rapallo Accord between Germany and Russia unraveled. This destroyed any potential for a cooperative alliance of technological advance between Germany, Russia and the U.S. By 1923, the conditions for another devastating world war were in place.

Then to rearm Germany, the British began to make secret agreements designed to get around the restrictions imposed on Germany by the Treaty of Versailles. And in Germany, fascists proceeded to ignore the Versailles provisions that called for dismantling German industry. Instead, with the help of the British, they recapitalized German industry and then seduced the government into inflating the German currency to reduce the value of the German war debt. As a result, the German peasants and lower class workers suffered horribly.

The only European country to emerge in tact from World War I was Britain. France had been ravaged by continental warfare and after the war she had limited options for recovery. Without getting her war debt payments reduced, obtaining credits for rebuilding, or collecting her reparations payments from Germany, she was destined to flounder. She made an appeal to the League of Nations for help, but British Lord Balfour intervened and prevented it, so France then insisted that Germany make good on her reparations payments. Then the British applied high tariffs to both German and French exports to their country. Desperate, the French then invaded the German Ruhr Valley and occupied it. France's year-long occupation of the Ruhr then collapsed the German economy while it did little to help the French, but the British Empire thrived.

Then, under the Dawes Plan, the Morgan banking interests went to work to further destroy Germany by mortgaging German railroads to raise revenue for the payment of German debt. Then they placed the management of the efficient German state railroad into the inefficient hands of private companies that pocketed most of the profits. Meanwhile the Reichbank received only meager war debt payments. Then railroad carrier rates were raised ostensibly to procure more money for debt payments and this further destroyed the German economy.

All this destruction had been orchestrated under the watchful eye of Hjalmar Schacht, student of British economy. Once German unemployment became very high, Schacht eliminated civil service jobs, slashed state budgets, and drastically increased taxes—devastating the German workforce. With these measures in place, Schacht then called for a Hitler coalition government and went to the U.S. to seek backing for Hitler from pro-fascist American banking and business interests. With funding from the Wall Street bank, Brown Bothers Harriman, Prescott Bush, father of former President George H. W. Bush and an officer of that bank, then helped fund the bankrupted Hitler coalition.

Then, in 1933, with the help of London financing, Schacht orchestrated a sham recovery based on the issue of MEFO bills and they were used to rearm Germany. Because they left no paper trail, these bills allowed Germany to run a greater deficit than it could have done under more normal circumstances. Savings and commercial banks had to convert thirty percent of their deposits into these bills. Other rates were set for municipalities and insurance companies who also had to comply. Then, when German rearmament was complete, Schacht further inflated the currency and this lowered German buying power even more. Once he was in power, Hitler then enforced the negative growth economy Schacht had created and this further increased the suffering of the German people. Schacht had been placed in power by the British Empire and he remained in power behind the scenes in Germany until 1939 when the British broke faith with both Hitler and Schacht. By building a German war machine, the empire intended to wage another war in order to further their long-range plan for One World government.

1922-1939

52

THE SECOND WAR

"The moneychangers have fled the temple. We may
now restore the temple to the eternal truth."

FDR, FROM HIS FIRST INAUGURAL ADDRESS

After World War I, the elite secret British intelligence planning organization, the
British Round Table, sent emissaries to the Versailles peace conference. There,
they made key contributions that helped insure that the shape of the post World
War I world would coincide with their long-term geopolitical goals. They insisted on
incorporating German reparations payments into Wilson's Fourteen Points. Without
them, they said, the peace treaty would not be "adequate." Designed to purposely keep
Germany de-industrialized, those reparations payments set the conditions that led to a
second devastating British-sponsored war.

In anticipation of that coming war, the British Empire brought Hitler to power and
secretly planned to use him to prosecute their planned war against Russia. They promoted
him from three levels of British society. From the first level, they openly endorsed him.
Then, through a second group of appeasers led by Neville Chamberlain, they appeared to
negotiate with him even though they were really secretly aligned with him from the top
levels of government. Then, there was a third group composed of the supposed "foes" of
Hitler—men like Churchill, Lord Robert Cecil, and Lord Mountbatten, but they, too,
were all covertly aligned with him. In the empire's initial war plan, Britain was to remain
on the sidelines and use Hitler to crush the growing might of Russia, but when empire
forces lost control of Hitler, Britain entered the war to defeat him and later appealed to
the U.S. for help. They had to then put the conquest of Russia on hold. Later, they would
regroup and plan again. The empire has always advanced its plan for world domination

through long-range planning that takes into consideration the need for a two steps ahead, one step back approach.

As factions in Britain were sanctioning Hitler's aggression and others were negotiating with him, the German people were largely opposing him. Five days before a scheduled Chamberlain press conference, General Beck, the German army's chief of staff, made an appeal to German military leaders opposed to Hitler. In that appeal, he urged all sincere and responsible Germans to prevent Hitler's 1939 invasion of Czechoslovakia. He maintained that it would lead to a world war of awful proportions and end the existence of Germany as a nation. Acting together, he insisted that the German army could avert war, and so he urged the generals to take action!

Chamberlain then held a well-timed press conference that undermined Beck's initiative by sanctioning the invasion of Czechoslovakia. Beck was then forced to resign, but his successor, General Franz Halder, prepared to work with him to continue to take action against Hitler. Their plan called for seizing the Reich Chancellery by a surprise assault on its SS guards. In possession of the Chancellery, Halder's forces were then going to occupy radio communications centers and other strategic points in Berlin. Then they were going to arrest Hitler, Goering, Goebbels, and Himmler, and remove them from that city. The generals had the support of the Berlin chief of police, but instead of immediately moving to carry out their coup, they made a critical mistake. They sent Ewald von Kleist-Schmenzin to London to inform the British government of their plans. There, he saw Churchill and others and, arguing against the coup, they instead urged a compromise with Hitler. Britain fully knew that Hitler would probably be removed from power if they lent support to the German generals, but they refused this support because they were secretly aligned with him.

Even after the war was well under way, in 1942, the Germans tried again to overthrow Hitler and once more appealed to the British for help, but they were again turned down. Then, in July of 1944, high-ranking German military leaders tried to kill Hitler by placing a bomb in his headquarters, but he unexpectedly left his seat, so this initiative also failed. Hitler then initiated a roundup of suspected conspirators and had 20,000 men killed. When Churchill was asked why the British did not help rout Hitler, he said that his government had a policy of not cooperating with German nationalist leaders. He said that he considered them a greater evil than Hitler.

Throughout the war, Churchill maintained communication with Himmler, Hitler's liaison. From Geneva, U.S. envoy, Allen Dulles also negotiated with him and kept covert allied intelligence lines of communication with Germany open. Intent upon using Hitler to defeat the Soviets, the British had always been open to the possibility of joining the German army in its drive to the East.

Throughout the war, the secret British Round Table held regular meetings at which they documented their plans to use Hitler to defeat Russian nationalism. The aristocratic members of the Round Table considered Britain to be the world's policy maker and the U.S. its subservient enforcer. During times of peace, in conjunction with their agents in the U.S., the British liked to inaugurate pacifist-appearing agencies and pseudo-religious organizations to help further their plans for world domination. In conjunction with British secret intelligence, these established agencies had successfully coordinated the entry of both Britain and the U.S. into World War I.

Before the Second World War, the openly pro-Nazi King of England, Edward VIII, opposed Britain's entry into that war and told British Prime Minister Baldwin that he would abdicate if Baldwin embarked on that path. Baldwin then began to push for the King's abdication. Churchill took a position of publicly defending the King, but secretly urged his removal by stirring up opposition to his intended marriage and used it as a superficial cover for the real reason he wanted him out.

As we have seen, in his role as British agent, Hitler had to contend with long-standing progressive nationalist German factions dedicated to the U.S. industrial model that had been spreading throughout the world as a result of the legacy Lincoln left behind. Nationalism had long been quelled in Britain, but it was strong in Germany. To advance the plan for a world federation opposed to the U.S. industrial model, from 1923 on, Britain began pushing for the organization of a fascist Pan European Union—the precursor of today's EU. Both the Rothschild and the Warburg family banks initially financed the beginnings of the Pan European Union and a German branch was established with Hjalmar Schacht as its leading member. The League of Nations had also been created for this same purpose.

The Pan European Union was behind the resignation of Chamberlain as Prime Minister and the installation of Churchill as his replacement. Then, after the planned second European war took on a broader scope, the PEU sent emissaries to the United States to address the American branch of the Round Table as well as the New York Council on Foreign Relations. Publicly, they urged the entry of the U.S. into the European war, ostensibly to defeat Hitler, but their secret goals were more pernicious. They wanted to enlist the aid of the U.S. in their plans for a fascist world. The American patriot, FDR, however, made it clear that he stood in opposition to their plans.

Even after waging two world wars, the enemy failed in its plan to use Germany for the defeat of Russia. Then, after World War II, in the absence of FDR, they regrouped to form a third plan for world conquest. It would involve the re-implementation of their earlier plan for a post-war European Union, so that they could raise an army larger in size than any army the Russians could organize. The actual implementation of their long-range goal of one world rule, though, would require the covert conquest of the United States because, in no other way, could Americans be enticed into giving up their historical heritage of opposition to empire. To see to it that the proposed Pan European Union was not conquered by the American System of Political Economy, Americans would need to be demoralized and then, forgetful of their heritage, they could be expected to go along with the relentless enemy plan.

Churchill was not a war leader dedicated to saving the world from Hitler. The true facts no longer sustain that false version of history. During World War II, British secret intelligence was always focused upon its covert geopolitical goal of One World government. The covert plan subtly surfaced on several occasions. In one particular instance, in 1942, General Marshall suggested opening up a "second front" in Europe to relieve pressure on the Soviets, but really to lengthen the war. Slyly, the British initially opposed this plan saying that it was not feasible, but that was a just a manipulative ploy to deflect attention from their war-extending goal.

Then, again in support of lengthening the war, in this same year, in Dieppe, France, under the guidance of Mountbatten, the British deliberately sacrificed three elite Canadian units when they were fired upon by Nazi troops who had been forewarned of the planned assault. This planned defeat then further worked upon the psyche of the American military, so the American General Staff backed down from its plans for a concerted unified push from the West and instead accepted plans for a diversionary African offensive. As a result, German pressure on the Russians again failed to be relieved and the war was protracted.

In 1941, the British had also actually turned German planes on their own city of London by placing these planes in direct radio communication with British-recruited Germans who worked in Britain and they instructed the Germans to bomb London. The London bombings were orchestrated so that Britain would then have a reason to bomb and devastate the civilian population of Germany. The whole scheme was also used to gain the sympathy of Americans. Privately Churchill justified the London bombings by claiming that the raids were a morale-builder for the British population. At the same time, he justified the British bombings of Germany by saying that they would break German civilian morale and force an early surrender. But, as we have mentioned, the British actually never wanted an early conclusion to the war. For geopolitical reasons, they wanted a long war. Long wars break civilian morale, make British prey controllable and advance the covert geopolitical agenda of the empire.

In 1940, on the beaches of Dunkirk, when Hitler was still covertly allied with the British, under protest by his generals, he purposely stopped the German advance at the Battle of Dunkirk just at the point when he might have wiped out the British army. The British army then escaped by sea. Then, when it appeared that Hitler might overwhelm England, Roosevelt intervened in the internal affairs of that country to prevent the British from surrendering. This saved the world from eventual domination by the Nazis. The original British plan had called for Hitler to move east to attack the Soviets. Then, after Hitler had made deep inroads against the Soviets, the British and the French were secretly going to attack him from the rear and defeat both Germany and the Soviet Union. Hitler's generals, however, intervened and instead insisted that Germany first mount a western attack. This modified plan then changed the scope of the war.

You will remember that Japan had enjoyed a long-standing alliance with Britain that dated back to the days when Prince Edward Albert had become King of England. This alliance was secretly maintained well into the 1920s and included a planned Japanese attack the U.S. Naval base at Pearl Harbor. It was not, however, until 1941 that the Japanese, then aligned with Hitler, launched this planned surprise Pearl Harbor attack and effectively brought the U.S. into the war.

Strategically, World War II was a military failure in terms of British geopolitical goals as long as FDR remained alive. During that war, FDR held a series of meetings among the Allies where he guaranteed post-war help to the Soviet Union, so that they might rebuild their war-torn economy. He also publicly stated many times that, after the victory, he was going to defeat the British Empire for good by economically subduing it. But, with his untimely death in 1945, the British unfortunately had the opportunity to regroup and revive their plan for One World government. For the success of their long-range plan, the enemy would rely on covert agents within the United States—agents who had been silenced while the British needed the help of the United States during the war. Harry S. Truman then became the U.S. puppet-president after the death of FDR and he complied with British plans to inaugurate the Cold War. Had FDR, in his bid for re-election to a fourth term, not been pressured into accepting Truman as his running mate, his popular vice president, Henry A. Wallace, would have succeeded him as president and, he would surely have continued FDR's post war peace plans. Single covert enemy decisions have too often sadly derailed American plans for economic progress. Yet the actions of FDR demonstrate, too, that the decisions made by a right-minded patriotic American president have also temporarily defeated the British Empire.

1940-1945

53

HITLER AND
THE NAZI CULT

"Three hundred men, all of whom know one another, direct the economic destiny of Europe and choose their successors from among themselves."

WALTER RATHENAU, GERMAN NATIONALIST ASSASSINATED IN 1922 AFTER HELPING TO ESTABLISH THE RAPALLO TREATY

Hitler was a twentieth century product of nineteenth century Bavarian-centered British paganism. Although he was born in Austria, Hitler served in the Bavarian army during World War I. Later, he was recruited as a low-level Bavarian intelligence agent. Other Nazi officers like Goering, Himmler and Hess came from the same background. Rudolf Hess was, in fact, actually ushered into German politics while he was a student of Karl Haushofer, Munich University professor of British geopolitics. Haushofer had introduced the British policies of Sir Alfred Mackinder to Germany after World War I. Under the guise of making Germany a world political power, the British intended to use Germany to defeat the industrialization of Russia. Hess later helped mold Hitler's thinking and his speeches.

The British-organized Nazi cult that originated in Bavaria was directed by the Jesuit black oligarchy, a feudal remnant of Catholicism that had long served the forces of empire. The Bavarian House of Wittelsbach had ruled in Bavaria for over seven hundred years and, for generations, they had been inter-marrying with the Habsburgs, the Hohenzolleans and the British House of Hanover. All of this interbreeding created severe mental incapacitation among the Wittelsbachs, so they became easy prey for the Jesuit black oligarchy. The Nazi SS was later modeled upon the black oligarchy.

In the seventeenth century, the black Jesuit oligarchy intelligence network had provoked the Thirty Years War in Europe. As a result of this religious warfare the German Empire was broken up into a squabbling group of duchies. The empire has always engaged in the promotion of religious warfare for the purpose of breaking up large kingdoms. It is a traditional empire scheme that destabilizes societies and makes the people easy prey to manipulation.

In the eighteenth century, to further the spread of empire counterinsurgency, the black oligarchy had created a university in Munich as a locale for the promotion of British ideology. Under the guidance of the black oligarchy, when the British brought Napoleon to power, the Wittelsbachs quickly became allied with him. Then, after Napoleon's defeat, the British Empire maintained Bavaria as a backward area, so that they would have a breeding ground for paganism. By the nineteenth century, the Jesuit black oligarchy, commanded a huge intelligence network in Bavaria. When Bavaria joined the German Empire in 1870, it did so under the condition that it would be allowed to maintain its own army. Then, during the advent of American-inspired industrialization in Europe, the backward area of Bavaria became a seat for British intelligence operations. There, the British promoted the rise of anti-Semitism and the cult of the supremacy of the Aryan race. These evil ideologies did not arise with Nazism. They were British ideologies that pre-dated Nazism.

After Hitler was imprisoned for inciting the Beer Hall Putsch in Munich, he wrote Mein Kampf, as an expose on British ideology. He did not write it alone. He had the help of both Karl Haushofer, his constant visitor, and Rudolf Hess who was imprisoned beside him. Mein Kampf began as a tirade against the Rapallo Accord, a German/Russian agreement for renewed industrial cooperation between these two countries. Mein Kampf's propaganda was a British tool for the defeat of European nationalism.

Mein Kampf was an expose aimed at brainwashing the Germans into believing that they were superior to the Russians. It declared that Germany needed to conquer the Russian heartland, displace the inferior Slavic peasant workforce, and replace them with Germany's "superior" Aryan peasants. It also falsely declared that Bolshevism was a Jewish movement designed for the defeat of Germany when actually it had been a British plan to defeat Russia. Mein Kampf's racist philosophy was just a disguised version of the old British aristocratic slave ideology.

Mein Kampf extolled the virtues of England and her colonial empire in India. It also depicted the Teutonic German "type" as superior to other races and claimed that, with the help of the noble Englishman, the Germans would rule the world. Then it compared the old British system of imperial conquest to modern-day industrial buildup, claiming that modern methods were unreliable. By contrast, it nonsensically asserted that the old regressive British aristocratic system was reliable because it "brought the soil in harmony with the population."

Through the evil brilliance of this <u>Mein Kampf</u> "bible," many demoralized Germans were brain-washed by British rhetoric. Then, with the backing of police enforcement, when the Nazis seized power, many secretly fascist-oriented Germans outwardly began to cooperate with Nazi evil while other Germans tried to defeat it. In 1932, just before Hitler seized power, General Schleicher, one of the architects of the Rapallo Accord, assumed the office of German chancellor and tried to keep Hitler at bay. Hitler's margins in the polls, never really huge, were slipping. Hoping that Hitler might lose his window of opportunity in the approaching election, Schleicher then appealed to both the British and the French and asked that restrictions on the size of the German army be lifted, so that he might quickly recruit a citizen's militia to wipe out Hitler's band of street terrorist thugs. The French agreed, but the British objected. Then, British banks covertly increased Hitler's funding and this gave his street thugs command over the population. In the face of this power, Schleicher could barely hold on until the 1933 elections. In that election, Hitler became chancellor of Germany even though he garnered less than forty percent of the vote. After the election, Schleicher tried to take away some of Hitler's support by pushing the Strasser faction into bringing the national industrial Rapallo Accord back, but he was unsuccessful. During the "Night of the Long Knives," Schleicher was murdered.

Then, in 1940, after Hitler had invaded the Low Countries and they lost control of him, the British deserted the Nazi leadership. The Nazis, however, tried to covertly maintain this alliance because Hitler believed that the earlier Second Reich had failed because it had opposed British Empire trade. Therefore, to plead for Britain's support, Deputy Fueher, Rudolf Hess, flew, under tracking by the British Royal Air Force, to Scotland to see a former Nazi collaborator. Hess had been authorized to present a whole list of concessions. Among them was an agreement for the evacuation of German-occupied territories in both northern and western Europe. The Nazis were also prepared to allow Norway, Denmark, Belguim and Holland to re-establish their sovereignty. And, they agreed to withdraw from all French territory except Alsace-Lorraine, but they were even open to negotiating on that point, too. In order to realign with Britain, Germany was prepared to focus exclusively on waging war in the East on behalf of the British as originally planned. Hess requested to speak with Churchill, but, instead, he was transported to the Tower of London to be imprisoned. At that point, the British prime minister was not interested in peace. He had already become determined to fight a long protracted war in Europe. Hitler, on the other hand, remained committed to trying to reconcile with the British right down until 1943.

Later, Hess was transferred to a camp where the British chief of the Tavistock Institute ordered an assistant to administer drugs to him in order to bring on the symptoms of mental illness. All the while, in conversations with FDR, Churchill insisted that Hess was sane. During this same time, Hess wrote that he was being deprived of sleep and threatened with harm to his family. Despite his induced mental problems, Hess later stood trial at Nuremburg where he was convicted of war crimes. Despite the fact that Hess had fulfilled his assigned role in forging British plans for the establishment of a Greater Germany in service to the empire, he spent the last forty six years of his life in prison as a fallen victim to British treachery.

1923-1943

54

FDR'S WARTIME CHALLENGE TO CHURCHILL

"When we've won the war, I will work with all my might and main to see to it that the United States is not wheedled into the position of accepting any plan that will further France's imperialistic ambitions, or that will aid and abet the British Empire in its imperial ambitions."

A PRIVATE COMMENT MADE BY FRANKLIN DELANO ROOSEVELT TO HIS SON, ELLIOTT, AT THE CASABLANCA CONFERENCE IN 1944

When the United States entered World War II to bail Britain out of the mess she had gotten herself into in Europe, Franklin Delano Roosevelt was well-aware that the British Empire was the long-standing pervasive enemy of freedom-loving people everywhere. FDR then took advantage of the fact that Britain could not win the war it had created without the help of the United States, and held a series of wartime conferences dating from 1941, until just before his death in 1945. At those meetings, he ardently pursued plans for an empire-free post war world.

In the first of these wartime meetings, he met with Churchill at Argentia, in Newfoundland, Canada, to draw up the Atlantic Charter. FDR knew that Churchill understood that, without the entry of the U.S. into World War II, Britain could not possibly win the war, so, he shrewdly began to work on maneuvering him into accepting U.S. terms for the post-war world. During this meeting and all successive ones, the life of the British Empire was at stake. Churchill knew it and FDR knew it.

During the Atlantic Charter conference, British advisers tried to convince FDR to divert more lend-lease supplies to the United Kingdom, so that the Soviets would get fewer supplies. Britain had an ulterior motive. She wanted the Soviet Union to be militarily weak, so that the Nazis and the Soviets would destroy one another in a long protracted battle. Then Britain would step in to prevail over Europe. But Generals Marshall, King and Arnold pressed for giving the Soviets as much help as could be spared and, aware of the game the British were playing, FDR concurred.

A back and forth dialogue between FDR and Churchill ensued when FDR boldly announced that he spoke for the American people when he said that the U.S. would not help England win the war just so she could emerge from it in the same position as before and continue to run roughshod over colonial peoples. Churchill quickly retorted, saying that England did not propose to lose its favored position among her dominions, but FDR said that those British trade agreements were backward. When Churchill insisted that they had made England great and that they would continue under conditions prescribed by England's ministers, FDR asserted that a stable peace had to involve the development of backward countries. It could be done and, he insisted, it would be done. It was time, he said, for the British to give up eighteenth century methods and substitute twentieth century methods instead. Twentieth century methods would involve giving colonial peoples a return on their resources by bringing them industry, educating them, bringing them sanitation and generally raising their standard of living. Freeing the world of fascism, he insisted, was also going to involve freeing the Third World from backward colonial slavery. Churchill knew that every idea Roosevelt entertained involved the destruction of the British Empire and he silently abhorred the thought of FDR being in charge of the post-war world. He was in a difficult position, though, because the U.S. would not tolerate empire and, without the U.S., Britain would be destroyed in the war.

Two years later, again hoping to overwhelm FDR, Churchill brought Mountbatten, Supreme Allied Commander of the Pacific Theatre, to the Casablanca Conference and together they argued for an assault of landing craft in Southeast Asia. In order to promote continued empire control in that region, they wanted to initiate a regional war in Burma. To British thinking, Burma had to remain subservient to the empire. If she gained her freedom, it would affect India, French-Indo-China, and Indonesia. Freedom in one colony would mean eventual freedom to all.

Always one step ahead of the British, FDR then let them know that he had other plans. After the war, he suggested that France preside over her old colonies, with a qualified pledge that they would properly administer them and keep colonial freedom as the eventual goal of their occupation. Under the empire's colonial system, the native Indo-Chinese had been down-trodden. What would happen if, after the war, colonial peoples were allowed to slide back into their state of pre-war semi-slavery? It would, he insisted, make a mockery of American involvement in the war and he was not going to let the loss of American lives be in vain. With this pledge, FDR made a bold announcement of his post-war intent to systematically destroy the empire's colonial system of exploitation.

At that conference, FDR also held a meeting with the Sultan of French Morocco. Churchill was present, but he remained quiet while FDR engaged the Sultan in a meaningful conversation about the future of French Morocco and the wealth of its natural resources. There were rich possibilities for Morocco, FDR said, if the country itself was allowed to develop them. FDR told the Sultan, that in order to do this, after the war, he would need to prevent imperial interests from obtaining concessions within the country because these concessions would drain off the greater part of the profit. Then FDR remarked that, in the post-war world, he would be preventing French and British financiers from maintaining their self-perpetuating syndicate—a syndicate that had been dredging the riches out of colonial lands.

They also spoke of Morocco's oil deposits. The Sultan wanted to develop them, but, his country lacked trained scientists and engineers. FDR suggested that a post-war reciprocal arrangement might be made between the U.S. and Morocco that would involve the training of Moroccans at U.S. universities. Or, he said, it might even be practical for the Sultan to engage U.S. firms to carry out the development program for a fee or percentage basis. With such possibilities, the Sultan became exuberant. After the war, he said, he would petition the government of the U.S. for help. He could foresee a new bright future for his country.

In his book, As He Saw It, FDR's son, Elliott, documented many conversations he had in private with his father when he accompanied him as his aid to these wartime conferences. In one particular conversation, FDR had explained to him that down through the centuries, the British had historically used others for empire aggrandizement. By getting others to fight their imperialist wars, they perpetuated a hold on the markets of the world. FDR said that he had strived to make it clear to Winston and others, first in Argentia, later in Washington, and then in Casablanca, that while the U.S had become Britain's ally in war, and would be their ally in victory, they must never get the idea that the U.S. was just in the war to help them hang onto their outdated medieval empire. He said that he hoped that the British did not think that they were senior partner in an imperial relationship with the U.S. The U.S., after winning the war, did not intend to sanction the British system and watch it continue to inhibit the development of the world! Britain had signed the Atlantic Charter and he intended to make her live up to it.

At the Cairo conference, spirits were high because the Allies had just learned of the Stalingrad victory, but FDR knew that the U.S. still had much work to do. Not only was she going to have to mediate between England and the U.S.S.R. after the war, but she was also going to need to mediate between the British Empire and China. FDR was anticipating the need for two separate Cairo meetings—one with Stalin and another with Chiang Kaishek because relations between the U.S.S.R. and China were tense. The Soviets had not declared war on Japan and China was hoping that she would. Relations were also tense because the Soviet Union had not yet ceded her rights in Manchuria to China and, as a result, Chiang was keeping thousands of Chinese up on the country's border, guarding that province from the Soviets.

With all their shortcomings, FDR knew he had to depend on the Chiangs because the war had changed. Rather than remaining a war of survival against fascism, it had become a British geopolitical war because the British were resisting the American suggestion for a unified Allied assault from the West in order to speedily conclude the war. Instead, they were pushing for an invasion through the "soft underbelly" of the Mediterranean, so that they could bring Turkey into the war and pit the Turks against the Soviets. A protracted war favored their geopolitical interests. By contrast, FDR, wanted an immediate victory, so that he could get busy with his post-war peace plans.

After the conclusion of the war, Chiang wanted the Americans to guarantee that the British would not move into Hong Kong, Shanghai and Canton with the same rights as before the war. FDR gave him this pledge and he fully intended to keep it. In return for this guarantee, Chiang pledged to form a democratic government once the Soviets ceded their rights to Manchuria. That was going to be negotiated in the upcoming Tehran conference.

At the second Cairo conference FDR met with Stalin and he agreed that Manchuria would remain a part of China. He also agreed to help the U.S. back Chiang against the British because FDR made it clear to him that the U.S. was not allied to Britain and would never side with the British against the Soviets. He did not want the post-war world to be divided along those lines. FDR anticipated that the Big Three—the U.S., Britain and the U.S.S.R, would work together in the post-war world. Any military action against acts of world aggression would require the unanimous agreement of the Big Three. He said that he saw the U.S. as a world referee and he guaranteed to Stalin that U.S. foreign policy would be separate from that of Britain. Through the establishment of the United Nations, FDR intended to integrate both the British and the Soviets into his peaceful post-war world plans. FDR was optimistic that this could all be accomplished.

When he met with Stalin again at the Tehran conference, in 1945, FDR elaborated upon Chiang's agreement to unify his people by allowing Chinese communists into his government before any national Chinese elections were held. The elections, he had promised, would take place as soon after the end of the war as possible. Churchill then changed the subject and began to argue for British balkanization through an invasion of Europe from the Mediterranean. With this diversionary ploy, FDR and Stalin both knew that he was trying to balkanize Europe in order to strengthen the empire.

At Tehran, FDR also privately received the Shah of Persia (Iran), Mohammed Reza Pahlavi. With him, he discussed the barren dessert that made up so much of the Shah's country. The Shah told FDR that, in the ancient past, the land had been heavily wooded. It had become a dust bowl rather quickly. FDR proposed a giant reforestation project. Then they discussed the economic grip the British Empire had on Iran's oil wells and mineral deposits. They also discussed steps that could be taken to protect Iran's natural wealth. Then FDR put his aids to work drawing up papers that would guarantee Iran's independence from Britain after the war.

In 1945, at Yalta, in the Crimea, FDR attended his last conference. He was anxious for a meeting that would force the British to accept the need for world progress. After the war's end, he was going to place the U.S. military in charge of the peace. The cartels were not going to be built up again.

At Yalta, it was determined that Germany would be divided into zones. The control and administration of these zones was going to be a cooperative operation between the Big Three. Both German militarism and Nazism were going to be destroyed by dismantling German industry. German reparations were also determined. A U.N. conference was also set up to meet at Dumbarton Oakes, in San Francisco. The big question to be determined there was whether or not a veto by one of the Big Three would be able to halt action by the U.N. Security Council. FDR and Stalin were both in favor of a unanimous Big Three veto power because they believed that this was the only way to maintain a viable peace.

At Yalta, agreement between FDR, Stalin and Churchill was stronger than at Tehran because FDR dominated Churchill more completely than before. Stalin, too, was prepared to heed his counsel. After the war, FDR knew he would need to be wary of the advice coming from his advisers. He particularly distrusted the men in the State Department and often referred to them privately as "the boys in the striped pants!" Many times they had tried to conceal messages meant for him. Many of these career diplomats, he said, weren't in agreement with him at all. It seemed as if they should have been working for Churchill because they were convinced that American foreign policy should be a mere copy of British foreign policy. FDR said it didn't matter whether they were Democrats or Republicans. The phenomenon crossed party lines. He said he should have cleaned out the department when he was counseled to do so because it was like the British Foreign Office. Had he lived, he might have done so!

Not only had the press and the Department of State become infiltrated by the enemy, but the military had become infiltrated, too, and, so, after the death of FDR, deprived of his leadership, the army was never used as FDR had envisioned. He wanted to use it to help elevate the standard of living in the Third World. With his death everything fell apart.

During the war, because the British needed the U.S. to win the war for them, fascist-oriented elements in the U.S. government had been silenced. But, after FDR's death, they quickly emerged to again assume control over American foreign policy. With FDR as president during the war, the G.I.s, too, had had a patriotic leader to rally around, and so they happily served in a cause they believed in. But, after FDR's death, sensing that his patriotic mission would soon be abandoned, they just wanted to go home. Not until John F. Kennedy was elected president in 1960, did the United States have another patriotic president to rally around, but, he was ruthlessly murdered. His story shall be the subject of later chapters.

1941-1946

55

THE WORLD LOSES ITS PEACE ADVOCATE

"This time when we clean out the enemy, we are going to clean them out thoroughly, so they can't start another war....Even if we have to keep peace by force for a while, we are going to do it."

FDR AT THE SECOND CAIRO CONFERENCE IN 1945

Upon the death of FDR, Truman began to dismantle Roosevelt's policies. United States armed forces, equipped with the latest rockets, were then placed in Europe. The U.S. also adamantly refused to share the secret of the atom bomb and, so the world began to be suspicious of her. The world climate had changed. Washington gossip circles had even begun to predict a war with the U.S.S.R. by 1948—before the Soviets could perfect their version of the bomb. FDR had been the articulate voice for integrity in the world. When he died, the world lost its peace advocate.

Chiang Kaishek had been guaranteed that after the war only American warships would enter Chinese ports. British warships were not to enter the area. But, what happened? After the war, the first warships to enter Chinese ports were British. Faced with a broken American promise, Chaing Kaishek then broke his promises. The British also went into the Dutch East Indies and ruthlessly used American equipment to suppress the struggle for independence of those native peoples. The United States stood by and did nothing. With French troops and French administrators, the British also went into Indo-China and quickly took over that area, too.

Then British enemy peace saboteurs, in an attempt to dismantle Roosevelt's Big Three veto power, began to lie about the Soviets saying that they could not be trusted. Convinced that no nation could work with the Soviets, the U.N then abandoned FDR's veto rule. Yet while FDR lived, the Big Three unity had worked, and, after the war, the Soviets stood by all their promises. It was the U.S., in the absence of FDR and under the sway of the British, who reneged on promises.

After the Foreign Ministers conference in Moscow in 1946, U.S. representative to that conference, Secretary of State Jimmy Byrnes, was criticized and accused of selling out the U.S. because he had suggested that the atom bomb be placed under United Nations control. He knew that the bomb was creating suspicion. Then the press launched a "get tough with the Soviets" campaign and Byrnes succumbed to some kind of pressure because he quickly changed his position on the bomb. Then, he too, began to also promote the "get tough with the Soviets" policy.

Only one week later, Churchill gave his now famous Iron Curtain speech at Fulton, Missouri. In that speech, while Truman looked on admiringly, Churchill called for a fraternal association of the English-speaking peoples to counter the British-created Soviet "threat." In the absence of FDR, Churchill had shrewdly reverted back to promoting the empire's policies. With that speech, he was testing attitudes—testing to see if the world would buy into the British plan to create a new world enemy.

Months after the end of the war, an Anglo-American military alliance was still meeting in Washington to further the breakdown of the Big Three unity. That breakdown can first be dated to before the end of the war. Three weeks before the Nazi defeat, the war ministers of the Big Three nations had drafted a memo on the terms of the surrender. The Soviet's had circulated a copy of the memo to their forces in the field, but the Allies forwarded no memos to Eisenhower, so he surrendered under different terms. With this "mishap," unity disappeared and the Soviets wondered why. Later, they began to resent the fact that neither American nor British troops withdrew promptly from Europe as agreed to at Yalta. Then, at Fulton, Missouri, when Churchill called for an "iron curtain" to drop between the East and the West, in the face of abrogations to Ally peace promises, Stalin began to seriously consider erecting it. Under Truman, the U.S. had abdicated its role as peacemaker to line up behind the British Empire. There she remains today!

Despite protests by the British people, British soldiers later went into Greece and shot down Greek anti-fascists. The U.S. sided with the British in this action and then pronounced the mock elections that followed to have been democratic. The power of the empire was restored in Greece.

The U.S. supported the British in Turkey, too. Geographically, Turkey and Greece controlled the Dardanelles. But in the cooperative spirit of a post-war free world, FDR had proposed that the Soviets be allowed commercial access to these straits. Then, after the war, as the U.S. lined up solidly behind the British, this proposal was abandoned. There was then no one to intervene in the British-created hostility between Turkey and the U.S.S.R.

Post-war, the British continued to guard its oil concessions in southern Iran. From before the war, they had had a 51:49 agreement with Iran—the largest share, of course, going to Britain. The Soviets offered a 50:50 deal to the Iranians for a concession in Northern Iran—near their Baku oil fields. The Security Council of the United Nations then began to wage an anti-Soviet propaganda campaign over this proposal. Brain-washed by British propaganda, the American people then began to believe columnists who relentlessly accused the Soviets of being imperialists! Enemy agents in London and Washington had succeeded in creating a new hostile world climate. The Cold War ensued! An atmosphere of hatred toward the Russians had been so quickly created that everyone forgot that they had borne the largest share of the sacrifice in winning the war. The British Empire propaganda machine, with the help of the very traitors in the State Department that FDR had mistrusted, helped reverse the peace. These traitors were the very same people that Joseph McCarthy later mistakenly labeled as communists. The establishment considered them to be foreign affairs experts, but they were actually British enemy agents! So long as the British had needed the U.S. to win the war they had created, fascist elements in the U.S. government remained silent, but, after the war was won, they emerged again as a viable political coalition. In 1944, this coalition pushed Roosevelt into taking Truman on as his running mate. That story shall be told in an ensuing chapter.

1945-1946

FRANKLIN DELANO ROOSEVELT
32ND PRESIDENT OF THE UNITED STATES

*On one of his final campaign rallies in 1936, FDR
unleashed the following attack upon the reckless banking
practices of Wall Street: "I should like to have it said of my
first Administration that in it the forces of selfishness and
lust for power met their match. I should like to have it said
of my second Administration that in it these forces met their
master."*

56

LIKE A SECOND PRESIDENT

"Some have spoken of the 'American Century!' I say that the century on which we are entering—the century which will come out of war—can be and must be the century of the common man. Everywhere the common man must learn to build his own industries with his own hands in practical fashion. Everywhere the common man must learn to increase his productivity so that his children can eventually pay the world community all they have received. No nation will have the God-given right to exploit other nations. Older nations will have the privilege to help younger nations get started on the path to industrialization, but there must be neither military nor economic imperialism. The methods of the nineteenth century will not work in the people's century which is now about to begin."

HENRY A. WALLACE IN A SPEECH TO THE AMERICAN PEOPLE, 1946

In his role as vice-president to Franklin D. Roosevelt, Henry A. Wallace was given more executive power than any other vice-president in the history of the United States. After having served FDR as secretary of agriculture for two terms, in 1940, despite protests by Democratic Party bosses, FDR so admired Wallace that he insisted on having him as his presidential running mate. He even refused to run again if he was not allowed to have Wallace on his ticket.

Henry Wallace came from an extraordinary Iowa farm family. His ancestors had emigrated to the U.S. from Ireland, in 1822, to settle in Pennsylvania. Later, his grandfather, the first Henry, had moved west to Iowa. There he took over a small livestock journal of little profitability and turned it into the start of a profitable farm journal called the *Wallace's Farmer*. This journal eventually made him a local Iowa legend.

From the start of their bustling career as farm journal editors, the Wallaces were spokespersons for anti-monopoly interests and proponents of government aid to the farmer. Their journal was unique. It had something for everyone—-articles by, for and about farmers, and inspirational poems, recipes and homemaking tips on Aunt Nancy's Hearts and Home page. However, nothing in the twenty-four page journal was as popular among the people as Uncle Henry's Sabbath School Lessons. Back-logged at the time of his death, they survived Uncle Henry by two decades.

The *Wallaces' Farmer* became the most influential farmer's journal in the Midwest and it supplied the family with a way to promote their passion— counseling farmers. With this journal, the Wallaces became prosperous almost effortlessly, but the acquisition of money never seemed to be a priority with any Wallace. From the time of their establishment in the farm belt, they were a family motivated by the urge to help people.

Henry A. Wallace was the third generation Wallace to enter the family business. As a child he had been a prodigy. Serious by nature, he never seemed to waste a moment of life's time. From his youth, he was consumed by a love for plants and gardening and, by the age of ten, he had his own sizable garden "plot." After college, a family-sponsored trip across the West for the purpose of getting a first-hand look at farms, initiated him into the family business as his father's co-editor. He worked in that capacity for two decades. During that time, he gave the journal an unmistakable intellectual flair by putting his genius to work making incredible planting forecasts! Graphs that tracked trends in commodity prices also appeared in the journal along with reports on scientific farm experimentation.

By 1921, the Wallaces were not only knowledgeable in farm matters, but they were also politically influential. This influence secured the appointment of Harry Wallace to the post of secretary of agriculture in the Harding administration. Harry Wallace also served successive presidents Coolidge and Hoover in that same capacity. Even before that, using his political influence, Uncle Henry had succeeded in getting Jim Wilson of Iowa nominated as secretary of agriculture under President McKinley. Henry A. Wallace had an extensive reputation as a farm expert and scientist when Franklin Roosevelt appointed him secretary of agriculture in 1932.

As agriculture secretary, Henry Wallace served FDR well. A creative thinker, he not only understood FDR's New Deal plan, but he suggested ways to implement it. As editor of *Wallaces' Farmer*, Wallace had learned of the political obstacles that always seemed to surface when legislation favorable to the farmer was proposed. Armed with this understanding, as secretary of agriculture, he was well-prepared to fight these political obstacles.

Towards this end, he began a complete overhaul of the Department of Agriculture. Then he addressed the need for farm credit by creating credit-extending government agencies that by-passed the Federal Reserve. This government-sponsored credit succeeded in raising the income of farmers. As secretary of agriculture, Henry A. Wallace finally happily succeeded in winning a battle on behalf of the farmer that his family had waged for two generations.

By his own admission, though, Wallace's proudest accomplishment as secretary of agriculture was the establishment of the Ever-Normal Granary. That granary established and maintained food reserves for times of emergency. Wallace's inspiration for the idea had come from reading a book by Confucius. In 54 B. C., Confuscius had established a grain storage system in China that survived there for fourteen hundred years. Wallace's granary proved useful during the World War II war effort and it later influenced the UN Food and Agricultural Organization.

As agriculture secretary, Wallace also worked to create locally-managed conservation districts across the nation. Through them, farmers organized both water management and soil erosion prevention projects. Federal money became available for all approved projects. This resulted in a partnership between local farmers and the government.

Wallace also worked with the large-scale government infrastructure projects inaugurated by FDR—projects like dam-building and the Civilian Conservation Corps. He also wrote and lectured extensively on the need for full employment. In his book, <u>Sixty Million Jobs,</u> he discussed the issue of building both a domestic and an international peacetime economy. In that book, he claimed that the U.S. survived the 1930s depression only through the bold and brave actions of FDR.

When, in 1936, FDR was facing reactionary opposition to his New Deal policies, Wallace wrote his influential book, <u>Whose Constitution? An Inquiry into the General Welfare</u>, and demonstrated that FDR's policies were a continuation of the policies prescribed by Alexander Hamilton, chief architect of the U.S. Constitution. Wallace also claimed that the Constitution had laid the groundwork for a profound new basis of government and he made convincing arguments for a return to that constitutional system. Then he went on to systematically denounce not only fascism and communism, but capitalism, too, saying that all three systems originated with the British imperial system—the dead system of the nineteenth century. He concluded his book by saying that the general welfare could only be served if "We the People" returned to the vision of Hamilton.

On the international scene, Wallace was an ardent supporter of FDR's post-war international policies. He voiced his whole-hearted support for the Bretton Woods agreement. With this plan, speculative foreign exchange rates, he said, would receive a badly needed defeat.

FDR sent Henry Wallace on several international tours. Wallace loved traveling on behalf of his country. It afforded him a chance to see foreign peoples and cultures up close. In 1941, he drove his own car down to Mexico and, in 1943, he also toured several other Ibero-American nations. Greeting the people in their own language, he was warmly received.

Then, just before the 1944 Democratic Convention, he asked FDR for permission to visit Siberia. Like all the great patriots before him, he had been dreaming of a future cooperative world community. The development of Asia, he said, had to be part of this plan. His dream was not an idle one, but a practical one. He envisioned a world community linked by a great highway that would start in Buenos Aires and go northward through South and Central America, into Mexico and on across the United States and Canada into Alaska and finally across the Beiring Strait to Asia. Over time, this great highway would bond the peoples of three great land masses into a peaceful fraternity of limitless opportunity. His heart thrilled at the thought of the magnificence of the upcoming "Century of the Common Man."

Eager to see Asia first-hand, Wallace received FDR's permission to make this goodwill journey to Siberia and a brief diplomatic visit to China to consult with Chiang Kaishek. FDR's enemy-affiliated consultants insisted that Wallace was not schooled in diplomacy and, therefore, should not make the trip, but FDR said that he would do just fine. Wallace left for Asia in May, 1944, and returned to Washington fifty days later. This was just nine days before the scheduled opening of the Democratic National Convention.

The majority of Wallace's time in Asia was spent in Siberia. There he visited twenty-two cities, traveling with a bare-bones staff of just three other people. The Soviets held lavish banquets for him, but it was all quite unnecessary as far as he was concerned. He was there to learn as much as he could about the region's agriculture and science. Whenever possible, he strayed from the working schedule in order to visit with the rural people whom he found to be not unlike the farm people he knew back in the United States Midwest. Wallace had prepared for his trip by studying the Russian language and so, in the native tongue of the people, he was able to convey a wish for cooperation between the Soviets and the Americans. Endeared by the fact that he had bothered to learn their language, his audiences received him well. Before leaving the country, he left a personal letter for Stalin.

When Wallace went into China, he found a different country—one that was both deprived and corrupt. Sharecropper farmers in debt to wealthy landowners were struggling to scratch a living from the land with primitive tools and a few water buffaloes. There was no science at all behind their farming because the Chinese national leadership was controlled by power-loving thugs. Not only did Generalissimo Chiang Kaishek hate the Chinese communists, but he was also full of antipathy for the people of both Japan and Russia. Sadly, Wallace did not, therefore, see much hope for cooperation between the Chinese and the Russians.

Wallace returned to the U.S., to hear critics call his trip counterproductive and amateurish. The British Foreign Office derided it, too, because Wallace had used the trip to repeatedly denounce imperialism. Wallace, on the other hand, felt that the trip had been a success. He claimed that it had done much to lay the groundwork for a post-war peace by suggesting the exchange of agricultural and scientific information between the U.S.A. and the U.S.S.R. In an extensive report compiled for FDR, he disclosed his findings and looked forward to continuing his work.

Instead, he returned home to find treachery a foot in Washington. Enemy operatives in the Democratic Party had organized the bosses for the defeat of the popular support for Wallace's re-nomination as vice-president. That story shall be the subject of our next chapter.

1940-1944

57

DERAILING WALLACE

"The highest joy of life is complete dedication to
something outside yourself."

HENRY A.WALLACE

After his trip to Asia, Henry A. Wallace returned home to the United States feeling like an accomplished man. Having succeeded in charting the beginnings of a mission of cooperation with Russia, in true statesman-like fashion, he wasted no time revealing his accomplishment to the American people by making a Sunday night national radio broadcast. On the air, he announced his faith that, in the post-war world, American leadership would help bring a great material benefit to the people of the world's Pacific region as the U.S implemented the peace plans laid out by FDR. With U.S. help, that region would develop its great natural resources and there would be an elevation of the standard of living of the area. The prospects for the future were bright, he said. With victory ahead, the American people were "on their way" to building a peaceful cooperative world.

By the time Vice-President Wallace had spoken these words, the conspiracy to dump him from the 1944 Democratic ticket was well under way. The enemy had shrewdly concluded that President Roosevelt was not well. Should he die in office, they reasoned that Henry Wallace was set to succeed him as president. Wallace, they knew, would continue Roosevelt's American system program at home and would also bring it abroad. Then, their old feudal system of empire would crumble and die. Wallace had to be stopped. His re-nomination as vice-president had to be prevented.

Popularity polls had demonstrated that Henry Wallace was far and away the popular favorite among potential vice-presidential candidates. Americans loved him. Able, experienced, and patriotic, he had been groomed to carry on FDR's policies. But, fearful of his popular appeal and his commitment to world progress, the enemy united in an all-consuming effort to destroy his political future. Many people participated in the campaign to derail Wallace. Some of them were out-and-out British agents. Others were unwitting accomplices to British intrigue. Henry A. Wallace stood apart from them. Largely above political haranguing, he did not peddle influence, trade in favors or otherwise seek to covertly influence men. He just did his job thoroughly and well. The enemy was aware of his qualities and they knew that he was not one of them. So they first tried to derail him by mounting an unsuccessful media campaign aimed at destroying his influence with the American people. They often accused him of being a communist or a scientific socialist, but, in reality, he was simply the embodiment of the true American.

Wallace had written a pamphlet entitled, *Our Job in the Pacific*. In it, he expressed his post-war goals—international control of airways, economic aid for Third World development, the demilitarization of Japan, and self-determination for colonial peoples, including the people of India. These goals alarmed the British. Before the pamphlet could even be printed, a British secret service agent who had "befriended" Wallace found a manuscript copy of the pamphlet, sequestered it and sent it off to his superiors. They quickly copied it and had it replaced before Wallace could miss it. The copy was given to Churchill. When he read Wallace's call for the liberation of colonial peoples in Asia, he was said to have become "stirred to cataclysms of wrath."

During this whole period, FDR had undergone a great decline. His doctors had insisted that he take a rest away from office, but it didn't improve his health. With Wallace in Asia, his wife traveling much of the time, and Harry Hopkins, his trusted adviser, ill— much of FDR's circle of support was missing. When he was approached to consider Truman as his vice-presidential running-mate, FDR initially hesitated because Wallace was his trusted confidant. But, later, because he was ill, in the face of a changing political climate, where once he would have argued and insisted on his own way, he then was more inclined to go along with what others wanted. When finally the bosses threatened him by saying that they would expose his poor health and prevent his re-nomination, FDR gave in. He knew he still had important work to do and he didn't know that he would soon die, so he reluctantly agreed to take on Truman.

Initially, the party bosses had tried to get Henry Wallace to quit office without a fight, but that didn't work. Wallace went straight to the President to ask him how he felt about running with him again. FDR made it clear that he supported Wallace, but he also wavered and said that he would not insist on his candidacy like he had done during the last campaign. Wallace offered to resign, but FDR wouldn't let him.

Once the enemy had Roosevelt's assurance that he would not oppose the party's wishes, the bosses began to plan the manipulation of the convention. Wallace hadn't even planned to attend the convention. He was just going to wait out the whole process at home in his apartment. Backroom deals were not his style. Even his re-nomination organization was unprepared for the convention. Placards weren't even made until last minute. Eventually his organizers sensed the importance of Wallace's presence at the convention, so they insisted that he attend. Even though he was tired from his trip, Wallace relented and went to Chicago.

The Culver and Hyde book, <u>American Dreamer, the Life and Times of Henry A. Wallace,</u> gives a startling depiction of party maneuverings at the 1944 Democratic Convention. The chapters on the convention begin with Wallace's arrival. From his first moments at the convention, Wallace's popular appeal was evident everywhere. People were exceptionally friendly and photographers sought to capture his picture. People even wanted his autograph. In preconvention meetings, delegates looked to hear from him. He was being accorded the respect he had earned.

The first few days of the 1944 convention rank among the most extraordinary in American history. On the first night, when Wallace walked on to the convention floor, he was greeted by a spontaneous outburst of applause that lasted for a quarter of an hour. When many otherwise hearty supporters of the President had learned of FDR's reluctance to insist on Wallace as his running mate as he had done in 1940, out of admiration for Wallace, some of them even considered pulling their support for FDR.

Behind the scenes, the party bosses were at work trying to convince Harry Truman that the President wanted him as vice-president. Truman really didn't want the nomination, so to convince Truman of FDR's desire to run with him, they got the President on the line and quizzed him about the matter. Then, just as the President was about to acknowledge his endorsement of Truman, they quickly handed the phone to Truman who could hear FDR's distant ascent. Surprised, Truman asked why FDR hadn't indicated his wishes to him personally.

On the second night of the convention, amid loud cheering, Wallace stepped up to the podium to address the crowd. Bluntly, he laid America's future on the line by telling the convention that the American people had come to the most important election of their history. FDR had waged a war to free the world of fascism. Now, he said, he needed to be re-elected so that he could forge a lasting peace. Issues that would shape the future of the world were at stake and FDR had to be allowed to finish his work. His speech electrified the convention. Many were moved to tears.

The popular response of the crowd to Wallace's convention address made it perfectly evident that the enemy had been promoting a very big lie by claiming that Wallace was unelectable. So, to actually defeat him, the bosses knew that they would have to out-maneuver his delegates. At the time, many knew that Truman was the candidate of the bosses; while Wallace was the candidate of the people.

The keynote speech for the evening was a radio-dispatched shipboard address by Roosevelt who was away on a peace-planning trip. The convention received his address amidst cheering and the waving of placards. Then, at its conclusion, a curious thing happened. The convention galleries spontaneously erupted with a call for Wallace.

"We want Wallace! We want Wallace," they began to cry. Then the convention organist began playing the "Iowa Corn Song" and everyone began to chant its rollicking chorus. The bosses began to panic. In a move to incite pandemonium, they then opened the doors and allowed hundreds of additional people to enter. Wallace standards were waving everywhere. Fearful, that Wallace might be nominated on the spot, the bosses tried to stop the convention from proceeding by sending for city workers. They even ordered firemen to cut the cables to the organ, so that the music would stop.

Soon delegates began to demand recognition from the chairman, so that they could move to nominate Wallace, but the chairman would not give it. With his microphone dead, a delegate from Florida approached the podium in order to be recognized, but the chairman quickly adjourned the convention. This ploy had been used effectively in the past to prevent popular candidates from being nominated. The bosses successfully used it again to put a halt to the momentum that had arisen for Wallace. Then they scrambled to use the overnight time-delay to organize delegates for Truman. Had the political apparatus not convened the convention that evening, Henry Wallace would surely have been re-nominated as vice-president.

Overnight the bosses worked feverishly to secure delegate commitments for Truman's nomination. All kinds of bargains and promises were made. Cold hard cash even changed hands. Every state chairman was called that evening and erroneously they were assured that Roosevelt wanted Truman. The next day, policemen prevented full access to the hall, so thousands of Wallace supporters were denied entrance. The few supporters that did gain entrance were widely scattered throughout the hall. Large portions of the galleries were empty. There were no further explosions in the hall and the organist did not play the Iowa Corn Song.

Wallace maintained that he was in the fight to the finish, and so his forces never gave up! In a spirited speech, they nominated him and he was enthusiastically applauded. Other nominating speeches followed, but the dictate of the bosses were at work still. So Truman's name was eventually placed in nomination along with other favorite-son candidates. Seventeen names in total were submitted and things began to go as planned. The bosses had shrewdly calculated that, with the submission of a long list of nominees, no one would be nominated on the first ballot. This insured Truman's staying power. The prospects for "Project Missouri Compromise" were looking good.

Despite all the political haranguing that had occurred, Wallace made an impressive showing on the first ballot. He led Truman in votes, but he did not have a majority, so the speaker proceeded to the second ballot. He would allow no dinner break—no chance for the Wallace forces to make calls. On the second roll call, Wallace's number went higher, but fell one hundred votes short of the number required for victory. Then, on the third ballot, his strength broke as delegates began to switch to Truman as planned. Photographers surrounded Truman and began to snap pictures. In a show of victory similar to that of a boxing match, boss Kelly held the Senator's arm high. Then other delegates followed the prescribed lead and the convention lined up behind Truman.

With the nomination of Truman for vice-president, enemy opposition had stopped Henry A. Wallace from eventually becoming President of the United States. The bosses had engineered their coup. An FDR election victory followed. Then, his subsequent unexpected death altered the course of American history by making Harry S. Truman President of the United States. Soon American nationalism experienced another defeat as Truman canceled the plans for world peace and prosperity that FDR had chartered and Wallace had so eloquently advocated. The Truman-inaugurated Cold War followed. Per order of the enemy, not only had the political future of Henry A. Wallace been hijacked, but the world's cooperative future had been hijacked, too.

1944

HENRY A. WALLACE
Genius Botanist, Secretary of Agriculture and United States Vice President

As a brilliant nationalist, Henry A. Wallace well-understood the historic problems that confronted FDR when he was elected President in 1932. In his appointed capacity, first, as FDR's Secretary of Agriculture and, later, as Vice President, he helped FDR wage a fight on behalf of the nation against fascism. He once said: "If we define an American fascist as one who, in case of conflict, puts money and power ahead of human beings, then there are undoubtedly several million fascists in the United States." This statement will cause a thoughtful person to wonder if fascism, as an ideology, might not still be thriving today.

58

ENTER TRUMAN

"These economic royalists complain that we seek to overthrow the institutions of America. What they really complain of is that we seek to take away their power. Our allegiance to the American institutions requires the overthrow of this kind of power. In vain they seek to hide behind the flag and the Constitution. In their blindness they forget what the flag and the Constitution stand for."

FRANKLIN DELANO ROOSEVELT

As we have seen, a coalition of Wall Street-allied Democratic Party bosses recruited Truman to the vice presidency in 1944, so that he would become president should FDR die. Strangely though, Harry S. Truman never aspired to be vice president, nor did he ever want to be president. Initially, he went to the 1944 Chicago Democratic convention to try to get out of the deal. He was worried that the campaign might be hard on his family. He did not want the Republicans to start digging up "dead horses from the past"—things he had tried to thoroughly bury. Truman was a small-time politician and wanted to remain as such.

Put into office by the Kansas City mob in the 1920s, Truman came from a Missouri family with ties to the political tradition of the old-time pro-slavery political faction that had engaged in Kansas-Nebraska-style terrorism in the 1850s. In order to get elected to political office, he had even flirted with joining the Klu Klux Klan. He could easily be manipulated into doing the bidding of the enemy, so they viewed him as the perfect puppet-president and sought to promote him politically.

Initially, when Truman acceded to the presidency, he kept Wallace in his cabinet, but as he began to dismantle the New Deal program of FDR, a clash ensued between the philosophical former vice president and the politically-savvy Truman. As vice president, Wallace had enjoyed the loyalty of many New Deal Democrats. Truman characterized these same men as "the lowest form of politician," and so he rapidly thinned them from the ranks of his cabinet. Then he began to heed the advice of those around him who were about to redesign foreign policy. In 1945, in response to reports made to him by the enemy-aligned U.S. ambassador to Moscow, Averill Harriman, Truman became convinced that the U.S. and the Soviet Union had irreconcilable differences and that he should get tough with them. So, in his first meeting with the Russian foreign minister, V. M. Molotov, Truman bluntly opposed Soviet requests for loans to rebuild their war- torn country.

The FDR-designed Bretton Woods system had called for the dismantling of the ages-old imperial system that dominated world trade. We have seen that during the war, FDR had had many discussions with Churchill about the need to bring twentieth century methods of development to the world. FDR knew that the British Empire was an out-dated evil system and that it was in need of dismantling. Many Americans knew this, too. A gallop poll conducted in 1945 had shown that, at the end of the war, sixty percent of Americans were anti-British.

In 1945, the U.S. ambassador to Britain, Joseph Davies, warned Truman of the conspiracy to break up the FDR wartime three- power alliance. The British, he said, were scheming to pit the U.S. against Russia. Churchill had shrewdly reverted to the old British divide-and-conquer scheme—the same doctrine that Hitler and Goebbells had espoused. Thoughts of cooperation between the Americans and the Russians terrified the British. They knew an alliance between these two nations would conquer their old imperial system. Nuclear war, Davies said, was even part of their strategy for continued world dominance.

The British post-war attack upon the Soviets was pushed on the American people despite the fact that they had long held the Russians in high regard. After the war, Americans collectively viewed Russia as a valuable wartime friend. She had sacrificed much to win the war. Why, they reasoned, couldn't she be a peacetime friend, too? The United States had never engaged in a war with Russia and Americans saw no reason to think that she ever would.

Yet, despite popular opinion, Truman embraced British plans to dismantle all of FDR's post-war plans for peace. Instead of issuing credit to build peacetime economies, as FDR had envisioned, under the new Wall Street takeover, the International Monetary Fund (IMF) and the World Bank eventually became agencies of world destruction. Even though the bank's staff and boards were initially eager to issue credit, Eugene Meyer, the bank's first president, enacted a program of strict austerity, claiming that the issue of credit was fiscally irresponsible. When Meyer abruptly resigned after a short time as president, he was succeeded by John McCloy. A typical Wall Street lawyer, McCloy brought all the board members of his Chase Manhattan Bank with him to oversee the World Bank. Then he moved to have the disbursement of all bank monies placed in his hands.

The World Bank had eight billion dollars in capitalization, but McCloy would not lend any of it. By April, 1947, Chile, Poland, France and other countries had all applied for loans. France received a loan, but only under terms that infringed upon her sovereignty.

France protested the conditions, but McCloy held firm. To rid France's government of people unsympathetic with the enemy's plans, McCloy labeled these people as communists and had France oust them from her government. Then, while the Marshall Plan was being submitted to Congress, he denied aid to the rest of Europe saying that Europe needed to assume responsibility for her own problems.

His policy toward the Eastern bloc countries was even worse. Poland had become a communist country by 1947, but she wanted to work with the anti-communist West. In 1946, she had applied for a loan of 600 million dollars to buy coal-mining equipment, but she received an amount much smaller than requested. When McCloy made a trip to Poland to evaluate the situation first-hand, he stopped in to see Churchill and he convinced McCloy not to make any more loans to Poland. Churchill said that he was opposed to lending to the "enemy" Eastern bloc. Then, in 1948, Truman officially ordered the veto of all loans to Poland. Critical of the U.S., the Poles then accused the United States of waging economic warfare against them. She also charged that loans made to both France and the Netherlands correlated exactly with the size of their foreign military budgets in Vietnam and Indonesia. In other words, the World Bank was funding imperialist measures designed to further the colonial system of empire. The enemy had subtly hijacked World Bank money in order to fund her imperialist plans.

In Ibero-America, countries like Chile had received loans so small that they did hardly any good at all. When Chile applied for a second loan, she was told that no more money would be available until her previous loan was repaid. Most of the loans that were dispersed in Ibero-America went to dictators like Somoza in Nicaragua because McCloy believed that dictators kept their nations in "superior condition."

When the Marshall Plan went into effect, it, too, proved to be nothing more than a program for furthering the enemy's plans for a cold war. It had been designed by the same cabal of pro-British globalists who were running the World Bank and they intended to forge an Anglo-American bloc in Europe. By rebuilding West Germany and depriving East Germany of any loans, a tense stand-off between East and West would be created. It was all part of a carefully designed strategy to keep the world imprisoned and backward.

While American foreign policy was being redirected in support of imperialism, at home, the Truman administration deliberately launched a domestic "red scare" diversion to draw attention away from the enemy's scheme to dismantle the world vision of FDR. There had been leftish sympathizers in the New Deal during FDR's administration and there had also been traitors in the State Department. FDR knew it, but he chose to ignore them. He didn't need to create diversionary witch hunts. He was too busy fighting the war.

By contrast, in 1947, Truman launched a loyalty campaign—followed by a National Security Act. Timed to coincide with the advent of the Cold War, it inaugurated background checks of all federal employees without exception. As Truman launched this trumped-up witch hunt, the most dangerous real national enemies—double and triple spy agents, were engaged in treasonous work in the State Department. Yet, they were routinely being given clearances and promotions. This charade gave way in 1950 to an investigation by Senator Joseph McCarthy. He labeled the enemy as communist, but, in fact, they were really British agents who had infiltrated the government of the United States. From this position, they were engineering the downfall of the country. For his courageous work in exposing this treason, in typical enemy style, McCarthy was vilified, slandered and discredited. With American support, the British continued to give away the peace FDR had forged.

1944-1947

59

THE BOMBINGS OF HIROSHIMA AND NAGASAKI

"He who trusts by the atom bomb will perish by the atom bomb or something worse.....To make Britain the key to our foreign policy would be... the height of folly."

HENRY A. WALLACE

FDR had stirred Americans to new heights and new ideals. He taught his people to confront their fears and he gave his pledge to fight the "Wall Street Tories" that he had identified as having caused the Great Depression. He had also labeled these Tories as enemies of progress. In a stand to free the world from Nazi tyranny, he had come to the wartime aid of the British, but he had made himself clear—he would not accept their old ways in the post-war world. Then, when he unexpectedly died, the British puppet-president, Harry S. Truman, assumed the reigns of the U.S. government and presided over the nuclear bombing of Japan. Americans then, once more, became gripped with fear. A climate of mistrust quickly ensued.

After FDR died, Truman, in conjunction with the British and the Dutch and others, sent Japanese troops into Indo-China to reoccupy it until the British and the French could get back into the area. Freedom in Africa was bloodily put down and a war was fought in Indonesia to suppress the freedom gained there. The liberation of India from British imperialism was also postponed.

In the spring of 1945, General Douglas MacArthur sent General George Kenney to Washington to report that Japan was on the brink of surrender, but Kenney failed to convince his superiors in Washington. Japanese ships, he reported, could not get in or out of the main island of Japan, so, hopelessly stranded, Japan's surrender was inevitable. From before FDR's death in 1945, Emperor Hirohito's diplomats had been seeking terms of surrender and they had negotiated an armistice agreement through a special office of the Vatican. Then, after his death, they continued to try to negotiate, but Secretary of War, Henry Stimson, kept on insisting upon the use of the bomb.

Truman was told that the nuclear bombing of Japan would save American lives by preventing the need for a land invasion. He was also told that the bombings would target only military bases. Truman was fed lies and he believed them. When Japan made peace overtures, Stimson made sure that no follow-up action was taken. He had also delayed the convening of the Potsdam meetings, so that nuclear tests could be completed in New Mexico. When Stimson conspired with the British to drop the bomb on Japan, she was already a defeated adversary.

On May, 31, 1945, Stimson chaired the Manhattan Project, a committee organized to meet with scientists, and later with industrialists, about the bomb. At that meeting, he bluntly opposed giving Japan any advance notice of the planned bombings. He also rejected a proposal that the bomb be first dropped on an uninhabited Japanese island. Robert Oppenheimer, the bombs inventor, is said to have favored that approach, but Stimson objected to it. The Japanese were to be given no warning. The whole scheme was intentionally planned to intimidate the Soviets and everyone else into accepting the enemy's new imperialist plans for a return to oligarchy. Despite opposition to the bombings, the mission went forward. In shock, afterward the West then "fell" to the enemy by proceeding to take political directives from them.

Oppenheimer was in agreement with Wallace and some others in the Truman administration who favored sharing information about nuclear power and channeling it for peaceful purposes. Oppenheimer had openly claimed that any country with top nuclear scientists could develop nuclear power, yet, despite his opinion, the U.S. acted like it was a big military secret.

Wallace thought that the U.S. nuclear program should be placed in the hands of the U.N. military establishment. As secretary of commerce, before Truman fired him, Wallace had written the President a memo. In it, he counseled the President about Britain's plans to destroy the Big Three alliance by creating an irreparable break with the Soviet Union. Then he reminded Truman that Britain's game had always been intrigue and he cautioned him not to play that game. But Truman was no patriot. Firmly in the British camp, he instead chose to follow his marching orders and dropped the bomb on Japan. This orchestrated the U.S. entry into the enemy-planned Cold War.

As part of the enemy's post-war strategy, the bombings were a Truman administration policy intended to prepare for the next British-planned world war. That policy had actually been devised by the perverse British geopolitician, Bertrand Russell. The intention was to build up the U.S. nuclear arsenal for a pre-emptive "preventative" strike against the Soviet Union in order to compel her into submitting to British long-term plans for One World government. It didn't work, however, because U.S. nuclear weapons production became stalled. The Soviet Union then developed the bomb sooner than expected. They also went beyond the U.S. to develop thermonuclear weapons, so the U.S. had to be given time to catch up. Unpopular with the American people, Truman later decided not to seek re-election. He was then replaced by Eisenhower who was more of a nationalist and he was followed by JFK, who was a true patriot. As our story continues, we shall see why the enemy resorted to murdering JFK, the last of our string of great U.S. patriot presidents.

1945-1963

JOHN F. KENNEDY
THIRTY-FIFTH PRESIDENT OF THE UNITED STATES

In referring to his science-driver space program and his commitment to promoting the general welfare, President Kennedy liked to say: "A rising tide lifts all the boats."

60

WHO KILLED PRESIDENT KENNEDY AND WHY?

"Before my term has ended, we shall have tested
anew whether a nation organized and governed such
as ours can endure. The outcome is by no means
certain. The answers are by no means clear.

JOHN F. KENNEDY

John F. Kennedy became president of the United States in 1960 largely through the efforts of Eleanor Roosevelt. When Kennedy contacted her, she noticed his candor. As he spoke, she noticed that he shared the perspective of her late husband. Like FDR, JFK was an American nationalist, so, when he became president, he clearly indicated that he would pursue a path of opposition to British geopolitical interests. Like the assassinated patriots who preceded him, John F. Kennedy was also an idealist.

As president, Kennedy had done four progressive things that alarmed the entrenched oligarchy. To build a new vibrant economy, he had inaugurated an investment tax credit to encourage industrial development and he faced down the J.P. Morgan interests when they tried to initiate an increase in the price of steel. To promote technology and invention, he created a space program and announced his intention to put a man on the moon within ten years. And, by extending the hand of friendship to the Soviets, he expressed an interest in world cooperation.

Then he did another thing that the British found highly objectionable—he conferred with retired General Douglas MacArthur about the Vietnam War and took the general's advice when he told him to avoid a land war in Southeast Asia. With his decision to oppose this war, he boldly challenged the enemy's plan to destroy the United States by escalating her national debt through an involvement in an expensive imperialist war. Then, before he went to Dallas in 1963, with the stroke of a pen, he further restricted the enemy by issuing presidential executive order 11110. This order restored to the U.S. government the power to issue its own currency based on the amount of silver held in the U.S. Treasury. When he departed for Dallas, he had already circulated ones and fives and tens and twenties were set to go to print.

Why did this last move prove fatal to the President? Under the guise of a federal agency, a cabal of private bankers had usurped the constitutional authority of the U.S government by creating the Federal Reserve as a private central bank with the power to print U.S. currency. They then enriched themselves by charging the U.S. government interest on the currency. This effectively destroyed the government's constitutionally-sanctioned power to control its own finances.

By first refusing to engage in the enemy's planned imperialist war, and then by refusing to let them finance it through escalating the nation's debt, the President had taken some first critical steps that aimed to place the nation on a new course of freedom from the entrenched oligarchy. Remember that Lincoln had boldly taken this same stand against the cabal when he became president by issuing sovereign greenbacks as the initial step in his plan to independently finance the coming Civil War. The London enemy banking cartel tried to bribe Lincoln into letting them finance this war, but he steadfastly refused any bribes or loans from them. In the tradition of Lincoln, President Kennedy, too, steadfastly opposed the same scheme and he was killed for the same bravery. As Lincoln once said, banking "denounces as public enemies all who question its methods or throw light upon its crimes."

The assassination apparatus that killed President Kennedy can today be traced to the British Crown. Lee Harvey Oswald was a patsy. He worked at FBI Division Five, in New Orleans, where the FBI covertly trained Cuban subversives and supplied them with weapons. Throughout 1963, the year Kennedy was assassinated, that office had been frequented by Clay Shaw and David Ferrie.

After he discovered that Lee Harvey Oswald had been based in this New Orleans secret political intelligence office, and discouraged by the "findings" of the Warren Commission, two years after the assassination of President Kennedy, New Orleans District Attorney, James Garrison, brought Clay Shaw to trial for conspiring with David Ferrie and Lee Harvey Oswald, to murder the President. Of the three, only Shaw was still alive. Oswald had been shot by Jack Ruby and David Ferrie had died under suspicious circumstances. Judge Edward Haggerty presided over the trial. Garrison called many witnesses, but his best evidence was Shaw's self-styled confession to the Dallas police. Under their interrogation, Shaw had admitted that he knew Ferrie. But Judge Haggerty ruled that Shaw's statements to the police were inadmissible because the police had violated the law while interrogating him.

One decade before the assassination, David Ferrie had recruited Lee Harvey Oswald to U.S. intelligence, so their association was established. Shaw's conviction depended on proving beyond a question of a doubt that he knew Ferrie. That would have established a conspiracy of three. But, under oath, Shaw lied and claimed that he never met Ferrie. At the time, photos had appeared in a local New Orleans gossip weekly that showed Shaw and Ferrie together at a bizarre party. Garrison never presented these photos at the trial, so the jury ended up deciding that there was insufficient evidence to convict Shaw. Had the photo been admitted as evidence, further questioning might have effectively established Shaw's association with Ferrie.

Clay Shaw was a member of the board of Major Louis Mortimer Bloomfield's Permindex Company (Permanent Industrial Expositions,) a Canadian front company that expedited British intelligence operations. Shaw's involvement with Permindex would have been the subject of a follow up probe had his connection with Ferrie been substantiated at his trial. This probe would undoubtedly have established a connection to the British Crown.

Permindex had a shaky background. By 1967, it had been thrown out of Italy, France, and Switzerland because the French had determined that it had paid for assassination attempts against the life of French president, Charles de Gaulle. Under an agreement made between FDR and Churchill during World War II, Bloomfield had served as counterintelligence adviser to J. Edgar Hoover. Then, from the close of World War II, he worked through Division Five as the liaison between British Crown intelligence and the FBI. Bloomfield and Hoover had collaborated intimately for twenty years.

Oswald sent a personal telegram to Hoover just forty-eight hours before the assassination. In it he warned of the plot to kill President Kennedy. Hoover treasonously suppressed the telegram and ordered FBI offices across the country to bury any documentation linking informant Oswald to the FBI. Up until the moment when he was shot by Jack Ruby inside the Dallas Police Department, Oswald had been denying that he shot the President. Had Oswald lived to go to trial, his testimony would have undoubtedly incriminated the Permindex assassins and exposed the relationship of the British Crown to the Permindex Company.

Today, there exists evidence that Major Bloomfield, the late British intelligence operative, was a charter member of the super-secret British elite 1001 Club. A Canadian by birth, he was also an early member of the Canadian branch of Prince Philip's World Wildlife Fund (WWF.). Today the WWF is a widely misrepresented organization. It claims to be concerned with the environment and endangered species, but that is a masquerade. Launched in 1961, it is actually a powerful European oligarchical network committed to promoting One World government. It opposes American-style nationalism and is committed to population reduction.

Like Lincoln, Garfield, and McKinley before him, JFK was murdered by the British oligarchy because he was advancing U.S. national interests. Like FDR whom he admired, he had inaugurated an era of profound American optimism. Undoubtedly, he had identified the British Empire as the long-standing enemy of the American people.

Time has given us a look at all the connections between the above-mentioned nefarious operations—the FBI, British Secret Intelligence, the Permindex assassin bureau, District Five, the World Wildlife Fund, the 1001 Club, and the British Crown. The lone assassin theory has realistically been ruled out. Perry R. Russo, who was called to testify at Shaw's trial, had related that he had been at a house party where Ferrie and Shaw discussed the planned assassination of Kennedy. He had even heard them speak about creating a triangulation of crossfire and alibis.

Clay Shaw had been associated with the British from his days as an OSS liaison to the office of Prime Minister Winston Churchill and he was on the board of the Permidex Company. Bloomfield himself had co-authored an assassination strategy manual called "Crimes Against Protected Persons: Prevention and Punishment." Other members of the Permindex board included various members of the European "nobility"— people who had been associated with the governments of both Hitler and Mussolini.

After the murder of JFK, a string of outspoken American patriots arose to public prominence—his brother, Robert, Martin Luther King, and Malcolm X, but, they, too, were all murdered. After that culture shock, the United States was engulfed by a spirit of pessimism as the baby boomers lost sight of the focus JFK had provided them. Having forgotten about his call to service, they became victims of the enemy-created drug, sex and rock and roll counterculture. They also became engulfed by a spirit of greed. Deprived of his leadership, the great national start that JFK had re-initiated came to a close. Americans then suffered a sad retreat as Lyndon Johnson, fearful that he, too, might also be killed, compromised with the enemy.

1960-1963

61

THE GEORGE WASHINGTON OF INDONESIA

"The world cannot exist half-poor and half-rich. Yet
the gap between developed and less developed is
year by year becoming greater rather than less."

HOWARD JONES, U.S. AMBASSADOR TO INDONESIA, 1958-1965

Long before the existence of European settlements on the North American continent, the imperial forces of empire had sought to rule over the Indonesian Islands in order to acquire a monopoly of trade in its rich fabrics and spices. Finally in 1750, the Netherlands established control over the islands and subdued the island of Java, but the outer islands of this vast archipelago were not subdued until 1900. Then, during World War II, the Japanese invaded Indonesia and easily overpowered the Dutch. During all these years of colonial occupation, the Javanese suffered terribly. Then, with the Japanese surrender following World War II, a charismatic Indonesian leader named Sukarno emerged to lead his people to a military victory over the Dutch. Following this victory, he declared Indonesian independence and became the country's first president.

With the intention of uniting the diverse warring archipelago, one of the first things Sukarno did as president was create an easy-to-learn language for common use throughout Indonesia. But, even after creating this common language, ruling the diverse archipelago of 17,500 islands proved to be a grueling task.

When John F. Kennedy became U.S. president, he began to promote improved relations with Indonesia by hosting a meeting with Sukarno at the White House. Then he put his foreign advisers to work convincing the Dutch to completely give up the Indonesian island of Java and conditions began to improve in Indonesia. The U.S. also withdrew its support for British subversive activities in Indonesia.

Sukarno then undertook the formation of a political confederation that he called The Maphilindo Project in order to reunite the long separated Malay people—living in Malaya, the Philippines, and Indonesia—around issues of common concern. President Kennedy heartily supported this project, but the British were unhappy with it because it impaired their long-standing British plan for an imperialist Federation of Malaysia. So, to sabotage the Malphindo Project, in 1962, the British fomented a Malay revolt and created an opportunity to eliminate Sukarno. Sukarno then used force to clamp down on prevailing violence and, in 1963, after surviving a two year British-orchestrated attempt to create a coup, he suspended the Parliament and had himself installed as president for life. He then procured military equipment and training from communist countries and sent troops into the British-occupied stronghold of Malaysia. In conjunction with British secret intelligence, John Foster Dulles and his British-allied cronies in the U.S. State Department tried to inaugurate a second coup against Sukarno, but it failed.

The many traitors in the United States Department of State had tried to push their dangerous Cold War mentality on President Kennedy, but aware of the false charges the establishment was leveling on Sukarno, he did not comply. He had come to believe that the British Cold War strategy of attempting to divide the world into warring blocs was dangerous. In a private conversation with his able Ambassador to Indonesia, Howard Jones, Kennedy had disclosed the fact that he considered Sukarno to be like an Indonesian George Washington. Patriot that he was, Kennedy was committed to supporting Sukarno's efforts to free his people from British imperialism.

In conjunction with his European allies, Konrad Adenauer in Germany and Harold Macmillan in Britain, Kennedy had planned to revive FDR's worldwide anti-colonial policy. In response to this challenge, the enemy then launched the Profumo scandal in Britain, a minor, yet sordid little affair of the kind that the British traditionally sweep under the rug. In this case, though, the scandal was intentionally given wide-scale notoriety in order to derail Macmillan's conservative "winds of change" government. This brought the staunch enemy-aligned Harold Wilson labor government into power in 1964. By this time, Kennedy had been murdered and Konrad Adenhauer was being forced into retirement. There had also been attempts on the life of French President Charles de Gaulle, and so he would soon retire. Treacherously, the enemy had successfully orchestrated the removal of an international coalition dedicated to an anti-colonial world and instead substituted leadership that was sympathetic to their post-war imperialist agenda.

Jones met with Kennedy's successor, Lyndon B. Johnson just a few days after JFK's death, but Indonesian sovereignty was not a priority on his list of concerns, so nothing was concluded. In subsequent days, under the advice of administration advisers and through the counsel of the Southern Democrats, LBJ quickly acquiesced to the British approach in Indonesia. Soon he, too, began to accuse Sukarno of being a communist and adopted a policy of punishing him for his association with them. He also punished him for his resistance to the British intention to organize Malaysia out of three of her Asian colonial protectorates. And he refused to supply Indonesia with the financial assistance Kennedy had pledged to her. With this betrayal, U.S./Indonesian relations were compromised. Secretary of State Robert McNamara concurred with this plan to curtail aid to Indonesia and then began to promote the escalation of the war in Vietnam. Afraid that the enemy might also kill him should he also oppose the war, against his better judgment, LBJ then pledged his support for the war's escalation.

When Richard Nixon was elected to the presidency in 1968, he did so with the political backing of the Southern Coalition, the long-time southern British-sponsored counterpart to the Wall Street-aligned Tory enemy tradition in America. Nixon was elected under a promise to end technology development in the United States. In 1971, under the direction of the enemy-agent, George Shultz, in response to the British devaluation of the pound-sterling, he pulled the U.S dollar off the gold standard. This destroyed the remnants of the old FDR-sponsored Bretton Woods system and led to an era of speculation at the expense of the physical economy. The International Monetary Fund then forced the devaluation of specifically-targeted world currencies. Then the United States embarked upon a path of complicity with the British and moved further away from the Kennedy-inspired nationalism that had held so much promise.

1961-1971

62

HIJACKING THE WORLD'S WEALTH

On one of his final campaign rallies in 1936, FDR unleashed the following attack on monopoly and reckless banking: "Never before in all our history have these forces been so united against one candidate as they stand today. They are unanimous in their hate for me—and I welcome their hatred. I should like to have it said of my first Administration that in it these forces of selfishness and of lust for power met their match. I should like to have it said of my second Administration that in it these forces met their master."

The fraternity of men who desire to rule the world is close-knit and clandestine. They and their agents move easily between corporate board rooms and halls of government. Former World Bank president, Robert McNamara was a perfect example of the kind of agents that run this world coalition. Before assuming that office in 1968, he was president of Ford Motor Company and then he was secretary of defense under Kennedy and Johnson. Part of a clique of agents—enemy agents of empire—who rule from the high echelons of a pyramid of power, these men grow rich at the expense of ordinary people. Accountable to no one, they run the modern-day British Empire. Vast in scope, it rules over international finance and continues to be the cause of wars, poverty and all kinds of backwardness—from genocides, to starvation and famine. The British Empire is still the pervasive enemy of the United States republic.

The National Security Association (NSA), a U.S. Department of Defense spin-off of the military signals section of U.S. military intelligence, serves a clandestine function. Among the least known and least understood of United States agencies, it is virtually a large spy organization that covertly facilitates the joint operation of big business and government. This operation has grown into a grand "corporatocracy" that employs hundreds of men and women worldwide. Students of British ideology work for consulting firms scattered around the world and these firms, in turn, use FDR's hijacked world government agencies to promote the system of empire. Although larger and more complex, the modern-day relationship between government agencies and these international consulting firms is akin to the relationship that once existed between the British East India Company and the British Crown. In fact, it is the evolution of this relationship.

This is how the modern-day empire operates: At the insistence of the World Bank, international consulting firms hire themselves out to Third World countries where they go to conduct studies to determine whether the World Bank should fund infrastructure projects and other improvements. Taking advantage of a system that FDR put into place to advance the economic welfare of the Third World, this modern-day substitution for the work of FDR instead burdens the Third World with unreasonable debt that they are unable to pay off. Once enslaved, the poor people of these nations grow poorer. FDR's noble plan would have freed them.

In his 2004 best-selling book, Confessions of an Economic Hit Man, John Perkins describes in detail how "engineering" firms purposefully create indebtedness in the Third World through a process they call economic forecasting. This involves over-stating the growth of planned infrastructure projects in order to jack up the size and costs of loans. These companies outwardly appear to be engineering firms, but they are really just involved in forecasting. They do not construct anything. Many employees of these international consulting firms are ex-military people, yet they do not contract with any departments of defense or any military agencies. They just manipulate statistics to produce forecasts that serve the corporate/government allied covert system. These people keep a low profile and see to it that money is funneled back to huge corporations such as Charles T. Main, Bechtel, Halliburton, Stone & Webster and Brown & Root among others. After the forecasting work is complete, huge construction companies then do the building.

A large part of the job of these international forecasting companies involves bribing the leaders of Third World countries into becoming part of this vast system. In this process, by becoming pawns of the system, they enjoy a share in the wealth that the system creates. As part of the deal, they police their part of the empire's vast imperialist network. Thus ensnared, they can be called upon to serve the empire's needs by providing political, economic or military assistance. These Third World leaders are usually part of extended families. They get all the trappings of wealth along with the benefits of parks, power plants and airports, but, their country's poor never benefit from anything. They just grow poorer. Through this system, the long-term financial enslavement of the Third World is assured. The larger the loans, the deeper the enslavement!

Throughout the history of the world, military force largely built and maintained the system of empire, but at the close of World War II all that changed. It all began in Iran in 1951. There, a British oil company—the forerunner of British Petroleum (BP)—was exploiting the people of Iran through the control of that country's natural resources. In defiance of this, the democratically elected popular Iranian Prime Minister, Mohammed Mossadegh, nationalized all Iranian petroleum assets. Outraged with what they considered to be rebellion in Iran, the British then sought the military aid of their post-war ally, the United States, and together they considered launching an invasion of Iran. Both countries, however, hesitated because they feared that Iran's neighbor, the Soviet Union, might intervene. So, instead of sending in the Marines, the U.S. dispatched CIA agent and grandson of Teddy Roosevelt, Kermitt Roosevelt, to Iran. Through payoffs and bribes, he enlisted the aid of eager corrupt Iranian government officials and had them organize street riots and other displays of violence. Pro-British Iranian government agents then removed Mossadegh from office and placed him under house arrest. Kermitt Roosevelt then installed Mohammad Reza Shah into place as the puppet-dictator of Iran. Without firing a shot, Kermitt Roosevelt had organized a successful coup. In the process, he laid the groundwork for a new covert strategy of empire-building. Kermitt Roosevelt's approach was subtle and for a while this covert approach was used elsewhere behind the backs of the Soviets. In his brief tenure as U.S. president, Kennedy fought this system, but, after his death, presidents Johnson and Nixon cooperated with the empire and advanced its interests in this quiet and bloodless way.

Then the empire began to consider the risks of this CIA approach to hijacking the resources of Third World governments. Kermitt Roosevelt had orchestrated the overthrow of a democratically elected government. What if he had been recognized as a U.S. CIA agent? The U.S. would have been discredited. A more discreet approach was sought. Instead of involving the CIA, why not revive the old World War II international cartels and let them work directly with world agencies like the World Bank and the International Monetary Fund (IMF.) In this way, government could stay behind the scenes, yet bolster the system. You may recall that the old British East India Company had used the British Crown in the same way. In conjunction with modern day governmental agencies, the "corporatocracy" would do the same thing, but on a much larger scale. Multinational corporations could interface with the World Bank and it would appear like the governments of Britain and the U.S. were uninvolved. Employees of the multinationals could approach the governments of Third World countries and personally bribe the officials themselves. Trained government intelligence operatives would be needed only when this approach failed. If suspicion of government involvement arose, the corporations could be charged with greed and no one would ever suspect government complicity. They had come up with a plan that was both workable and safe.

1951-1953

63

SENDING OUT THE ASSASSINS

"Regarding the Panama Canal Treaty negotiations, they will find us standing up or dead, but never on our knees. Never!"

OMAR TORRIJOS, PAST PRESIDENT OF PANAMA

In an attempt to help the British steal the wealth of South America, in 1902, Teddy Roosevelt presided over an enemy-orchestrated coup that stole land from the nation of Columbia in order to build a canal under imperial control through the Isthmus of Panama. Following that coup, TR sent the United States warship, *Nashville*, to Panama and U.S. soldiers killed a popular local militia leader and declared Panama an independent nation. A puppet government was then installed in Panama and a Canal Zone treaty was quickly signed. This established an American trade zone on either side of the waterway that was thereafter ruled by an oligarchy of wealthy local families and right-wing dictators. With their help, populist movements were then ruthlessly subdued while big business interests like Rockefeller's Standard Oil and United Fruit were protected. The ruling families were well-protected, too, as U.S. military forces intervened regularly on their behalf.

Then in 1968, after many years of enemy rule, a nationalist coup in Panama overthrew this unbroken string of Panamanian dictators and placed Omar Torrijos into power as head of state in Panama even though he had not orchestrated or participated in the coup. Handsome, charismatic and courageous, Torrijos was very popular with middle and lower class Panamanians. He had grown up in rural Santiago where both his mother and father had been school teachers. As a young man, he enlisted in the Panamanian National Guard and rose through its ranks. Possessed with empathy, he often walked through his county's shantytowns to converse with the poor and disenfranchised. He helped many of the unemployed find jobs and, although not a rich man, he often gave money to tragedy-stricken families.

As president of Panama, Torrijos turned his country into a haven for fugitives from persecution in other lands. It didn't matter what side of the political spectrum they embraced, Torrijos welcomed them all. A true agent of peace, many considered him to be the long-awaited liberator of South America. Torrijos planned to help Panama escape the clutches of empire by announcing her sovereign rights and demanding that they be respected. He also objected to the School of the Americas and the U.S Southern Command's tropical warfare training center that had been established in the Canal Zone. For years, the U.S. had been inviting Latin American dictators to send their military leaders to these facilities where they learned covert operational skills and interrogation techniques as well as military tactics, all under the guise of fighting communism. In reality, though, these facilities were used to protect the assets of the oil companies and international corporations that were looting the hemisphere. Latin Americans generally hated these enemy-sponsored facilities and understood them to be agencies for the training of the death squads that helped install dictators. It wasn't long before Torrijos made it clear that he did not want these training centers within the borders of Panama. He also insisted that the Canal Zone rightfully belonged to Panama.

Everything located in the opulent Canal Zone was U.S. property. All the businesses— from restaurants, supermarkets, barber shops, beauty salons, and golf courses— were exempt from Panamanian laws and taxes. U.S. post offices and courtrooms were located there, too. And more international banks were located in the Canal Zone than in any other South American countries. When depositors conducted transactions in these banks, very few questions were asked. Canal Zone influence sharply contrasted with the poverty of the rest of the country.

For a while, Guatemala, too, had a democratically-elected government. Jacob Arbenz had been elected that country's president in the early 1950s. At that time, only three percent of Guatemalans owned seventy percent of the land, but, after his election, Arbenz enacted comprehensive land reform. One of the largest and most repressive of Guatemala's land owners, United Fruit, opposed these measures. Founded in the late 1880s, United Fruit had grown into one of the most powerful forces in Central America. It also owned big plantations in Columbia, Costa Rica, Jamaica, Nicaragua and Santa Domingo. To unseat Arbenz, United Fruit launched a major public relations campaign to try to convince the U.S. Congress and the American public that Arbenz was a Russian- sponsored communist. Then, in 1954, in a CIA-orchestrated coup, American pilots bombed Guatemala City. Arbenz was then overthrown and replaced by Colonel Carlos Castillo Armas, a ruthless right-wing dictator. His new dictatorship then abolished both land reform programs and the taxes that had been levied on foreign investors. The secret ballot was also eliminated. Critics of the new government were then often jailed. No one could speak out against

Armas. In subsequent years, United Fruit, the CIA, and the Guatemala military promoted a climate of constant violence in Guatemala.

Torrijos was considering building a new canal in Panama, a sea-level one without
locks—one designed to handle bigger ships. Japan, one of the canal's biggest clients, had
expressed an interest in financing it. They also wanted to do the construction. It was to
be the biggest construction job in recent South American history.

Like Arbenz, whom he revered, Torrijos wanted to make his country a sovereign
nation. In order to do that, he knew he had to build up an economic base for his people.
And, like Arbenz, he was also interested in creating a model for other South American
nations to follow, so that they could obtain the same freedom. He wanted to bring electricity to the poor and he wanted the state to subsidize it. He also wanted the state to
sponsor transportation, communication and agriculture. To do this, he needed money—
World Bank money and money from the Inter-American Development Bank. Torrijos
knew that the foreign aid game was an empire-orchestrated trap designed to enslave the
Third World and that it had made many corrupt South American dictators rich. He did
not want to play the game. Like South American dead heroes before him—Che, Arbenz,
and Allende—Torrijos wanted to raise a standard for reform, but he knew he was under-
taking a dangerous mission.

After he came up with innovative plans to expand and improve agriculture and to
inaugurate infrastructure projects in his country, Torrijos determined to secure honest help
from the international interests that were fostering indebtedness among poor nations. To
do this, he consulted with Charles T. Main and got them to agree to arrange a World Bank
loan that was fair. Then, with the whole world watching, he set out to renegotiate the
Canal Treaty with President Jimmy Carter. Many Americans grumbled and called him a
socialist, but, in general, the world favored the return of the canal to Panama. As Torrijos
escalated the push for this return, many wondered, however, if the imperialists would
actually cede their vast commercial interests back to Panama.

The return of the canal to Panama had grave implications for the empire because it
threatened to create a new relationship between Panama and the U.S. by nudging the U.S.
republic back in the direction of the pre-1900 policy of cooperation with South American
republics. Remember that President McKinley had been determined to forge this kind of
relationship by establishing trade reciprocity agreements with South American countries?
These agreements would have helped build up regional economies through mutually beneficial commerce and trade. To prevent such progress, empire agents murdered McKinley.
Then the committed Anglophile, Teddy Roosevelt, immediately reversed McKinley's
pacifist policies. This policy reversal then set the United States upon a path of sad and
steady conversion to an imperial partnership with Britain. Today, few Americans understand that, under the leadership of Teddy Roosevelt, the United States began to oppose
her founding principles.

In an effort to stay the return of the canal to Panama under Torrijos, the United States
CIA began to bribe Panamanian officials. The bribery was so strong and forceful that
Torrijos, too, had to resort to bribing his military chiefs in order to stave off the CIA. But
his determination to help his people was very strong, so Torrijos held his course and in

1977, he negotiated a new Canal Treaty with President Carter. When the U.S. Congress ratified the treaty by only one vote, the Canal Zone was narrowly returned to Panama.

During this same period, Jamie Roldos rose to a position of similar influence in Ecuador. Possessed of charm and charisma like Torrijos, Roldos, too, strongly believed that it was the duty of politicians to rise to the heights of great statesmanship and elevate the living standards of the poor. Opposed to the status quo in Ecuador, when he began campaigning for his nation's presidency in 1978, Roldos captured the attention of the world by attacking the oil companies and their system of oppressive exploitation. In order to try to destroy Roldos, the enemy accused him of being a communist, but, of course, he wasn't. He was just a fierce independent nationalist with the courage to stand up to the forces exploiting his country.

Roldos knew that Ecuador's greatest potential was petroleum and so he campaigned on a program of social reform centered upon nationalization of hydrocarbons and was elected. Early, in 1981, Roldos presented his hydrocarbons law to the Ecuadorian Congress. It intended to reorient his country's relationship with Big Oil and stretch beyond the borders of Ecuador to the rest of South America. The oil companies then attempted to vilify Roldos. They also sent their lobbyists to both Washington and Quito in an attempt to bribe and threaten officials.

After Roldos gave a speech at the Atahualpa Olympic Stadium in Quito in which he condemned the conspiracy between politics and oil and even religion, the enemy knew he could never be bribed. In that speech, he said that unless foreign interests began to cooperate with him in his attempt to free his people, they would be expelled from the country. Then he boarded a helicopter to head for a vacation in southern Ecuador and died when that helicopter crashed on May 23, 1981. The empire had called out the assassins because Roldos had shown that that was the only way he could be defeated!

The death of Roldos shocked the world and Latin Americans were out-raged by it. Newspapers throughout the continent accused the CIA of murdering him. As more and more facts became known, assassination was suspected, but nothing was ever proven conclusively. Forewarned of an attempt on his life, Roldos had arranged to travel in a decoy helicopter, but, last minute one of his security officers convinced him not to board the decoy, so he instead boarded the one that blew up. The news of the death of Roldos hardly made the U.S. press. Osvaldo Hurtado succeeded him as president and he then launched an ambitious program that gave Texaco and other foreign companies increased drilling rights in Ecuador.

Torrijos eulogized Roldos and began to have nightmares about his own assassination. Determined not to back down, though, he refused to renegotiate the canal treaty with the Reagan administration. Then, on July 1, 1981, just two months after the death of Roldos, Torrijos, too, was assassinated. As a role model and leader, had he lived, Torrijos would have undoubtedly quelled the subsequent violence that erupted in South America.

Torrijos was succeeded by Manuel Noriega. Initially, Noriega tried to follow in Torrijos's footsteps by continuing with the Torrijos plan for a new sea-level canal financed and built by Japan. But, Noriega not only lacked Torrijos' charisma, he lacked his integrity, too. So, under pressure by Bechtel, a company that wanted to build the new canal, Noriega gave up on plans for a Japanese-built canal. So, Japan was forced out of the deal.

Dating back to his days in the Panamanian Defense G-2 forces, in his capacity there as colonel, Noriega had served as a liaison with the CIA. In this capacity, he had developed a close relationship with William Casey, the CIA director. Casey used his connection with Noriega to further the empire's agenda throughout the Southern Hemisphere. During the Reagan Administration, he had even used Noriega to warn of the U.S. invasion of Grenada. Impressed with the CIA's power and emboldened by his close association with William Casey, Noriega thought that he was invincible. So, in defiance of the empire, he boldly refused to renew a fifteen year extension of the School of the Americas in Panama.

Then, in 1986, Noriega closed down First Inter-Americas Bank in Panama after it was proven that that bank was owned by the Cali Cartel. Following this shutdown, under the lying pretext that Noriega was a drug-runner, President George H.W. Bush launched an assault upon Panama—the largest U.S. airborne assault since World War II. Many civilians died. Afterwards, four members of the board of the same bank that Noriega tried to shut down were placed in positions of power in the Panamanian government. Drug-running then increased in Panama.

The world was shocked by the magnitude of this unprovoked U.S. assault upon Panamanian civilians and widely denounced the U.S. for its actions. After all, critics said, Panamanians had posed no threat to the United States or to any other country for that matter. All the while, Americans, who had been brain-washed by the press about Noriega's alleged corruption and drug-dealing, remained largely oblivious to the real reason for the outrageous air assault—the promotion of a coup to oust Noriega and enhance the power of the drug cartels. Those cartels have, ever since, served destabilization interests in South America.

While enemy agents of empire, George Schultz and Casper Weinberger, went around the world justifying the U.S. attack on Panama, the real reasons for the attack received little publicity in the U.S. press. Americans remained unaware of the outrage expressed by the rest of the world. After the removal of both Torrijos and Noriega, the Canal Zone was then promptly returned to the United States even though the treaty was not renegotiated.

Today, all around the world, employees of huge international companies go into Third Word countries as agents of empire bent on exploitation. There, they levy over-stated debt payments on these poor countries. Then they put desperate people to work in factories where they work for low wages producing goods for consumption by the world's well-to-do. The empire's system is a pervasive one that threatens the whole world with the return of a new dark age. In forthcoming chapters, we shall demonstrate why this is so.

1954-1981

64

THE OPEC OIL EMBARGO

"The only thing that we can be sure rises faster than
the price of gasoline is the sky-rocketing profits of oil
companies.

ROBERT OWENS, JOURNALIST

Although it appeared to be a creation of the Arab oil-producing nations, from its beginnings in 1974, OPEC was really a British scheme designed to elevate the price of oil and then keep it high. This was not the first time the enemy had intervened to establish control over the "regulation" of oil. The Texas Railroad Commission had been organized in 1891 for the purpose of overseeing the empire-linked Harrison railroad interests. Then, in 1901, when oil was discovered in Texas, in typical empire style, that same commission got involved in setting the price of oil, so that maximum profits could be realized. Eventually it assumed complete authority over the regulation of oil.

Then in 1931, after independent oil companies had associated as Big Oil, Texas governor Ross Sterling, one of the founders of Humble Oil & Refining, and a former board chairman of that company, sent the Texas National Guard into the Texas oil fields to enforce oil production quotas. This resulted in a further increase in the price of oil. Years later, OPEC was established in order to implement an expanded global version of the same price-fixing operation that had earlier been established in Texas.

We have already documented the role played by John D. Rockefeller in forging a monopoly over oil in the U.S. when he bought out independent U.S. drillers for pennies on the dollar. Then, when his oil cartel became international in scope, it used this same policy worldwide to squeeze independent competitors out of existence. This gave the empire complete international control over oil.

The covert international control of oil has figured in the design of British geopolitical strategy for a long time. To gain control of Middle Eastern oil, the empire has promoted the destabilization of that area's ruling governments, and so the Middle East has never developed the means to distribute its own oil. In return for policing their kingdoms on behalf of the enemy, elitist Middle Eastern royal families have grown rich from oil, too. To continue to enjoy this status, however, they must submit to the conditions established by the empire and never challenge its authority.

Up until the 1970s the price of oil was quite stable. Big Oil was buying from the oil-producing countries at fixed prices over long-term price contracts. But in 1971, Nixon agreed to participate in an imperialist plan to dismantle the international fixed exchange rate system, so that speculation in the price of oil could occur. In 1973, the British then precipitated the Yon Kippur Arab-Israeli War and a disruption in the distribution of oil followed. A subsequent "Arab" boycott of oil to the U.S. and Britain ensued. Concurrent with this boycott, the enemy set up a spot market in Rotterdam that allowed oil from blacklisted Arabian companies to be sold at substantial markups. As a result of this spot market, oil prices went from $3.50 a barrel to $10 per barrel.

In 1979, with the overthrow of the Shah of Iran, more disruption in the flow of oil occurred and prices went even higher—from $19 a barrel to to $40 per barrel by 1980. Like the 1973 event, the crisis of 1979 was another British-orchestrated event designed to increase prices and further maximize profits. The American press then sold a lie to the American people by telling them that the Arabs had purposely engineered this price hike when it was really the British who were behind it all. Both of these dramatic spikes in the price of oil had nothing to do with supply and demand and everything to do with the emergence of speculative deregulated markets.

Following the 1973 crisis, the population was also inundated with propaganda designed to promote the idea of a world shortage of oil. In the U.S., a great charade was then conducted to further convince the people of the reality of these "shortages." Here is how it happened: The enemy undertook the promotion of a traveling road show that moved from one U.S. city to another. It would stop at various targeted locations where organized sham shortages of gas had been orchestrated. Long lines formed at gas stations and the news media moved in to show the lines on camera. Then the show moved on and normalcy returned to that locale, but lines emerged elsewhere. New lines were then also reported on the news leaving the impression that "shortages" existed everywhere all at once. Actually, though, the traveling road show, with the help of the press, was manipulating that impression! All the while, tankers full of oil were waiting just off the U.S. coast ready to bring in oil.

While empire forces were working on the minds of Americans to create the belief in shortages, the spot market pricing mechanism was causing a buildup of a huge pool of petrodollars and this allowed the British Empire to compile a huge war chest. With all of this oil speculation, empire elites got fabulously wealthy. The U.S. economy, however, dismantled from the fixed exchange rate system, suffered a great decline in productivity—a decline to about 50% of what it had been in the 1950s and 1960s. As empire-manipulated inflation soared, the world's "wealth" began to become detached from the real physical economy. That physical economy has never recovered! In subsequent years, one speculative bubble after another has ensued. All of this has led to an increasingly fragile world financial system—a system that will collapse unless it receives continuous feeding. This has brought the world to an existential crisis of immense proportions.

1971-1980

65

THE SAUDI ALLIANCE
WITH BRITAIN

"I like Mr. Gorbachev, we can do business together."

MARGARET THATCHER,
SPEAKING OF THE RUSSIAN COVERT BRITISH AGENT

When Egyptian president Gamal Abdal Nassar embraced nationalism in the 1960s, he terrified the British, so, in order to deter his nationalist push, the British organized a Geneva-based Islamic counter-movement. It moved to Jeddah, Saudi Arabia in 1969 to become the beginning of Islamic fundamentalist terrorism. As this informal organization held global strategy discussions in Saudi Arabia, a formal organization, the Muslim World League, was established to internationally promote the spread of British-inspired terrorism.

Then, in 1985, partly due to fear over the Iran-Iraq War, Saudi Arabia sought to purchase American-made F-15 fighter jets from the U.S. in order to build up its Royal Air Force. By law, this purchase of U.S. arms required congressional approval, so President Reagan submitted a bill to Congress requesting the sale. But when the American Israel Public Affairs Committee heard of it, they began to mount a massive effort to kill the bill. Enemy-allied agents surrounding Reagan then withheld information from him in order to stall the congressional process, so that the AIPAC could fully mobilize to defeat the bill. Then these same agents eventually convinced Reagan to withdraw the request all together.

The very next day, chief Saudi diplomat, Prince Bandar bin Sultan flew to London to consult with Prime Minister Margaret Thatcher about purchasing British-made fighters. Arms sales in Britain did not require Parliamentary approval or oversight. In fact, in 1966, the British government had actually created an agency, The Defense Export Services Organization, to facilitate the sale of British arms worldwide. Then, in 1981, when Prime Minister Thatcher privatized the British arms manufacturing industry, the giant arms cartel, BAE Systems, was established. Just four years earlier, the arms manufacturing industry had been nationalized under the former Labor government.

Bandar's trip to London had actually been planned months in advance. In 1984, the British had sought to do business with Saudi Arabia when that country was considering buying French mirage fighters. Bandar had deep ties to Britain. Trained to become a BAE pilot at an elite British Royal Air Force College, before finishing this training, he is even thought to have been recruited by British intelligence. Before the contract for the 1985 purchase of British fighters had even been finalized, the British delivered fighters to Saudi Arabia from the BAE inventory.

The arms deal between Britain and Saudi Arabia was structured as a barter agreement. The agreement, called al-Yamanah, stipulated that, in exchange for fighter jets, the Saudis would deliver a full tanker of oil to Britain every day during the life of the contract. Under a different agreement, cash was paid for bribes or "consulting services," to Bandar and other Saudi officials. Bandar's fees went into his account at the Riggs Bank in Washington.

The BAE-Saudi oil for weapons barter deal turned out to be a huge money-maker for Britain because the British sold the oil they received from Saudi Arabia at huge markups on the spot market they had created in Rotterdam. Over time, an off-shore, off-the-books slush fund of approximately $100 billion accrued. These funds have been used to finance British covert destabilization operations around the globe. Included among these covert operations were the 1980s Afghan Mujadiheen War against the Soviet Union, the Iran-Contra arms for hostages scheme, covert military operations in Africa and the 9/11 attacks in the United States.

When the al-Yamanah deal became public, the British Serious Frauds office launched an investigation of it. But, in December, 2006, before he left government, Prime Minister Tony Blair backed an order given by his attorney general to shut down the investigation. He said that it would compromise British national security and jeopardize the war on terror by interfering with Anglo-Saudi "anti-terror" operations.

Despite efforts to keep the details of al-Yamamah from the public, the British Broadcasting Corporation aired a story on the bribes paid to Prince Bandar bin Sulton. They then followed up this story with the results of their decade-long probe into the British- Saudi arms for oil deal in a one-hour TV documentary called "Princes, Planes, and Pay-Offs." Further investigation has revealed that al-Yamanah is part of a British/Saudi covert intelligence scheme—the biggest one in recorded history—and that the money from al-Yamanah helped fund the 9/11 attacks in the United States.

The cash spawned from al-Yamamah has circumvented any kind of government regulation—British or Saudi—and the covert forces of empire have used the money from its lucrative slush fund to pay for the creation of "Islamic" terrorism in Afghanistan. It all started in 1980, when the Saudis began funding radical Pakistani madrassas (seminaries) inside Pakistan for the purpose of arming thousands of foot soldiers for an enemy-funded jihad against the Soviet Union. Until 1994 no one outside Saudi Arabia had ever heard of the rising force the press labeled the "Taliban." Before the Mujidiheen-funded fight against the Soviets, Afghanis had never heard of the term either, yet they had been marked by the empire to become the Taliban. The word taliban means schooling. The goal of this particular schooling is the organization of terrorism for the purpose of suppressing the impulse toward nationalism in both Afghanistan and Central Asia.

Through both the al-Yamamah deal and the creation of the Taliban, the British Empire has obtained the necessary funding and the manpower to unsettle whole geopolitical regions. A hallmark of British influence in the world is destabilization. They infiltrate a region, foment unrest and displace cultures. Then they get the people to mistakenly identify each other as the enemy and fight one another. Through their manipulated wars, the empire prospers and maintains its reign in the world.

After the "Taliban" drove the Soviets out of Afghanistan and then captured Kabul in 1996, the Soviet Union broke up into a myriad of Soviet states—Uzbekistan, Tajikistan, Kyrgyzstan, Kazakstan and Turkmenistan. In collaboration with the British, the Saudis then financed the funding of teachers from radical Islamic sects housed in Britain and dispatched them to these states for the purpose of indoctrinating locals into the Sunni brand of violent Islam. Dedicated to the destruction of the nation-state, Sunni Islam wants to see a return to the Islamic caliphate.

Today, under the pretense of fighting terrorism, hate-driven soldiers schooled in Pakistan also protect the illegal opium crop that the British cultivate in Afghanistan. British troops are also on the ground there supervising the shipment of their opium to area laboratories where it is converted into heroin. The empire's American allies are there protecting this crop, too. All of this has resulted in the emergence of a huge market for cheap heroin. It has been taking the lives of fifty million Russians every year. And in Pakistan, where the drug used to be largely unheard of, the population has also become widely addicted. Russia has expressed an interest in eradicating the crop, but, with the U.S. puppet-President Barack Obama's support of the U.S. military on the ground in Afghanistan, the empire's opium crop remains protected. The empire has always dealt in drugs. The trade is enormously profitable. Addicted people are no threat to the empire!

1985-2001

66

DEFEATING IRAQ

"My belief is that we will, in fact, be greeted
as liberators."

VICE-PRESIDENT DICK CHENEY,
SPEAKING OF THE WAR IN IRAQ ON MEET THE PRESS, FEBRUARY 5, 2003

B ehind the search for weapons of mass destruction lies the true reason for the 2003 invasion of Iraq—the destruction of the government of that would-be independent nation. Iraq was never a threat to world peace and she was not becoming a hostile world power of immense danger to the world community. She was merely moving away from the grip of the British imperialist empire. For this crime, she was attacked.

Two previous wars had actually also been launched against her for the same reason. The first one began in 1980 when Iran, under British pressure, attacked Iraq. A long war ensued. Then in 1991, President George H. W. Bush launched a brief invasion of Iraq when Saddam Hussein, in defiance of the empire, marched upon Kuwait. President Bush launched this attack upon Iraq in order to protect the empire's hold over Kuwaiti oil. That attack was a warning to Hussein that he had better follow the example of other Middle Eastern countries and comply with empire guidelines. But thirteen years of sanctions had not motivated him to fall in line, so, in 2003, in a search for "weapons of mass destruction," the United States invaded Iraq. This third war entirely defeated Iraq by destroying its industrial capacity as well as its infrastructure. As a result, Iraq has been returned to her pre-1971 era of poverty, illiteracy and religious fundamentalism.

From 1971 on, Iraq had actually embarked upon a path of development of her natural resources and she was anticipating real economic progress. She had also built up her infra-structure and health care programs. And she had geared up for scientific research through a program of high-tech education that was poised to wipe out illiteracy. Opposed to nation-state building, the Anglo-American Empire used war to destroy all this progress.

Covert enemy intelligence also initiated an outbreak of bloody sectarian violence between Sunni and Sh'iaites that did not abate until the end of the long war. This sectarian fighting left deep scars on the Iranian psyche. So traumatized are the people of Iraq now, that a single instance of killing can trigger a chain reaction of more horrible violence. Many Iraqis have long suspected that this fighting is instigated by a third unidentifiable outside force. All those who understand historic patterns know that this violence bears the hallmark of British Empire counterinsurgency tactics. To help the British with planned Middle Eastern counterinsurgency, there is no shortage of mercenary groups and private sector firms that will work under the auspices of the British, the Americans, or the Saudis to destabilize the area. The Saudi Wahhabi net watches over it all.

It is almost impossible for the average observer to identify those who provoke this violence in Iraq. On the rare occasion that a British-promoted plot is uncovered, it is quickly covered over and forgotten. In one 2005 incident, two British special Air Service officers, wearing beards and dressed like Muslims, drove a car loaded with weapons, explosives and detonators into Iraq. There they were stopped by Iraqi police and detained. Then, in a desperate move to cover up the situation, the British attacked the police station where the prisoners were being held in order to secure their release. No serious investigation was ever conducted. Demoralized and deprived of its sovereignty, the Iraqi government didn't even protest. Only because some Iraqi reporters took photographs did the incident receive any attention at all. Yet, rare incidents, like the one at Abu Ghraib, receive all kinds of notoriety and this incites the average Iraqi into hating Americans. All the while, the true long-standing enemy of Iraq remains unidentified. Throughout history, the Iraqi people have shown a remarkable capacity to survive British-inspired upheavals in the life of their nation and, so, they have repeatedly recovered and rebuilt. But this last war was so devastating in scope and intensity that it seems impossible for the Iraqis to once again recover. Only a wide-scale awakening to the reality of British-funded terrorism and a move by the U.S. to reinstate the American System of Political Economy will save Iraq and all the countries like her that are suffering under the ravages of the new and improved modern-day empire.

In 2006, Iraqi Prime Minister Nouri al-Maliki took over the reigns of the Iraqi government. Then, under the guidance of the U.S., an artificial alliance was forged between Shi'a-Arabs, Kurds and some Sunni-Arabs. Taking his marching orders from the enemy, Maliki then sought to compensate the Iraqi people for their suffering, not by reinstating their sovereignty, but by providing them with subsidies for the purchase of cheap imports from China. With the wide-scale destruction of Iraq's manufacturing base, the empire has restored control in Iraq. Enemy control over the Iraqi economy has now advanced the global march toward One World government.

The agricultural base of the Iraqi economy has also been thoroughly destroyed. In the prolonged absence of maintenance and repair, water infrastructure systems have fallen into disrepair, so Iraqi farmers are producing poor crops. With tariffs on imported food non existent and no subsidies for farmers, the agricultural sector in Iraq has been left defenseless. Previously, the state had supported Iraqi farmers with free seeds and fertilizer, but, after the 2003 invasion, all this was withdrawn. Several years of drought have lowered the level of water in rivers and, because of a dysfunctional water pumping system, farmers can no longer even sustain animals. As a result, many farmers have moved to cities that are incapable of supporting them. There, health care is faltering and so are hospitals. Many physicians have fled the country to escape ethnic and sectarian killings.

Students are also dropping out of school in record numbers because they must work to help support their families. This has actually been the trend since after the close of the Iran-Iraq War. As a result, a country that was once poised to eliminate illiteracy is now rapidly becoming illiterate again. Widespread devastation has caused many Iraqis to flee their country and many Iraqi children now live in camp-like conditions in neighboring countries.

"Coincident" with this invasion of Iraq, beginning in 2003, Anglo-Dutch Royal Shell received a majority of the rights to the oil in the Majnoun oil fields in Basrah, in southern Iraq. A skyrocketing of production was anticipated by 2009. Other oil consortiums, all from countries that participated in the 2003 war, received similar contracts in the Rumaila oil field in southern Iraq and the al-Halfaya oil field in northern Iraq.

Following Saudi Arabia, Iraq has the second largest oil reserves in the world. Before the 2003 invasion, these oil reserves were in the hands of state-owned oil companies. Now this oil is in the hands of Britain and her allies. An Iraqi government, now focused on an increasing need for cash, is trying to keep its citizens satisfied with the flood of cheap goods that are coming into the country from China, but the prospects for civil war are great.

1980-2010

67

PRINCE BANDAR AND THE 9/11 ATTACK

"Whenever the government of the United States shall break up, it will probably be in consequence of a false direction having been given to public opinion...In a country where opinion has sway, to seize upon it is to seize upon power...as it is a rule of humanity that the upright and well-intentioned are comparatively passive while the designing, dishonest and selfish are the most untiring in their effort...few men think for themselves."

JAMES FENNIMORE COOPER, THE AMERICAN DEMOCRAT, 1838

We have already established how the al-Yamamah arms-for-oil deal created a British- Saudi offshore slush fund for the purpose of promoting international terrorism and world destabilization. In helping to sanction that deal, both British Prime Minister, Margaret Thatcher, and chief Saudi diplomat, Prince Bandar bin Sultan, furthered empire plans for One World government.

A devoted Anglophile, Prince Bandar has made a career out of money-laundering. While professing to be a passionate Muslim, he is really a thoroughly committed covert agent of the British financial empire. Covert enemy agents in the United States government have also aided and abetted the empire. After the U.S. Congress prohibited the funding of the Nicaraguan Contras in 1985, National Security Adviser, Robert

McFarland, approached Saudi Prince Bandar and asked him to fund them. Then, after securing these funds, McFarland gave orders to Lt. Colonel Ollie North that money for the Contras should be wired directly into Contra leader Aldolfo Calero's offshore account, so that a traceable money trail would not be established. Bandar wields enormous influence among covet intelligence circles and has long claimed that he was responsible for getting McFarland installed as U.S. National Security Adviser. Bandar and Cheney arranged the same kind of money transfers to help fund the Iraq War.

Prince Bandar is on top of covert world politics. Beginning in the 1980s, he helped fund anti-Soviet guerrilla operations in Afghanistan and, in the process, introduced the world to Osama bin Laden. He also played a key role in the defeat of the Italian Communist party in 1983. And, he saved the life of Yasser Arafat and the PLO leadership in 1982 when they were under attack by Beirut. Following that action, there was a horrific slaughter of Palestinian civilians at the Sabra and Shatula refugee camps. As we have seen, the British Empire has a history of funding both sides of armed conflict. They do so in order to destabilize areas and weaken the impulse toward nationalism.

Despite the fact that both houses of the U.S. Congress have conducted investigations of the 9/11 attacks in the U. S., like other investigations of the same sort, no definitive conclusions about the attacks have ever been established. But private independent investigations have corroborated both British and Saudi complicity in at least the partial funding of the 9/11 attacks. They have also documented the fact that leading agents in both Britain and Saudi Arabia and top officials of the Bush-Cheney administration, the U.S. Department of Justice and the FBI knew, in advance, of the planned attacks. **The attack upon the U.S. was not perpetrated by cave-dwelling terrorists in Afghanistan as we have been told.** It was a high-level British-Saudi intelligence operation aimed at dragging the United States into a war in the Middle East. If the U.S Senate could muster up the courage to sanction the truth about the 9/11 attacks, British-sponsored terrorism could probably be stopped!

Documentation also exists that shows that hostile Israeli intelligence teams were in the United States prior to the 9/11 attacks. Afterwards sixty Israelis were detained in the U.S. because they had intelligence information about the planned attacks that they did not disclose. Records of phone calls and FBI wiretap information were also uncovered that show that secret Israeli spy networks in the U.S. had the ability to circumvent U.S. law enforcement and intelligence investigations. It now appears that the Anglo-American-Israeli cabal, which includes rogue elements of the U.S. military-security establishment, could have been attempting a coup.

Prince Bandar has attempted to cover up the involvement of Saudi Arabia in the 9/11 attacks. Sections of the House and Senate intelligence committee report have also been blocked from public view and remain declassified to this day. Osama bin Laden, a member of a prominent Saudi Arabian family that owns that nation's largest construction company, was recruited to serve the British Empire in both Afghanistan and India. The problems in those regions are all British-created. They are not endemic to the region. There is no endemic Islamic problem! There is only an incessant British problem involving the manipulation and management of religious cults for purposes of destabilization.

The empire has also always trafficked in drugs. The immense profits from this trade has aided and funded world destabilization activity. Without this drug trafficking, world problems would abate. Wider recognition of this fact is sorely needed. An international commitment on the part of sovereign nation-states could eradicate the drug trade and shut down the terrorism that it finances. But it would need to involve a top-down targeted attack upon the big banks that launder the profits from the illegal trade. The revenue from drug trade is far-reaching and perverse. It supports all the governments of South America, with the exception of Columbia and Argentina. Those countries are run by drug kingpins covertly installed by the British Empire.

Here is the story of the empire's connection to the 9/11 attacks: During the period between 1998 and 2002, under the guise of charitable assistance, Prince Bandar and his wife provided traceable checks—of both the personal and cashier variety—to at least two of the suicide bombers involved in the 9/11 attacks. The documented money trail began in 1998 when Saudi National, Osama Basnan, wrote to the Saudi Embassy in Washington seeking financial aid for his wife who ostensibly needed thyroid surgery. Bandar then immediately wrote a check to him for fifteen-thousand dollars ($15,000.) He followed it up by sending him regular monthly checks of between two-thousand ($2,000) and three-thousand, five-hundred dollars ($3,500.) Many of these checks were signed over to Osama al-Bayoumi, another Saudi living in Southern California. Some of the funds came from Bandar's famous Riggs Bank account in Washington. The money in that bank had been financing the emigration of members of the Muslim Brotherhood to the U.S. throughout the 1980s and 1990s.

Around New Years Day, 2000, two other Saudis, Nawat Alhazmi and Khalid Almihdher, arrived at Los Angeles International Airport. There they were met by al-Bayoumi and were provided with cash and social security ID cards, an apartment and other needs. Al-Bayoumi later helped both men enroll in fight school in Florida. There they received training for their mission as suicide bombers. Two months before the 9/11 attacks, al-Bayoumi moved to England and then dropped out of sight. Before his disappearance, and days before the 9/11 attacks, agents of Scotland Yard, working with the FBI, raided his apartment in England and found tucked beneath the floorboards, the phone numbers of several officials at the Saudi Embassy in Washington.

Members of the Arab community in San Diego had long suspected that al-Bayouni was an agent of Saudi intelligence because he seemed to be keeping tabs on Alhazmi and Almihdher and he was also trailing Saudi students in the area. Basnan, too, was a suspected Saudi undercover agent. When Basnan was arrested for drug possession in Southern California, the Saudi government got the charges against him dropped.

Basnan had also befriended Alhazmi and Alimihdhar prior to their deaths on American Airlines flight 77. At one point, Basnan, al-Bayoumi and the two 9/11 hijackers all lived at the Parkwood Apartments in San Diego.

Bandar and his wife have denied any involvement in financing the 9/11 hijackers and have maintained that, with their financial donations, they were only providing charitable assistance to the Saudi community in the U.S. During the Senate investigative hearings, when the Senate wanted to probe the Basnan and al-Bayouni links to 9/11, the FBI refused to allow the agents that had worked on this case to be interviewed. Yet, Congress and U.S. law enforcement have maintained that all leads were investigated and no compelling evidence of Saudi involvement in the 9/11 attacks exist. President Barack Obama promised the families of the victims of the 9/11 attack that he would publically disclose the contents of congressional investigations into the attack, but he has reneged on those promises.

1985-2001

68

THE BREAKDOWN CRISIS
AND ITS SOLUTION

"It is time to send the practice of usury, including
monetarist dogmas, into permanent retirement in a
place where such intrinsically immoral practices shall
repose forever in harmless innocence."

LYNDON H. LAROUCHE, JR.

For hundreds of years now, the British Empire has been covertly attempting to destroy the United States republic because its constitutional guarantees, if properly applied, will completely defeat the system of empire. The roots of the system of empire go back to at least 700 B.C. Its ideology sanctions the inhuman enslavement of one human being to another. The U.S. Constitution is the only tool that can defeat this evil system.

In the year 2011, the world is now poised on the brink of an empire-imposed financial collapse. Demoralized, the people of the once-great republic of the United States have fallen asleep to enemy intrigue. Unaware of the source of the evil that has infiltrated their government in order to destroy it, they do not realize what the founders of their once-great republic knew—that lovers of good everywhere must join together under the authority of the U.S Constitution to vigorously defend it, so that the ages-old enemy of mankind can be defeated. That enemy runs the organized system of empire banking that now controls world finance from the City of London and its appendage, Wall Street. Because the world's financial center is located in London and because, in 1763, the British East India Company formed a deal with the British Crown that gave private bankers control over

Crown finances, we call this empire the British Empire. It is not to be confused with the British people who are as much victims of the scheme as any people in the world.

Today, through this City of London/Wall Street operation, the British Empire has grown into a world-wide financial empire of immense proportion. It has secured a monopoly over world financial speculation and it largely controls world commerce through free trade. London is also the headquarters of international terrorism. An incredible difference in taste and morals has always set the British monarchy apart from the U.S. republic until the days of her nearly complete subjugation under the British puppet-presidents Theodore Roosevelt and Woodrow Wilson. The quarrels between FDR and Winston Churchill, during World War II, were fueled by this difference in philosophy. Patriotic presidents Washington, John Quincy Adams, Lincoln, McKinley, FDR, and JFK knew the truth about the traditional enemy of the United States.

After the world emerged from the Dark Age into the era of the Fifteenth Century Golden Renaissance, enlightenment began to prevail in Europe, so the forces of empire, fearful that the people were becoming too smart, began to covertly reorganize. They also promoted a constant state of European "religious" warfare that did not abate until 1648. So, in order to free the world from the constant ravages of the empire, enlightened men, led by the sovereign nation-state philosophy of the great European Cardinal Nicholas of Cusa, began to plan for a settlement in the Americas, so that a wide ocean's distance could give the sovereign nation-state system a chance to flourish.

From its beginning, the establishment of the free republic of the United States was a planned counterintelligence move by republican forces in Europe. Among Americans, Ben Franklin figured predominantly in this cause. Then, after the American victory in her war for independence, the concept of establishing a government dedicated to promoting the general welfare became embedded in the U.S. Constitution. America was thereafter rightly declared to be a "beacon of hope for the oppressed." And, this was generally the case during the periods when Wall Street and traitorous Confederate agents were not in the seat of U.S. government.

In modern times, we find that the enemy-aligned financial rule of Wall Street has largely displaced the constitutional rule of government in the United States. That Constitution gives the U.S Congress the authority to print the nation's money and issue credit through a Bank of the United States. By law, imperialist bankers have no right to issue U.S. currency and then charge the United States government interest on it. This usurpation of the constitutional right of the U.S. to regulate its own financial affairs has been the cause of wars, depressions, assassinations, and all manner of unrest in the United States and in the world.

Under the legacy of the greatest heroes in American history—men like Washington, Hamilton, John Quincy Adams, Henry Clay, Lincoln, McKinley, FDR and JFK, America has enjoyed its greatest times and held its greatest promise. During these periods the nation has briefly rallied as a force for good only to be re-infiltrated by the enemy. Today, the United States is threatened because the American people have lost sight of their country's founding mission. Opinions proliferate, but American system understanding has largely disappeared from American life. The current world financial system is hovering under a speculative bubble of immense proportions and the system might collapse any day now to usher in a worldwide new dark age which will be of greater devastation than the last.

Yet there is a solution and a man with the understanding to implement it. His name is Lyndon LaRouche. Mr. LaRouche is a free man whose genealogy can be traced back to William Brewster, one of the original settlers of Plymouth Plantation in Massachusetts. LaRouche came out of nowhere, from an obscure New England Quaker background. Self-taught from his youth, through his acquired capacities as an original thinker, LaRouche emerged into prominence. He did not come up through establishment channels. He came from outside of the establishment and cannot be controlled by it. He has been invited to join the establishment, under the proviso that he accepts the kind of control they demand, but he has rejected those terms. For this, he has been denigrated, charged with leading a cult, and even unfairly imprisoned.

If one were to go back to the nineteenth century and imagine figures like John Quincy Adams, Henry Clay, Henry C. Carey and Abraham Lincoln living today, Lyndon LaRouche would easily fit in among them. He belongs to their tradition—the Whig tradition. He does not fit the mold of twenty-first century politicians—men with no real political orientation in the American system.

Larouche has dedicated his whole life to self-study in the classical tradition. He is a real economist—a physical economist, not a mathematician who fools around with numbers and tries to make predictions. His repeated successful economic forecasting takes numbers and anchors them to the real world and the real economy. Speculation plays no part for him in his studies. As a follower of Gottfried Leibnitz, he has made his own contributions to Leibnitz's science which began during the period of 1672-1716, when Liebnitz designed the principles of what was to become the industrial revolution.

The economic science of Leibnitz was adopted by the founders of the United States republic and later they became incorporated into the U.S. Constitution through the efforts of Alexander Hamilton. The United States republic adopted this system in explicit opposition to the doctrine of the British East India Company and its spokesperson, Adam Smith. During intermittent periods, when the U.S. adhered to the principles imbedded in her Constitution, she prospered. By the 1830s, all competent economic science was known worldwide as the American system.

Then a succession of enemy-aligned presidents came to power in the U.S. and they presided over the country's eventual bankruptcy. Fortunately, though, Abraham Lincoln came along to revive the republic, and even though he was quickly murdered, the results of his efforts endured for a while. Then, in 1879, under pressure by the enemy, after years of congressional deliberation, the treasonous Specie Resumption Act became law. The control of U.S finances then passed into the hands of foreign enemy bankers, expressly in opposition to the policy of the deceased hero, Lincoln. Tremendously fearful of the threat that the American system had presented to them, these foreign bankers then used their power to infiltrate and re-orient American universities. By the time Theodore Roosevelt became president, the suppression of the teaching of competent science had almost been completed.

One of the results of the suppression of science was a persistent decline in progress. Since the 1971 return to a floating world currency exchange rate system, begun under Nixon, the enemy has presided over a decline in real U.S. production. This zero-growth economy has prevailed throughout the world and, as a result, the world's population has been placed on a course of extinction because its productive base cannot sustain current levels of population growth. For the world to recover, U.S. banking must be immediately reorganized through re-implementation of the original Glass-Steagall standard that FDR inaugurated in 1933. That standard was repealed in 1999. It separates investment banking from commercial banking and prevents Wall Street from speculating with FDIC-insured deposits.

In 2007, Lyndon Larouche actually drafted and circulated legislation called the Homeowner and Bank Protection Act. It would have reintroduced the Glass-Steagall standard. Worthless paper assets would have then been separated from viable bank assets and canceled. Then a firewall of protection would have been placed around commercial deposits to protect them from speculative processes. This bill had wide support from over one hundred city councils, state legislatures, unions, etc. Then, last minute, through enemy-orchestrated intimidation, support for it was withdrawn and the bill was defeated. Currently, a new Glass-Steagall bill, HR 1489, sits in the House of Representatives. It has a wide range of support, but Congress will not bring it up for a vote because they know Barack Obama opposes it and they lack the courage to challenge him. They also lack the guts to impeach him for his many flagrant violations of the U.S. Constitution.

Hopefully that dynamic will change, then, on the heels of bankruptcy organization, the U.S. can launch a technology revival by building a new science-driver economy like the one President Kennedy tried to establish. This new economy can be funded by a return to a policy of low-interest, constitutionally-sanctioned, government-sponsored credit. This will authentically spark new attendant industries and employment will rise. Under the LaRouche plan, the new science driver economy will be realized through NAWAPA, a huge infrastructure project—the biggest one in recorded history! The North American Water and Power Alliance (NAWAPA,) designed by the Parsons Company, has been shovel-ready since 1964. This huge hydroelectric project will green the American desert and alter the existing climate in North America. If implemented, it will put seven million engineers and skilled laborers to work immediately.

Magnetic levitation rail systems as well as bridges and tunnels connecting the world's great continents are also part of the long-range revitalization envisioned by LaRouche. Our study of history has already documented that a unified cooperative world economy was the long-range goal of the U.S. founding fathers and their nationalist counterparts from before the American Revolution. NAWAPA will spawn this kind of world change.

The world is just waiting for the inauguration of this American solution to the empire-orchestrated world crisis. The nations of Russia and China have already proposed a mutual cooperative venture for the development of the Arctic. Certainly they would partner with the United States in a massive technology advance if given the opportunity. The U.S. must, however, first get rid of Barack Obama. Then, she can return to the Glass-Steagall banking standard. Then China and Russia can copy the U.S. bankruptcy lead and a new Three Power Agreement can kick-start a model for other would-be sovereign nation-states to emulate. The world will then be off to a fresh new start as the U.S. Constitutional system finally brings the ancient system of empire to a close.

To insure that the system of empire never becomes viable again, the Federal Reserve System must be completely dismantled and replaced by the establishment of a third U.S. National Bank which will operate under a credit policy as intended by the founders. In conjunction with Congress and the U.S. Treasury, the U.S. government will then once more direct the finances of the United States and this life-giving credit policy will promote the general welfare. With a revival of American nationalism, perhaps our schools will then teach true history. When the people of the United States re-embrace the truth about the founding of their republic, that truth will protect them. Thus armed, they will then never again be held hostage to the system of empire banking that aggrandizes private wealth at the expense of the general welfare. The U.S. Constitution shall then rightly prevail over the world as was intended and peace shall then be the condition of man upon the planet. Amen

2011

Few people understand that history moves forward by conspiracy on a one step forward, two steps backward basis. Therefore, on October 12, 2011, Lyndon LaRouche issued the following warning on his website, www.larouchepac.com: "President Barack Obama has created a secret committee that decides which Americans should be placed on a 'kill of capture list!' While moves toward a police state dictatorship were well underway during the Bush/Cheney Administration, they have been accelerated under Obama, as part of a long-standing British plan for a fascist coup d'etat against the United States."

EPILOGUE

Those who dare to suggest that history moves forward by conspiracy are often maligned or accused of being unbalanced. However, if you look the word conspire up in the dictionary, you will find that it has a simple meaning: "to plan secretly, as a group." From this perspective, conspiracy becomes a fact of life. People have always conspired—for both good reasons and bad ones. The establishment of the U.S. republic was part of a conspiracy that originated in Europe for good reasons—the elevation of man to a position of creative control over his environment through the establishment of a lawful independent republic dedicated to promoting his welfare.

By contrast, evil men committed to the principle of empire, have long conspired to defeat this lawful progressive American plan. In the modern era, they did so by initially trying to force their oligarchical system upon the sovereign independent community that had been lawfully established in the Massachusetts Bay Colony, under a charter issued by the British Crown in 1629. When these patriots later refused to give up their freedom to the encroaching Crown, a revolution ensued and victory by the colonists succeeded in forging the long-sought-after New World republic.

The roots of the conspiracy to forge this New World republic go back to Europe where Benjamin Franklin spent much of his adult life working on behalf of the American republic as a trans-Atlantic American counter-intelligence agent. There he helped wage a European war of ideas based on the inspired leadership of Gottfried Liebnitz, the German Platonic philosopher who espoused progress through scientific advance. As a member of that European circle, Franklin helped spur rapid industrial change in Britain prior to the year 1763. Then, when the British East India Company seductively usurped the power of the British Crown, industrial advance slowed to a crawl in Britain.

For helping to advance this European republican conspiracy from Ireland, Matthew Carey, an Irish revolutionist strongly influenced by the Irish nationalist circles of Jonathan Swift, was driven from his home for "defaming" the British. So, he went to France to join with Franklin and the Marquis de Lafayette to help organize a broad coalition from among the humanist-oriented monarchies of Europe. Intent upon destroying the British Empire's monopoly over world trade, that League of Armed Neutrality seriously considered launching an invasion of Britain from Ireland, but that plan was foiled, when, in 1789, the British covertly organized, under Lord Shelburne, to form a secret intelligence operation aimed at averting progress. Shelburne, along with Francis Baring, then used the British

East India Company and its legion of terrorists to advance the empire's interests by launching wars in order to pit nations against each other. All the while, secluded on her islands, Britain kept herself a safe distance away from the carnage. The empire also employed an army of spies and saboteurs—primarily based in Geneva, in an attempt to subvert the new United States. An organized successful Jacobin revolt in France later destroyed all European hope for defeating the British Empire.

Matthew Carey eventually immigrated to America where he settled in Philadelphia to collaborate with Franklin for the establishment of academies devoted to scientific progress. During the years 1671-1716, Leibniz had written a series of documents in which he proposed the organization of just such academies—academies that would do the research that rapid scientific progress demanded. Against enemy opposition, Alexander Hamilton successfully incorporated Leibniz's ideas into the U.S. Constitution in order to insure this rapid economic advance.

Hamilton and Washington, and then John Adams afterward, inaugurated early nation-building enterprises, but, beginning in 1801, the country was deliberately weakened when Jefferson became president and appointed enemy-agent Albert Gallatin as secretary of the treasury. From that post, Gallatin imposed a policy of fiscal austerity on the new nation in order to deliberately displace the policies of Hamilton. Then, in 1804, when Hamilton was murdered, scientific advance was stalled and a way was cleared for the successful promotion of British/Swiss intelligence plans. Traditional versions of U.S. history never mention the fact that both Burr and Gallatin were British operatives. After Burr's intentional murder of Hamilton, he raised a mercenary army in service to the empire and treasonously plotted to break up the Union.

A successful British conspiracy to harass U.S. merchant ships later ensued and this led to the need for a second war of liberation from the British Empire. Then, after a U.S. victory in that War of 1812, the United States became the battleground for a different kind of war—a trade war with the British. To successfully promote this war, the East India Company established a covert alliance with New York merchants that gave them junior partner status in that company. So, by British secret design, they began lobbying Congress for the repeal of tariff restrictions—restrictions which had created much prosperity at home in the United States despite the expense of the recently fought Second War for Independence. On behalf of the U.S. republic, Henry Clay waged a constant battle with these enemy forces that lasted right up until his death in 1852.

These British-allied American shipping merchants also revived Adam Smith's <u>Wealth of Nations,</u> a work of British free trade propaganda that had already been largely discredited among intellectual circles. Matthew Carey then tirelessly countered this revived propaganda by writing his own texts and pamphlets on the subject of political economy. With other nationalists, he also organized the Philosophical Association for the Promotion of National Industry, to revive the work of Hamilton. Membership in this society not only included manufacturers, but agriculturalists, scientists and skilled mechanics, too. Carey also republished Hamilton's <u>Report on the Subject of Manufactures,</u> even though he knew that Hamilton had already refuted all that Adams Smith had to say on the subject of economic progress.

By 1821, the country had recovered from the 1819 depression that the enemy-orchestrated repeal of protective tariff law had created. Then, beginning in 1825, under the leadership of the renowned patriot president, John Quincy Adams, the nation experienced a profound prosperity. Under his policy of inland development, the population expanded to the Mississippi Valley as new roads, canals and river improvements were forged. Whole new cities and towns rapidly arose in the West. Because high wages were paid to the laborers who constructed all of these improvements, their lives improved.

Canal-building captured the imagination of the people. The Erie Canal, in particular, made vast resources available to them. Railroads were then forged along the path carved by these canals and plans for new railroads were in the works. Driven by the government-sponsored sale of western land at fixed prices, land was settled with the anticipation that economic expansion would continue. Under President Quincy Adams, land was not a speculative commodity.

Then, sadly, John Quincy Adams was defeated in his bid for re-election through the enemy-created populist campaign that succeeded in making Andrew Jackson president. A popular legacy developed around Jackson that has largely survived until this day despite the fact that he was a very flawed man. When, in the summer of 1833, he undertook a tour of the northern United States and received a particularly grand welcome in New York, John Quincy Adams was appalled by the way the people worshipped Jackson despite all of the fraud and corruption that both his campaign and his administration had engaged in. Henry Clay, too, watched as Jackson, emboldened by his own popularity, assumed a dictatorial demeanor and, under a belief that he had a mandate from the people, rushed in, under instruction by his handlers, to override the Constitution and dismantle the Bank of the United States.

In the absence of government oversight, private banks then issued excessive loans and a speculative land-buying frenzy followed. When the speculative bubble collapsed, the worst depression in the history of the U.S. ensued. Then, over the course of three decades, under the leadership of a string of traitorous U.S. presidents, the American system was put on hold and progress was delayed.

Under the enemy policy of free trade, slavery then grew in strength as southern slaveholding representatives began to dominate Congress. With more than seventy-five percent of all southern cotton being exported, cotton then became the center of British world trade. An enemy-orchestrated North/South struggle over the issue of slavery ensued, so Americans quickly forgot about the all the prosperity that a protective system had afforded them. Under enemy leadership, southern slaveholders then began to eye western territories with the intention of spreading their system to that region, so that the nation could be returned to a British plantation economy.

Jackson's political handler and financial sponsor, Martin Van Buren, became the next enemy-aligned president. Unpopular, though, he served only one term, and then went back to working behind the scenes on behalf of successive enemy-designated candidates. We have already chronicled the role the British played in the election of James Polk in 1844. And, we have noted that in all the years leading up to the Civil War, only two nationalists were ever elected to the presidency. Both died under suspicious circumstances shortly after being inaugurated.

By the time Lincoln became president, the United States had been completely bankrupted as planned. In the span of years when the early nationalists were exerting their influence in American politics, Lincoln was in the back woods of Illinois educating himself in the principles of the American System of Political Economy. The work of John Quincy Adams and Henry Clay had taken a particular hold over his imagination, so he later entered politics only to be defeated for re-election after he bravely spoke up in opposition to Polk's war of imperial aggression against Mexico. Lincoln only later re-entered politics after Franklin Pierce conspired with Stephen Douglas to promote the spread of slavery to the Nebraska Territory through the enemy's popular sovereignty agenda.

Lincoln died a martyr to the American cause, but his policies out-lived him both at home and abroad and fueled the second phase of American progressive advance which lasted until 1880. Lincoln is renowned for prosecuting a civil war that saved the Union, but that is only part of what he accomplished. He also waged an heroic battle with the enemy banking cartel that few really understand. Those enemy forces had usurped the constitutionally-sanctioned right of the U.S. government to serve as its own bank. Lincoln restored that power to the government by issuing a paper currency, called greenbacks, on the credit of the United States. This paper effectively financed both the Civil War and the beginning of a huge technology start.

As intended, this prosperity captured the attention of the world. The German chancellor, Otto Von Bismark, was an admirer of the American system of high tariffs that Lincoln had put into place to fuel this American technology advance. Bismark's admiration for the American system began in his youth while he was a student at Gottheim University. There he became acquainted with a circle of American students who had been sent there to study by President John Quincy Adams who had intended to educate them in German classical culture.

William McKinley was a contemporary of Bismark. Out of a feeling of deep kinship for him, in 1890, as a newly-elected congressman, McKinley read a speech before the U.S. Congress that Bismark had delivered to the German Parliament. In that speech, Bismark extolled the American system of protective tariffs and urged Germany to emulate them. Because the German Parliament wisely chose to take the advice of Bismark, within ten years, Germany emerged as the most powerfully industrialized nation in Europe. When McKinley became the United States president in 1896, he reinvigorated the U.S. economy by putting the protective tariff policies of his hero, Lincoln, back into place. Afraid that all this spreading prosperity would dismantle their ancient oligarchical system, the British then conspired to assassinate the emerging world nationalists who were copying the American system. Sadly, the great U.S. statesman, William McKinley, fell victim to this murderous conspiracy.

Bismark was conscious that the British Empire was planning to encircle Germany and wage war on her in order to defeat her industrialization and halt the spread of Lincoln-style global advance. So, in response to an alliance the empire made with Austria, Bismark secretly formed his own alliance with the Tsar of Russia and used his diplomatic skill to try to avert this British-planned war. When British secret intelligence heard of Bismark's diplomacy, they used Prince Edward Albert, son of Queen Victoria, to bring him down. A little man with the bad habit of listening to gossip, the prince then spread nasty rumors about Bismark's nephew in an attempt to discredit the Chancellor. When Bismark became aware of the prince's scheming, he astutely predicted the outbreak of World War I, calling it another Seven Years' War and crediting the Prince with initiating it.

The outbreak of that war actually began in the 1890s with an agreement between Edward Albert, who had become King Edward VII, and Japan's Mikado. Seductively, on behalf of British colonial interests, the king enticed the Mikado to go to war first with China and then later with Russia. This decision followed on the heels of the ouster of Bismark and the assassination of French president, Sadi Carnot. While cruising on a yacht in the Baltic Sea in 1905, the dim-witted German Kaiser and the Russian Tsar rightly began to wonder if their uncle, King Edward VII, intended to drive them into a war with each other.

Two British-inspired world wars, incited by covert British geopolitics centered in the Balkans, erupted precisely as planned. During the Second World War, however, under the masterful leadership of U.S. patriot President Franklin Delano Roosevelt, the world was saved from a British-directed fascist takeover when FDR won that world war on behalf of the patriots. During the war, FDR crafted a post war agreement which reflected his understanding that the U.S. needed to forge a policy for cooperative world progress. His carefully-crafted agreement with Britain, the U.S.S.R. and China was set to be implemented when he suddenly died. Then the British puppet, Harry S. Truman, became president and, in conjunction with Churchill, dismantled the work of FDR. The world was then gripped by the threat of nuclear war.

Later, John F. Kennedy launched a renewed push to defeat the enemy by eagerly accepting FDR's challenge for world cooperation. The enemy quickly murdered him for this dedication. The United States entry into the British-planned Vietnam War then followed, and the debt incurred by the U.S., as a result of that long war, spurred a rapid decline in U.S. productivity. After Nixon dismantled the fixed exchange rate in 1971, the U.S. physical economy declined even more. It was replaced by a speculative economy suitable to British imperial interests. A state of increasing imperial financier control over the entire trans-Atlantic region has dominated the world ever since.

When the senior George Bush became president in 1989, in service to the enemy, he quietly began to make changes in the organization of the U.S. military in order to prepare for an eventual military coup against the United States. Fascist aligned elements in the U.S. government had tried to affect a coup once before, when Franklin Roosevelt was elected president in 1932. Prescott Bush, the father of George Bush, Sr., was a key mover in this first operation. General Smedley Butler was approached to lead an armed assault upon the Capitol, but he listened to the fascist organizers of the intended coup only long enough to garner the details of their scheme, then he exposed their conspiracy.

To lay the groundwork for the enemy's second planned coup, Bush, Sr., aided by his defense secretary, Dick Cheney, inaugurated covert plans to replace the regular government-controlled military with a secret military institution designed to operate with private soldiers. Cheney returned from his job with Halliburton, the huge Texas-based oil equipment company, to help with this covert work. He then handed his former employer a liberal contract to conduct a secret study of the feasibility of this plan to out-source the U.S. military.

The Bush-led privatization of the U.S. military has strengthened the military/industrial complex that Eisenhower warned of before he left office. In the absence of patriot leadership, throughout the 1970s, this military/industrial complex routinely conspired to subvert nationalist governments worldwide. With the sanction of Henry Kissinger, George Schultz and his longtime friend, Felix Rohatyn, chairman of the New York/London/Paris brokerage house, Lazard Brothers, promoted the enemy conspiracy to have the Chilean patriot president, Salvador Allende, murdered. The British-sponsored dictator, Augusto Pinochet, was then installed to a position of power in Chile.

When Clinton became president, Cheney returned to Halliburton briefly only to return again to "government service" when Bush, Jr. was elected president. In that administration, he directed the newly-elected British puppet-president to carry out enemy directives. In collaboration with defense secretary, Donald Rumsfeld, that administration then presided over a massive privatization of the U.S. military. The Patriot Act was also inaugurated under the cloak of a British-created terrorist "threat," to aid in the eventual establishment of the dictatorship being planned in the U.S. Obama was placed in office as part of this conspiracy.

Centuries ago, the British built an empire by deploying mercenary soldiers in their service, so military privatization schemes are not new to them. The orchestrated bankruptcy of the U.S. is the necessary precursor to the empire-orchestrated conspiracy to destroy the U.S. through dictatorship. Only definitive patriot action within the U. S., can avert this planned disaster. Sadly, though, to date, U.S. elected representatives have shown an appalling lack of courage in standing up to Barack Obama, the enemy's latest and worst enemy-aligned president. Obama has been flagrantly violating the U.S. Constitution, yet no one steps forward to initiate impeachment proceedings.

These latest perverse enemy actions have brought the United States to a critical juncture in time as the British Empire moves the world closer to destruction through its planned countdown to World War III. To bring about that third planned world war, the region of Southwest Asia has been targeted as the "New Balkans" and actions against Syria, or Iran, appear to be the detonator. The real targets, however, are the nations of the Asian Pacific—Russia and China—because they are poised for progress. Right now, the entire U.S. military has been deployed to both the Indian Ocean and the region of the eastern Mediterranean in preparation for this latest British-planned conflagration. While many crazed U.S. senators call for NATO intervention in Syria, under the pretense of a peace-keeping force, Syria's president tries to maintain regional peace. History is sadly repeating itself through renewed Sikes-Picot-style secret agreements.

Americans have an intuitive sense that something has gone wrong, but, because they have been denied proper schooling in real history, they do not understand the principles by which the United States is meant to operate. Neither do they understand the nature of the enemy. Widespread corruption has left them unrepresented, and so they are angry.

Under Obama, the U.S. has become a complete tool of the empire. Mistakes like those from the past are now set to be repeated if patriot circles within the United States do not act swiftly to remove Obama from office. He can be legitimately removed from the presidency through section four of the Twenty-fifth Amendment, which allows for the removal of a sitting president on grounds of mental illness or incompetence. Or, he might be impeached for his numerous constitutional violations. Then Congress can pass the Glass-Steagall bill, HR 1489. The enactment of that bill will cause the six largest Wall Street speculative institutions to go under, but it will save the Union. Then the U.S. must once more begin to operate under its constitutionally-sanctioned credit system. NAWAPA, the grand hydro-electric project that President Kennedy had intended to implement, can then be launched and the nation will then be poised for progress once more. It can then join the new Russo-Chinese Trans-Pacific Alliance and invite other nations to first undergo bankruptcy proceedings, and then also join this international cooperative alliance. International progress will then lead the world. A wonderful future actually awaits the world's people **if we can surmount all the British-instigated trouble that now faces us.** Man actually sits on the fringe of unprecedented possibilities which will be spurred by new discoveries in science—discoveries that will defeat the enemy. But we must **choose properly.**

This book has been written to school you—the current generation of American adolescents—in American system ideas. Now that I have told you the truth, my dear friends, you must decide to spread the word. Get others to read this book. Perhaps you will also be inspired to research and read. You might then want to write your own essays and carry on this work. Maybe you can even run for political office one day. A serious crisis now looms over us. I pray that we survive it. I also pray that your generation will become the first completely awake American generation—a generation destined to step forward to inherit the grand legacy prepared for the United States many hundreds of years ago by the great men of the past. It is a legacy that was carefully designed to bring forth a beautiful world peopled by happy beautiful souls engaged creatively in helping the universe unfold as it wills.

BOOKS YOU MIGHT WANT TO READ SOME DAY

In preparing to write this book, here is a list of some of the books and publications I read. As you mature, you, too, may enjoy reading them:

Adams, John Quincy, The Diary of John Quincy Adams, Allan Nevins, editor, New York, Frederich Ungar Publishing Co., 1928

Blaine, James G., Twenty Years of Congress, Hand, Avert, and Company, Boston, 1884

Executive Intelligence Review, fifteen years of periodicals found on www.larouchepub.com. (Search by subject.)

Chaitkin, Anton, Treason in America, From Aaron Burr to Averill Harriman, Washington, D.C., Executive Intelligence Review, 1998

Culver, John C. and Hyde, John, American Dreamer: The Life and Times of Henry A. Wallace, Norton, New York, 2000

Daugherty, Harry M., The Inside Story of the Harding Tragedy, New York, The Churchill Company, 1932

FIDELIO, a magazine published by the Schiller Institute, Washington, D.C

Goodwin, Doris Kearns, Team of Rivals, The Political Genius of Abraham Lincoln, Simon & Schuster, New York, 2005

Leech, Margaret, In the Days of McKinley, Harper & Brothers, New York, 1959

Lowry, H. Graham, How the Nation Was Won, America's Untold Story, Executive Intelligence Review, 1988

McPherson, James M., Abraham Lincoln, Oxford University Press, New York, 2009

Miller, Scott, The President and the Assassin, Random House, New York, 2011

Olcott, Charles Sumner, <u>William McKinley</u>, AMS Press, New York, reprint of the original from 1916

Phillips, Kevin, <u>William McKinley</u>, Times Books, New York, 2003

Roosevelt, Elliott, <u>As He Saw It, The Story of the World Conferences of FDR</u>, Duell Sloane and Pierce, New York, 1946

Perkins, John, <u>Confessions of an Economic Hit Man</u>, Berrett-Koehler Publishers, Inc., San Francisco, 2004

Salisbury, W. Allen, <u>The Civil War and the American System, America's Battle with Britain, 1860-1876</u>, Executive Intelligence Review, 1998

Unger, Irwin, <u>The Greenback Era, A Social and Political History of Finance, 1865-1879</u>, Princeton University Press, Princeton, New Jersey, 1964

White, Carol, <u>The New Dark Ages Conspiracy, Britain's Plot to destroy Civilization</u>, New Benjamin Franklin House Publishing Company, New York, 1984

INDEX

Polk, James as a student 95, loyalty to Jackson 95, as governor of Tennessee 95, 1844 presidential campaign 95, campaign financing 95 and Texas annexation 95, Mexican negotiations 100, urges Congress to declare war against Mexico 100, Whig press condemnation 100, and Lincoln's Spot Resolution 100, and his generals 100, character 100, 317
Potsdam Meeting 272
Powderly, Terrance 139
"preventative nuclear strike" 273
Princes, Planes, and Payoffs 298
Prioleau, Elias 66
Priuli family 66
privatization of the military 320
Profumo Scandal 280
"Project Missouri Compromise" 264
Puter, Stephen 194

Quitman, John Anthony 103, 105, 106, 115

Rapallo Accord 232, 233, 242
Rathenau, Emil 148
Rathenau, Walter 241
Reichbank 234
Renaissance ix, 6, 11
Report on the Subject of Manufactures 20, 316
Report on the Public Credit 18, 19
Reynolds, Maria 20
Rhodes, Cecil 187, 189
Rice, Cecil Spring 187, 189
Richlieu, Cardinal Armand Jean du Plessis de 8
Ritchie, Thomas 74
Rockefeller, John D. 142, 152, 155, 156, 182, 293
Rohatyn, Felix 320
Roldos, Jamie 290
Romero, Matias 149, 151, 353
Roosevelt Elliott, 247

Roosevelt, Franklin Delano and his opposition to British geopolitics 245, and the Casablanca conference 240, and the Sultan of French Morocco 247, and his son Elliott 247, the Cairo Conference and Chiang Kaishek 247, 248 the Second Cairo Conference 247, the Tehran Conference and the Shah of Persia 248, and the Yalta Conference 249, and his wartime challenge to Churchill 246 and the Atlantic charter 246, and Wallace 254, 255, 256, 257, 259, 263, 264, 268, 287, 289, and his assurances to Stalin 249, and Truman 253, and the Department of State 249.
Roosevelt, Kermitt 285
Roosevelt, Theodore 106, 167, 168, 169, 171, 172, 192, 194, 181, 182, 185, 202, 311
Rosebush of War, treatise by Louis xi, 8
Rothschild, Meyer Amschel 133
Rotterdam spot oil market 294
Round Table 232, 235. 236
Royal Africa Company 65, 189
"Rough Riders" 178
Ruby, Jack 276
Ruhr Valley 234
Rumalia oil fields 303
Rumsfeld, Donald 320
Rupert's Land 190
Russell and Company 92
Russell, Bertrand 272
Russo-Chinese Trans-Pacific Alliance 321
Russo-Japanese War 202, 203
Russo, Perry R. 278

Sanders, George 105
Saudi Wahhabi Net 302
Schacht, Hjalmar 234, 237
School of the Americas 288
Schultz, George 281, 320
Scott, Winfield 103, 120

A CHANCE TO TEST YOUR KNOWLEDGE

Test your knowledge, if you'd like, by taking the following T or F test. Be sure to write your answers on a separate slip of paper, so that you don't spoil the test for someone wanting to take it after you.

1. _____ Alexander Hamilton was an aristocrat who tried to convince the founders of the U.S. republic to copy the British system of economics.

2. _____ The greatest of U.S. presidents have sanctioned tariff law.

3. _____ The U.S Constitution gives the government of the U.S. the authority to be its own bank.

4. _____ In winning her independence from Britain, the U.S. established for all time her freedom from that country.

5. _____ Alexander Hamilton can rightly be called the chief architect of the U.S. Constitution.

6. _____Thomas Jefferson unwittingly played into British hands when he became President of the United States.

7. _____ When he dismantled the Bank of the United States, Andrew Jackson accomplished a great feat for the American people.

8. _____ The American Civil War was covertly planned thirty years in advance of its outbreak.

9. _____ Free trade is a wholesome U.S. policy

10. _____ The U.S. has a long-standing enemy that is still working to destroy her.

11. _____ All U.S. Presidents have been patriots.

12. _____ John Quincy Adams can be safely compared to Charlemagne,

13. _____ Barack Obama can safely be compared to Hitler.

14. _____ Alexander Hamilton thought that the young United States should walk away from her war debts.

15. _____ Fearful of U.S. aggression during the 1840s, Mexico opposed the U.S. annexation of Texas.

16. _____ Polk lied to Congress in order to get them to declare war against Mexico.

17. _____ Young America helped elect Franklin Pierce to the U.S. Presidency.

18. _____ The Knights of the Golden Circle helped arm the Confederacy in the years prior to the Civil War.

19. _____ Franklin Pierce and Stephen Douglas conspired to promote civil insurrection in the U.S.

20. _____ The U.S. Supreme Court Dred Scott decision was an act that would have pleased Henry Clay.

21. _____ Profits from the British-sponsored opium trade helped shut down the Bank of the United States in 1836.

22. _____ The 1845 U.S. war with Mexico was a clandestine operation designed to further British imperial interests in America.

23. _____ Abraham Lincoln challenged the legitimacy of Polk's war with Mexico

24. _____ The goals of the slave abolition movement contrasted sharply with those of slave plantation interests.

25. _____ A thorough knowledge of the ups and downs in American history will lead an informed person to suspect that Zachary Taylor was poisoned.

26. _____ Corporations are thoroughly nationalistic.

27. _____ John D. Rockefeller was an early proponent of price-fixing.

28. _____ The establishment of trusts was a scheme to consolidate business profits in the hands of an elite few.

29. _____ The Queen of England is the figurehead of a bygone empire.

30. _____ By virtue of its Constitution, the U.S. government can issue credit for economic development.

31. _____ Northern U.S. Tory merchants once conspired to create a separate northern confederacy in America.

32. _____ South Carolina was a colony modeled upon the earlier Massachusetts Bay Colony.

33. _____ The Cherokees were a highly advanced Indian tribe that coexisted peacefully with the white man while Thomas Jefferson was president.

34. _____ Andrew Jackson can safely be characterized as an opportunist.

35. _____ The Bank of the United States served the interests of Wall Street.

36. _____ Speculation in land following the shutdown of the Bank of the United States, brought prosperity to the United States.

37. _____ Caleb Cushing was a mentor to William Lloyd Garrison.

38. _____ John Tyler continued the policies of William Henry Harrison after he succeeded him to the office of president.

39. _____ The British pushed opium on the Chinese people in order to enhance their trade with that nation.

40. _____ Martin Van Buren was trained as an empire-aligned political operative within the United States.

41. _____ Under the monetarist system of empire, the accumulation of money becomes the sole intent of commerce.

42. _____ Under the constitutionally-sanctioned U.S. credit system, economic progress substitutes for the accumulation of money.

43. _____ Speculative bubbles help promote the general welfare.

44. _____ The Philadelphia Interests held the advancement of science and technology as their goal.

45. _____ The University of Chicago was funded by credit from the Bank of the United States.

46. _____ McKinley's planned trade policies with South America earned him the wrath of British imperialists.

47. _____ McKinley challenged the principles in the Monroe Doctrine.

48. _____ William McKinley and James Blaine had different political philosophies.

49. _____ McKinley held the opinion of his fellow Americans in high regard.

50. _____ Teddy Roosevelt was a true trust-buster.

51. _____ President Wilson was firmly on the side of strikers when the Fuel & Iron Company strike broke out in 1913.

52. _____ The owners of monopolies fared well during the Teddy Roosevelt administration.

53. _____ After World War II, President Truman redesigned U.S foreign policy so that it would coincide with British geopolitical interests.

54. _____ FDR's post-World War II policy was going to involve the extension of credit to war-torn economies.

55. _____ Credit extension is an historically American concept.

56. _____ Truman ardently sought the nomination of his party for vice-president of the United States in 1944.

57. _____ The chief architect of World War I was King Edward VII of England.

58. _____ Secret treaties had both caused and prolonged World War I.

59. _____ The British brought Hitler to power and intended to use him to secretly promote a planned war against Russia.

60. _____ In 1932, Hitler assumed power in Germany by garnering a majority of the votes in that election.

61. _____ The invasion of Europe through the "soft underbelly" of Europe, during World War II, was an American idea.

62. _____ Churchill looked forward to a Big Three unified collaboration after World War II.

63. _____ U.S. Constitutional banking is the most modern system in the world.

64. _____ JFK challenged the British Empire by refusing to get involved in a long war in Southeast Asia.

65. _____ Henry A. Wallace was the most effective vice-president in the history of the United States.

66. _____ Lee Harvey Oswald was the lone-gun assassin of President John F. Kennedy.

67. _____ Lyndon Johnson continued the nationalist policies established by JFK when he succeeded him to office.

68. _____ The British royal family orchestrated the ouster of Otto von Bismark from the German chancellory in 1890.

69. _____ The Bolshevik Revolution was a British-orchestrated happening designed to collapse Russian technology advance.

70. _____ Richard Nixon was indirectly responsible for the dramatic increase in the price of oil during the 1970s.

71. _____ Iran has never tried to establish a constitutional government.

72. _____ Both World War I and World War II were British-orchestrated events.

73. _____ After World War I, the U.S. considered Russia to be her greatest threat.

74. _____ Brown Brothers Harriman of New York supplied Hitler with funding just at the point when he was about to go bankrupt.

75. _____ Churchill was supportive off German nationalism.

76. _____ Speculative deregulated markets serve the interests of nation states.

77. _____ The British were covertly aligned with Hitler during the early part of World War II.

78. _____ During World War II, FDR gave assurances to Stalin that U.S post-war policies would differ from those of Britain.

79. _____ With the advent of World War II, a fascist faction in the U.S government was silenced.

80. _____ Churchill had no problem with FDR being in charge of the post-World War II peace.

81. _____ The empire control of the native indigenous peoples of Southwest Asia had improved their living conditions.

82. _____ Henry A. Wallace was, far and away, the popular choice of the American people for vice-president in 1944.

83. _____ Churchill admired Henry A. Wallace.

84. _____ Eleanor Roosevelt disliked JFK.

85. _____ President Kennedy understood American system economics.

86. _____ Lee Harvey Oswald worked for the FBI.

87. _____ The World Wildlife Fund is an organization solely dedicated to the preservation of endangered species.

88. _____ Following the dismantling of the international fixed exchange rate system in 1971, the productive U.S. economy declined by about 50%.

89. _____ When Indonesian president, Sukarno, began procuring military equipment from communist countries President Kennedy condemned his actions.

90. _____ Omar Torrijos was a communist-sponsored South American dictator.

91. _____ The enactment of the Homeowners and Bank Protection Act of 2007 would have prevented the US. financial crisis of 2008.

92. _____ The Brits and the Saudis were behind the 9/11 attacks in the U.S.

93. _____ Al-Yamamah is an Islamic terrorist operation.

94. _____ The covert purpose of the U.S. war in Afghanistan is the protection of the British opium crop.

95. _____ The legacy of empire goes very far back in time.

96. _____ British drug money funds international terrorism today.

97. _____ Osama bin Laden came from a wealthy Saudi-Arabian family.

98. _____ Price-fixing is an enemy-driven scheme that funnels extravagant profits to huge empire-aligned cartels.

99. _____ Oil pricing is driven by supply and demand.

100. _____ By reading this book and getting others to read it, too, you are going to become the first among a new generation of Americans trained to understand American system economics.

ANSWER KEY:

1. F
2. T
3. T
4. F The British Empire has been relentlessly and covertly engaged in working to destroy the United States ever since she legitimately won her independence through revolution.
5. T
6. T Jefferson became confused by enemy-organized Jacobins during his stay in France as foreign minister.
7. F The takedown of the Bank of the U.S. was an act of treason
8. T
9. F Free trade is a hallmark of the colonial system. It allows oligarchs to garner the legitimate profits of others.
10. T
11. F Many have been actual traitors while others have been unwilling dupes of the enemy.
12. T Like Charlemagne, John Quincy Adams was committed to developing inland waterways.
13. T Obama is a political tool of the enemy. They paid for his election to the U.S. presidency.
14. F Hamilton wanted to pay down the war debt through a program of national development financed by constitutionally-sanctioned credit.
15. T
16. T
17. T
18. T
19. T They did it through promoting the Kansas-Nebraska Act.

20. F That act helped promote the spread of slavery, something Clay opposed all his life.
21. T
22. T
23. T He did it as a congressman through his Spot Resolution.
24. F The enemy was behind the orchestration of both political platforms.
25. T
26. F Corporations are conglomerates designed to siphon off the profits from labor.
27. T
28. T
29. F The empire still exists and the queen sanctions its policies.
30. T See article 1, section 8 of the U.S. Constitution.
31. T
32. F South Carolina was settled by oligarchs.
33. T
34. T
35. F That bank served the interests of the people.
36. F It caused a depression called the Panic of 1837.
37. T
38. F Tyler opposed the nationalist program of Harrison and vetoed a bill designed to re-charter the Bank of the United States.
39. T The British coveted many products produced by the Chinese, but the Chinese initially had no interest in anything the British produced.
40. T
41. T
42. T
43. F
44. T
45. F It was funded by Rockefeller money.
46. T
47. F McKinley attempted to uplift the nations of South America. This was the intent behind the Monroe Doctrine.
48. F They were kindred spirits.
49. T
50. F TR's trust-busting was a phony charade.
51. F Wilson tried to ignore that strike.
52. T
53. T
54. T
55. T
56. F Truman wanted to remain in the Senate.
57. T
58. T
59. T

60. F Hitler's margin in that election was no greater than 40%.
61. F It was a British idea designed to lengthen the war.
62. F Churchill dismantled that alliance after the death of FDR by promoting the Cold
     War
63. T The takedown of Glass-Steagall in 1999 was predicated on the false assumption
     that banking needed to be updated.
64. T That is why they killed him.
65. T
66. F Oswald did not shoot the president.
67. F Johnson reversed JFK's policies out of fear that he, too, might also be killed. He
     later admitted it.
68. T Bismark was the only aware statesman in Europe. He knew that the British were
     planning World War I
69. T
70. T
71. F Iran tried once in the early 20th century when they paid for the services of Shuster
     and then again when they elected Mossadagh in 1953.
72. T
73. F It was Britain.
74. T
75. F Churchill openly opposed German nationalism
76. F They serve the interests of oligarchs intent on accumulating money. They do
     nothing to promote the general welfare.
77. T
78. T
79. T
80. F Churchill abhorred the idea of FDR being in charge of the peace because FDR was
     going to dismantle the British Empire.
81. F
82. T
83. F He hated him for promoting the general welfare.
84. F She helped elect him.
85. T
86. T
87. F That is a false front. It is actually intent upon reducing the world population fro
     7 million people to less than I million.
88. T
89. F JFK was aware that the British were promoting anti-communist propaganda in
     order to divide the world into warring blocks and he thought that it was dangerous.
90. F He was a Panamanian nationalist.
91. T
92. T
93. F Al-Yamamah refers to the 1980s British/Saudi arms for oil deal.

94. T
95. T
96. T
97. T
98. T
99. F It is fixed by an international cartel.
100. T

The author welcomes feedback on her book. Address all comments to patriotsandtories@yahoo.com.

And, of course, don't forget to check out the website: www.larouchpac.com.

www.ingramcontent.com/pod-product-compliance
Lightning Source LLC
Chambersburg PA
CBHW060834280326
41934CB00007B/781